# STRETCH

# STRETCH

## UNLOCK THE POWER OF LESS— AND ACHIEVE MORE THAN YOU EVER IMAGINED

## SCOTT SONENSHEIN

HARPER
BUSINESS

*An Imprint of HarperCollinsPublishers*

HarperCollins books may be purchased for educational, business, or sales promotional use. For information, please e-mail the Special Markets Department at SPsales@harpercollins.com.

FIRST EDITION

*Designed by William Ruoto*

Library of Congress Cataloging-in-Publication Data

Sonenshein, Scott.

Stretch : unlock the power of less—and achieve more than you ever imagined / Scott Sonenshein.

p. cm.

ISBN 978-0-06-245722-6

1. Resourcefulness—Psychological aspects. 2. Creative ability. 3. Adaptability (Psychology). 4. Success.

BF411.S66 2017

153.3'5—dc23             2016028800

17 18 19 20 21   LSC   10 9 8 7 6 5 4 3 2 1

FOR RANDI

# CONTENTS

# CONTENTS

# INTRODUCTION

## MY STRETCH

A recruiter from a Silicon Valley start-up cold-called me on a spring day in 2000. She had been searching to fill a position for months and was convinced I was the right person. At the time, I was barely a year into my first job as a strategy consultant in Washington, D.C. I had never heard of the company, Vividence, and didn't know anyone living in California. But I knew the area was "hot," and I didn't want to pass up on the chance to take a closer look.

The night before my flight, I bought a copy of Michael Lewis's exposé about Silicon Valley called *The New New Thing* to learn more about a region that seemed exhilarating but also a bit unnerving.

As soon as I arrived, the company went all out to persuade me to join the team. Vividence had the best venture capital backers and lots of money—how could it not succeed? It was an exciting and growing company, with new hires coming on board each week. The pantry was always packed with snacks, and there were free dinners catered nightly. I'd have my own team, a bigger title, and the potential to strike it rich.

How could I say no?

A month later, I started a new job that took me away from family and friends. It was easy to get caught up in the valley's booming growth and buzzing creativity. There were glittering parties and promises of transforming everything from how we shop and date to how we learn and interact, all backed by a surge of venture capital and a flood of eager people like myself coming for California's most recent gold rush. I exercised my stock options early, believing that it was never a question of if I'd strike gold, only a matter of how long it would take.

Vividence helped our clients' websites operate better by conducting research. In theory, we wanted to be a software company to command a higher market value. In reality, we blew through tens of millions of dollars, just like many of our dotcom clients, to build something unsustainable—until the money train screeched to a halt, venture capital dried up, and we desperately but unsuccessfully tried to adapt to no longer having a blank check.

In a matter of months, we went from a high-flying start-up backed by over $50 million from the most prestigious venture capital firms to a collapsing business whose employees were fired just as fast as they had been hired. I saw some of the smartest and nicest people I've ever known heartbroken from having to leave what they had invested so much of themselves in developing.

Worried about the longevity of our company and the security of my job, I regularly visited FuckedCompany.com, the website that had sprung up to predict failing businesses and speculate about the reckless mismanagement that led to their demise. It provided an early warning about our fate and a comforting feeling that we were far from alone in our troubles.

The spreading economic collapse in Silicon Valley unfolded during a serious tragedy that devastated the country. On September 11, 2001, terrorists attacked the United States, killing almost 3,000 people and changing the nation's psyche forever. Jeremy Glick, a colleague of mine at Vividence, was traveling on United Flight 93 back to our headquarters. Placed in the most harrowing circumstances, Jeremy quickly teamed up with several other passengers to resist the attackers. Short on time and tools, they mounted a brave fight with what little they had, saving many lives by forcing the plane to the ground in rural Pennsylvania, away from a major population center.

In the wake of the 9/11 tragedy, lots of people reflected on their lives—and I was no different. I questioned how I was spending my time and what I really wanted to achieve. I was ready for a change, and I knew I'd likely be out of a job soon.

I started a PhD in organizational behavior at the University of Michigan. As I arrived, its faculty members were in the midst of their own post-9/11 crisis of conscience. They were leading a scholarly shake-up that came to be called Positive Organizations, which emphasizes bringing out the highest potential in people and organizations though engaging a person's whole self and the organization's larger purpose. Career success and profits are critical—but so, too, are living a satisfying and meaningful life and building sustainable companies that make a difference. I had found a place to examine some of my biggest questions of the past couple of years:

Why do some people and organizations succeed with so little, while others fail with so much?

Why do we get caught up chasing what we don't have?

How is it possible to achieve more prosperous organizations, rewarding careers, and fulfilling lives with what's already in hand?

———

Fifteen years after I left Vividence, people and organizations keep falling into the same traps I experienced during the dotcom era.

# INTRODUCTION

Our most recent recession—caused by consumers and companies borrowing excessively to fund lifestyles and operations beyond their means—brought lots of damage: $19.2 trillion of household wealth destroyed, nearly 8.8 million jobs lost, and confidence in our country's major institutions—including banks, businesses, and government—eroded.

Today, we're just as prone to think we need more to do more, and just as likely to overlook the abundance right in front of us. From the oil bust to the most recent tech run-up in Silicon Valley, history has, and will, repeat itself—unless we intervene.

In the chapters that follow, I'm going to draw from over a decade of my own research on the science of resourcefulness to teach you how to stretch. I'll share with you a powerful mind-set and a skill set that allows you to work with the resources you have to become more successful and satisfied in business and in life. Once you learn how to embrace and expand on the untapped value right in front of you, you'll unlock exciting possibilities to achieve more than you ever imagined.

# STRETCH

# ONE

## A TALE OF TWO BEERS

WORK WITH WHAT YOU'VE GOT

n the fall of 1961, a headstrong teenager named Dick left rural Pennsylvania to attend a military high school 150 miles away. Its rigid schedule and strict rules required students to rise early, dress in naval-style uniforms, and salute instructors. It was a far cry from his hometown life, where friends called him "Party Boy"—a fitting nickname for the son of a regional brewery owner who'd begun working in the family's warehouse stacking cases of beer a few summers back.

When his parents visited a month into the term, Dick begged them to take him home so he could learn about the family business.

# STRETCH

They refused. With the industry struggling, they hoped their son's new surroundings would inspire him to pursue a more promising future away from beer.

Dick had other plans. After convincing a maintenance man to give him civilian clothes, he climbed a tree and jumped over a wall to escape the forty-acre campus. He hopped on a bus to Philadelphia before hitchhiking home, unable to stay away from the brewery he loved. His return home with little more than the clothes on his back would foreshadow the resourceful way he would ultimately go on to turn the struggling family enterprise into one of the country's most successful beer producers, becoming a billionaire at the time his chief rival squandered what could've turned into a $9 billion company.

Started in 1829 as the Eagle Brewery by his German ancestors, the business had outlasted scores of other brewers by the time Dick took over for his ailing father in 1985. The three major players—Anheuser-Busch, Miller, and Stroh—controlled 70 percent of the national beer market. Dick's brewery put out a modest 137,000 barrels annually, a drop in the bucket of the close to 200 million barrels produced nationwide. Faced with competition from these mega-companies, smaller producers typically took one of two paths. Some gave up as independents and sold themselves to competitors. Others tried to grow rapidly through acquisitions.

Dick rejected both options. He wouldn't sell, and he wouldn't buy. Instead, he'd find better ways to work with what he had to build a prosperous business he'd enjoy running.

Although big marketing dollars typically drove beer sales, Dick found ways to get more out of his modest advertising budget. He built awareness by tapping into his company's rich but underutilized history. America's oldest brewery had a type of appeal that separated its products from the three major producers.

Instead of entering as many markets as possible, Dick limited sales to only a handful of regions, creating a sense of scarcity that drove more demand. A cultlike group of fans would cross state borders to buy the hard-to-get beer, lending a mystique to the brand. Several enthusiasts became the beer's best, and free, advertisers, and even started campaigns to appeal to the company to come to their part of the country.

As his business grew, Dick purchased used tanks, bottlers, and labelers—giving them a second life.

By 1996, Dick's efforts to get the most out of his 150-plus-year-old factory were so successful that the five hundred thousand barrels the company brewed finally maxed out the facility, which had been built to produce only about half as much.

Before investing in another plant, he consulted with his most important partners—his four daughters. With only 3 percent of family businesses making it to the fourth generation or beyond, he wanted to gauge their passion for becoming sixth-generation owners. Only after they enthusiastically expressed interest did Dick see a purpose in continuing to grow the business.

Dick's company, D. G. Yuengling & Son, grew into America's largest domestically owned beer producer. But that was never his goal. "We were not in any race to be the largest domestically owned brewer," he reflects. "Our game is longevity. . . . My daughters . . . are in the business now and we want their kids to be able to run it some day. That's what's satisfying to us."

*Forbes* estimates the blue jeans– and sneaker-wearing leader of the beer giant has a net worth of close to $2 billion. Even with all his wealth, he still drives a modest car and regularly turns off lights left on at the office. "They say I'm cheap," he told me, "but I'm economical."

His motto—to work with what he has and make the most out of it—helped him achieve the elusive goal of creating a thriving and sustainable business he enjoys running alongside his children.

# S T R E T C H

What made Dick so successful and satisfied when so many other brewers went bust, running themselves and their companies into the ground?

As a social scientist and Rice University professor, I've spent over a decade studying what makes organizations more prosperous and the people who work inside them better off. I've researched, consulted with, or worked at organizations in industries as diverse as technology, manufacturing, banking, retail, energy, health care, and nonprofits, spending time with top executives at Fortune 500 companies, entrepreneurs launching their businesses, front-line employees trying to make a difference, and everyone in between. I've had the privilege of teaching thousands of people from all over the world—executives, engineers, teachers, doctors, working parents, and young people just starting their professional lives.

What I've found in my research, and what a growing body of scientific evidence supports, is that how we think about and use resources has a tremendous influence on professional success, personal satisfaction, and organizational performance. The problem is: *We routinely overestimate the importance of acquiring resources but even more significantly underestimate our ability to make more out of those we have.*

Whether adapting to major changes, going about everyday routines, or trying to carve out meaningful careers and lives, my research explains how people and organizations can expand their resources to achieve great things and feel fulfilled—to stretch. Stretching is a learned set of attitudes and skills that comes from a simple but powerful shift from wanting more resources to embracing and acting on the possibilities of our resources already in hand.

Before stretching, we first need to break free from attitudes and habits that propel us down a dangerous path. When embarking on our most important efforts, from how we build businesses and cultivate careers to how we raise families and find happiness in our lives, our instincts are to follow a basic rule:

## Having More Resources = Getting Better Results

When you want to complete a project faster, so the logic goes, add more staff. If you want to have a higher impact at work, get a fancier title and a larger office. To prop up a declining product, spend additional marketing dollars. To make schools more effective, hire more teachers. For government to work better, provide a bigger budget. If you want to improve your relationship, buy an expensive gift.

There is a comforting intuition to this approach. It seems only natural that the more you have, the more you can do and the better you'll feel. But as alluring as this sentiment may seem, it regularly fails to produce the best outcomes because it leads us to go after resources we don't need and to overlook the full potential of the resources we already have at hand.

At the time Dick Yuengling expanded his beer business, his chief rival followed the conventional thinking of having more resources = getting better results. Started in 1849 by the German immigrant Bernhard Stroh, the Detroit brewery grew into one of America's largest and most prestigious beer producers. At its peak, it made 31 million barrels annually, ranking it third in the nation.

Peter Stroh, the founder's Princeton-educated great-grandson, became president of the brewery in 1967. The Stroh family had a lot riding on Peter's results. Although many family members did not hold regular positions at the company, each nevertheless collected up to $400,000 in annual dividends (equivalent to about $1 million today). As Frances Stroh tells in her recent memoir, "For decades, the money was flowing and the Strohs lived like kings."

Peter's philosophy on business—"we have to grow or go"—couldn't have been more different from Dick's work-with-what-you-have approach. Peter told his business partners that they needed to become "as big as we can get. We *have* to keep acquiring other brands," borrowing hundreds of millions of dollars along the way.

Even as family members continued to drain the company's profits, the brewer was already on life support. Weighed down by its debt and unable to fully utilize its existing resources, especially its products and brands, the company started rapidly losing market share. Greg Stroh, a former employee and fifth-generation member of the family, said, "It was like going to a gunfight with a knife."

The company closed its one-million-square-foot brewery in Detroit. Peter just couldn't see any way to make it viable. "No combination of civic and labor concessions, even coordinated with capital investment, could make the antiquated Detroit plant cost-efficient," he said.

Not making enough progress on its turnaround, in 1989 Stroh set itself up for a sale to Coors, but shortly after inking an agreement, the potential white knight got cold feet. A decade after its failed sale to Coors, Stroh's liquidated, squandering a family fortune that could have approached $9 billion. As Dick put it, "They'd gotten so big, so fast, it overwhelmed them."

With so much of the industry under pressure, few brewers had the means to take advantage of Stroh's misfortunes. Except one.

Dick Yuengling swooped in to purchase a former Stroh's factory in Tampa, Florida, paying dramatically below its market value. The new facility let him continue to expand while his formerly outsized competitor collapsed under the load of its overexpansion. He upgraded equipment at the plant and had it operational in a mere three months—at a fraction of the cost of a new factory. Under Dick's leadership, the Tampa facility ran with far fewer staff members than comparable plants, and it transformed its beleaguered and disempowered employees inherited from Stroh's into problem solvers who implemented their own ideas for how to make the factory even more productive.

As one of the top three players in the industry, Stroh's had access to tremendous resources. In principle, it should have fared better in the turbulent beer market than the smaller, and more vulnerable, Yuengling operation. But Stroh's faltered because its managers couldn't figure out how to use what they already had to weather stormy conditions. A strong urge to accumulate more in the form of competitors, brands, and workers turned the company's ambitions of rapid expansion into rapid contraction.

There is no doubt that having resources is important. Without talented staff, skills, knowledge, equipment, and the like, it becomes hard to get things done—and get them done well. Yet it's difficult to be productive with what's already in hand when we're distracted by always looking for something in other people's hands. Still worse, it's an awful feeling to think we're always empty-handed.

The approach followed by Stroh's exemplifies what I call *chasing*. Chasing, and those who frequently rely on it, *chasers*, orient themselves around acquiring resources, overlooking how to expand what's already in hand. Their decisions and actions might appear very reasonable on the surface, but I will expose the harmful consequences that lurk deeper and ultimately upend success and make people miserable.

A real difficulty with overcoming chasing is finding an alternative approach. We're surrounded by people who try to convince us that more is better in all aspects of our lives. This brings me to my first aim in this book: to convince you that people like Dick Yuengling and companies like the one he runs turn out to be remarkably successful and satisfied by stretching. Rather than focusing on getting more, people and organizations that stretch build more with what they already possess. For people like Dick Yuengling, how they approach resources looks quite different from chasers:

**Better Use of Resources = Getting Better Results**

To convince you of the benefits of stretching, I will introduce studies and stories that explain how to find success and satisfaction that's hard to get from chasing. People who routinely stretch, those I call *stretchers*, ask what more they can do with what they have, instead of asking what's missing.

## THE NEED TO BE RESOURCEFUL

In 1978, geologists in Siberia stumbled upon a family that had disappeared forty-two years earlier. The six-member Lykov family had fled life-threatening religious persecution and settled within a five-million-square-mile plot of largely uninhabited and treacherous land in the Sayan Mountains. Before they had fled, their life was nowhere near opulent, but exile 160 miles from anything remotely

resembling civilization exceeded any of the challenges they had previously encountered. World War II started and ended without their
knowledge. With typical temperatures near –30 degrees, the physical conditions of their makeshift home rivaled the psychological
challenges of isolated living. In summer, reaching the Lykov family
would have required a weeklong canoe trip. In winter, the harsh
conditions made traveling to the family's location impossible without a helicopter.

The parents, Karp and Akulina, raised two sons, Savin and Dmitry, and two daughters, Natalia and Agafia. The youngest children,
Dmitry and Agafia, entered the world during the family's isolation,
never meeting anyone beyond their parents and siblings until the
geologists' discovery.

Cut off from civilization for decades without modern-day con-
veniences and social interactions outside their immediate kin, the
Lykov family had little choice but to make do with what they had.
Lacking what most of us take for granted, the group of six built a
house with floors made of potato peels and pine nut shells. They
made clothes from hemp seeds and galoshes from birch bark. Without proper hunting equipment, a barefooted Dmitry chased his prey,
sometimes for days, until the animals succumbed to exhaustion.

The Lykov family had learned to adapt to their constraints
and found a way to transform what few things they had into life-
sustaining essentials. But they didn't have a choice. Their very survival depended upon it. Although we might marvel at their ingenuity and feel grateful that our circumstances are far easier, the Lykov
exile, in its extremeness, underscores that people can accomplish
incredible, unimagined things by being resourceful in times of need.

Almost all of us face some type of constraints or limitations. People vary in their desired goals—long-term aims such as achieving
career success, launching a business, finding challenging work, balancing work and family priorities, and raising good kids—as well as

short-term goals like completing a project, learning something new, running a meeting, or helping a child with homework.

People also differ in the resources available to achieve these goals—including time, money, knowledge, skills, connections, and tangible objects.

We regularly encounter gaps between what we want to accomplish and what we have at hand. For some of us, constraints boil down to financial limitations; for others, it might be professional contacts, information, skills, or staff. People who are resourceful act despite these shortcomings and instead ask: How do I take what I have and get the job done?

There's a lot that we can learn from people who overcome constraints. Constraints can motivate us to be resourceful, act in more creative ways, and solve problems better. Importantly, we can harvest these same benefits in *all times* by stretching: making the decision to approach our organizations, jobs, families, and lives in ways that see possibilities in what we have and creatively build on and transform them for the better.

## THE CHOICE TO STRETCH

The French anthropologist Claude Lévi-Strauss observed two different approaches to how people can go about getting stuff done—one called "engineering" and the other "bricolage."

The engineering approach he described involves searching for a specific tool. Chasers endorse this method because they take a narrow view of what resources can do. So if they need to put a nail in the wall, they go buy a hammer. In the absence of a hammer of the right size, shape, and weight, the engineering approach starts to break down. To anticipate their challenges, chasers try to get as

many tools for their toolbox as they can, even when those t[
meet an immediate need. Over time, their toolbox gets l[
larger, eventually making it difficult to remember what's inside.

The bricolage approach favored by stretchers makes good use of
the tools around, experimenting and testing the conventional limitations of what's at hand. If a rock is the only thing around, a stretcher
can pick it up to bang a nail into the wall—or an available brick, can
of beans, high heel, or heavy flashlight.

People can use engineering or bricolage to competently get a nail
into the wall, but with very different consequences. For engineering,
the solution appears elegant and comforting because it conforms to
a typical way to get a nail into a wall. You might find it bizarre if a
carpenter came to your house with a rolling pin to do his work. But
what happens when we extend this reasoning to many of the decisions we regularly make? There's going to be a lot of effort involved
in always securing the right tool for every job. Most of our time and
energy get spent looking for tools and not actually putting nails into
walls. And without the right tool, we are lost. When others have
better tools, we not only feel bad but also think we can't get things
done with our inferior-equipped toolbox.

For bricolage, the challenge depends on breaking free from mental traps that push us always to want to use a hammer, even when
we don't have one handy. There's a certain level of psychological
discomfort that can come from using things in different ways, making our first instinct to go out and buy a hammer and to turn to
bricolage only as a last resort—such as when the hardware store is
closed. But what if we intentionally avoided the hardware store and
forced ourselves to make the most of what we have? We would end
up living a very different type of life, one I'll argue is much more
enjoyable because it calms us with what we already have and teaches
us to use it in better ways. That's why there's a lot more to stretching than simply being resourceful in overcoming constraints. It's an

outlook on life that influences not just how we solve problems but also how we regularly obtain success and live better.

———

The Van Man, as some affectionately refer to him, lives in a beat-up 1978 Volkswagen Westfalia microbus camper nicknamed after the *Scooby Doo* character Shaggy. When the van's engine fails, he tries to repair it with duct tape to avoid the hassles and the cost of taking it to a mechanic. Van Man's portable stove helps him prepare fresh and healthy meals.

In 2015, he spent part of the year parked behind the Dumpster of a Walmart in Dunedin, Florida, which offered the convenience of an on-site general store. In the daytime, the gym, courtesy of the "pull-up" bar that hangs from the shopping cart receptacle, keeps him in top-notch shape. Although Shaggy is not spacious, it does have enough storage to hold Van Man's only pair of jeans, sleeping bag, and journals, which he pens in the evenings when not reading literature. Despite his bizarre living arrangement, Van Man enjoys it because it lets him appreciate what he has without the distractions of what others have. It also brings him closer to the outdoors he cares so much about.

Curious shoppers occasionally stop by his parking space at Walmart, wondering about the seemingly odd person who lives in a van. Some take sympathy on the man's plight, offering him food or money. He politely declines these overtures. When they stop and talk to him, they learn something rather startling.

Van Man is a multimillionaire. He could easily afford one of the spacious homes in the neighborhood. He has chosen the Walmart parking spot not because he's a vagrant but because it puts him in the right head space to stretch to achieve his life's dreams. "When you live out of a van," he says, "you have to appreciate what you have." His personal philosophy: "Life is like the ocean to me. It's gonna send you some good and bad waves, but at the end of the day you're gonna ride whatever comes your way."

The Walmart parking lot also offers the convenience of a three-mile commute to work, where he proudly parks the van next to his colleagues' luxury sports cars and decked-out SUVs. After enjoying some coffee brewed on his stove, he works a job many young kids hope for when they grow up.

Van Man is <u>Daniel Norris</u>—a major league baseball player.

In 2011, Norris was the number one pitching prospect for the Toronto Blue Jays. After receiving his $2 million signing bonus, he did what many people who come into money do. He went shopping. One of his new teammates, who himself had just cashed his own bonus check, organized a three-hour spree at a local mall. Norris's teammates spent tens of thousands of dollars on gadgets and gear. Norris's sole purchase: a Converse shirt he bought on sale for $14. "Just cuz money's there doesn't mean that you gotta have nicer things than you used to," he says.

After signing on for a large salary, Norris worried that having so much money would ruin his lifestyle and distract him from his work and love: playing baseball. He had his financial advisers deposit only $800 a month into his checking account to cover his living expenses, while conservatively investing the rest of his paycheck. His monthly stipend provides income equivalent to roughly half the amount of someone working full time at a minimum wage.

With money tight in his family when he was a child, Norris watched his friends receive new gloves and bats each season, while he kept using his old stuff. He didn't begrudge his parents for not buying him new equipment, reflecting, "Never once did I not have everything that I needed. As a kid, you always have wants. Slowly but surely, I learned to appreciate the things that I did get. I'm so thankful that they raised me that way."

# STRETCH

Even as he pulled in millions of dollars, Norris did what few of his fellow sports players would even consider. He got a second job. He worked during the off-season for forty hours a week at Mahoney's, a local outdoors store in his hometown of Johnson, Tennessee. He didn't need the money to live but simply enjoyed the work. He also spent part of his off-season traveling through Nicaragua, staying in hostels and hiking in the jungle. At first, this puzzled Norris's managers, who wondered why the rising star did not follow his teammates' off-season practices of luxury travel or partying in ritzy South Beach, Florida. The team came to recognize that his way of living kept him focused on what he really cares about: playing baseball.

For Daniel Norris, his life's dream includes excelling as a baseball pitcher and experiencing the wonders of the outdoors—none of which depends on spending millions of dollars. By holing up in his van, Norris escapes the chasing mentality that leaves many sports stars bankrupt and depressed.

In the summer of 2015, the Blue Jays traded Norris to the Detroit Tigers, and a few weeks later, Norris donned the number 44 jersey in his debut at bat in the major leagues. Approaching the plate in the second inning as a hitter for the first time since high school, he knocked the ball out of the park, becoming the first-ever American League pitcher to hit a home run at Chicago's Wrigley Field and only the nineteenth pitcher in baseball history to hit a homer in his first at bat.

When you first learned about Daniel Norris, you likely didn't expect him to be either a multimillionaire or a sports star. You also likely wouldn't have predicted that Dick Yuengling's beer empire exceeded a billion dollars in value. Sports stars should drive fancy cars. Businesses should ramp up as quickly as possible. Multimillionaires should live in spacious homes. More marketing dollars should equate with greater sales. People should buy things simply because they have the money to spend. The makeshift solutions to their work and lives might be what we expect from those who have little, but what Dick Yuengling and Daniel Norris have learned and can teach the rest of us is that stretching helps us achieve great results all the time—no matter how little, or even how much, we have.

Making the most of what we have is what many of us might already do when our backs are against the wall, but I want to convince you to *choose* to stretch in good times just as much as in bad times. My second objective in this book is to teach you how to avoid chasing and to embrace stretching at all times—without living in a van! It's an approach that goes far beyond getting out of difficult situations—it's an entirely different way of living and working to achieve success and fulfillment.

## AVOIDING COMPLACENCY

When we're already successful and satisfied, our natural instinct is to stay the course. We follow routines about how to use resources because that's what has worked in the past. But as we stay the course, the world around us constantly changes: jobs evolve, customers' tastes advance, competitors grow or shrink, families age, and technology shifts. In these situations, our once valuable and cherished resources quickly decline in value, as an apparently flourishing company based in Sweden called Facit learned. It grew into a large and profitable maker of machines and office furnishings. It had many product offerings, but its executives saw the greatest promise in its calculators.

They turned out to be right.

Facit started dominating the market so much that its top managers brushed off suggestions to pursue other opportunities. Instead, the company focused intently on improving the quality of its calculators and lowering its costs. To accelerate its prospects, the company took on a large amount of debt to expand capacity. The company became so good at manufacturing calculators that it rarely encountered product defects.

Customers were happy. Managers were happy. Employees were happy.

In an eight-year period, the company's workforce grew by 70 percent, and profits more than doubled. At its peak, Facit employed fourteen thousand people between its twenty factories, which spanned five countries, and its sales offices, which spread across fifteen countries.

Then, almost without notice, a crisis struck. The company's revenues substantially shrank, its previously stable management team turned over, and its employees were out of work. Even though the quality of its products remained high—some might say the best in its class—no one wanted a Facit calculator. They wanted other companies' calculators instead.

In a matter of years, Facit went from a stellar standout to near bankruptcy, forcing its managers to quickly sell off its remaining assets to a competitor.

It turns out that while Facit continued to make a darn good calculator, it made *mechanical* calculators. In the 1960s, times were good for mechanical-calculator producers such as Facit. The great accomplishments of the company convinced its managers they were on the right track and knew what they were doing. But in the 1970s, Japanese companies started mass-producing electronic calculators. Top managers at Facit shut down efforts to start manufacturing their own electronic calculators, writing off the technology as a distraction to its core mechanical-calculator business. Yet no matter how good Facit's mechanical calculators were, they couldn't match the features of an electronic one.

Success blinds us and reinforces what made us successful in the first place. We stick to what we know and do well, echoing the cliché, "If it ain't broke, don't fix it." Indeed, a host of research in economics and psychology regularly shows that people naturally prefer the status quo. Maintaining the current state of affairs—coasting through a job, putting a team on autopilot, or exploiting a successful market—can work in the short term. And when it works remarkably well, like it did for Facit, it becomes even harder to give up.

The problem, as Facit unfortunately learned, is that the world around us always moves even when we stand still in complacency. Our once valuable resources—an in-demand skill, a high-performing team, a unique product, and the best mechanical calculator—can quickly become worthless.

Doing nothing while the world around us changes makes us an inevitable victim to outside forces. This takes me to the third goal of the book. As uncertainty about our businesses, job, lives, and the world increases, the case for stretching becomes only stronger. I'll show you how stretching equips us with the abilities to adapt and change when facing a less predictable set of circumstances.

## THE PATH TO STRETCHING

When following the pursuits we care about, we rarely have everything we think we need. Whether leading or working in organizations, nurturing families or serving communities, people from all walks of life can become successful and satisfied by embracing stretching and the possibilities it unlocks. Let me tell you how we'll get there.

In the first section of the book, I'll focus on shifting our mind-set from chasing to stretching. We'll need to break free from the typical attitudes and beliefs about resources before moving on to a better way. I will introduce you to people from all walks of life who came to stretching—from those who grew up with very little to those who had too much. We'll learn from their remarkable accomplishments as much as from their everyday activities to find common patterns in how to stretch. I will review the scientific evidence about how chasers get into a costly game of constantly seeking out more, which, over time, diminishes their ability to be resourceful, realize their life's goals, and find fulfillment. By shifting to a stretching mindset, we can better appreciate what we have—recognizing its inherent value and making it even more valuable.

The middle section of the book will introduce a skill set that activates the stretching potential we all have but may not fully recognize or feel permission to use. We'll see the value stretchers have in knowing less than others and learn why it's sometimes smart to build teams by asking those who know the least to do the most. Next, we'll uncover when planning makes it hard to achieve our goals and how stretchers instead spontaneously act without a script. I'll also explain how to grow talent with seemingly so little by asking people to rise to high expectations. The last part of the section will examine how stretchers routinely combine things that don't appear to gel—mixing competition and friendship, work and home priorities, and economic development and environmental responsibility.

Like any approach based on science, stretching has important limitations. For this reason, in the final section of the book, we'll consider the downsides of overstretching—times when we're too cheap, unfocused, quick to act, cursed by high expectations, and responsible for bad combinations of resources. I will conclude the book with some simple but powerful exercises to strengthen a stretch.

The benefits that come from giving up the chase and learning to stretch are well within reach. You've likely already acted resourcefully in some aspects of your life. Have you ever opened a package with your keys instead of a pair of scissors? Have you ever worked beyond your formal responsibilities to make a bigger impact? Have you ever completed a project that no one else thought was possible with what you had? These, and countless other things you may have done, are examples of acting resourcefully.

I want to increase the frequency and potency of these experiences and show you that stretching is a work style and lifestyle you choose to accomplish goals, pursue opportunities, and live better by using and growing what's right in front of you.

# TwO

## THE GRASS IS ALWAYS GREENER

THE CAUSES AND CONSEQUENCES OF A

CHASING MIND-SET

Tucked away in Silicon Valley lies Woodside, California, a charming and posh town of five thousand or so residents ribboned with horse trails and redwood trees. Local stores dot a tiny business district, and the pastoral setting is worlds away from the nearby commercial mega-complexes that house some of the country's largest—and most successful—technology companies. The likes of Steve Jobs, Larry Ellison, and Neil Young have called this exclusive community home. Its spacious mansions sit on top of lushly landscaped lots complete with sparkling swimming pools—the kinds of estates that fill the pages of *Architectural Digest*. A median household income nearing $200,000 makes it one of country's most prosperous areas, but the opulence of the neighborhood masks a great irony.

It's a rich place that is poor in a critical natural resource—water. California's worst drought of the modern era has done little to convince some residents to change their behaviors, with thousands of gallons of precious water devoted to keeping up the lawns of these estate houses at a time of great scarcity. Three hundred of the community's tony homes use more than seventy-five thousand gallons of water a month. In nearby but far less affluent East Palo Alto, homes average about fifteen hundred gallons a month. Some Woodside families have largely ignored the water crisis, but others have adapted in resourceful ways, from funneling wastewater from washing machines to their backyards to hiring workers to spray paint their grass green.

This is not the first time some moneyed Californians have ignored a water crisis. The state's last major drought, which peaked in 1990, saw the billionaire Harold Simmons—who gained notoriety for bankrolling the swift-boat advertisements that sank John Kerry's 2004 presidential hopes—publicly wrestle with his municipality over water usage. The business tycoon paid $25,000 in fines to consume nearly 10 million gallons of water a year on the estate he rarely visited. The astounding usage could have supplied an average family of four with water for almost three decades. After the municipal water district restricted his supply, he hired tanker trucks to import water to keep the sprinklers running.

California may be the epicenter of the current water crisis, but in communities across the country, homeowners regularly go to great lengths to keep their grass green. Why?

Researchers at Vanderbilt University interviewed a demographically representative group of residents of the greater Nashville, Tennessee, area about their lawn-care practices. It turns out that a desire to keep up with the neighbors motivated homeowners to direct so many resources to get greener grass, a finding that held up after accounting for age, education, and property values. Homes represent the ultimate marker of success, and are high-profile places to show off that success—the richness of the lawn reflects the wealth of the people who live inside.

The ways people maintain their lawns tells us a lot about ourselves and the choices we make. When chasing, it's easy to get caught up in pursuing things because others have or want them. As resources get scarcer, chasing becomes more difficult, expensive, stressful, and even impractical. Eventually, the well runs dry (in this case, it literally did), and the constant stream of resources ends.

In this chapter, we'll examine the psychological foundations of chasing, which is not just found in the pursuit of green grass but in many domains that shape our well-being and prospects for success. We'll start with the social comparisons that drive us constantly to want what others have and underappreciate the value of what's already around. Afterward, we'll look at a psychology phenomenon called functional fixedness that prevents us from viewing resources as capable of more. The consequence of this is we look to acquire as many resources as possible to meet challenges or realize opportunities, which is a distraction from getting things done. We'll then turn to understanding our tendency to accumulate resources mindlessly and conclude by examining how having too many resources can lead us to squander them. Understanding how chasing unravels our functioning and fulfillment is a first step to embracing stretching.

# S T R E T C H

## IT'S ALL RELATIVE

Every four years, the world's greatest athletes gather in a new city to compete in the Summer Olympics. When the *Daily Mail* newspaper photographed Olympic medalists during the 2012 summer games in London, its staff observed a surprising pattern among some of the winners. American swimmers Nathan Adrian, Michael Phelps, Cullen Jones, and Ryan Lochte somberly wore their medals on the podium for the 4x100 freestyle relay. Colombian cyclist Rigoberto Urán Urán looked disappointed. American gymnast McKayla Maroney's face twisted up as if she were unimpressed by her medal. Spain's triathlete Javier Gómez looked incredibly sad, and China's top badminton star, Wang Yihan, struggled to hold back tears of sadness when receiving her medal.

What did these champions have in common, besides their dour expressions?

They'd won silver medals.

This observation is no surprise to Northwestern University researcher Victoria Medvec and her colleagues, who studied videotape from NBC television footage of the 1992 Summer Olympics in Barcelona, Spain. They captured the reactions of athletes upon finishing their competition as well as during their award ceremonies. Afterward, the research team asked twenty university students without knowledge of what happened during the games to view the tapes and rate each Olympian using a ten-point scale, anchored from agony to ecstasy, for the type of emotions they expressed at the end of their competition and, if relevant, on the awards podium.

It turns out that bronze medalists had a much higher tendency to be close to ecstasy compared to silver medalists, even though the bronze medalists did objectively worse in the competition. To explain these results, the researchers acquired additional NBC footage of interviews with the medalists immediately after their events. They then had ten different university students assess the extent to which the athletes expressed thoughts and sentiments more closely resembling "at least I" or "I almost." The "at least I" statements represented a focus on what the athletes had accomplished, whereas the "I almost" statements emphasized what they had failed to accomplish. The students also assessed the extent to which the athletes explicitly made comparisons to those competitors who finished worse, comparisons to those who finished better, or no comparisons to other athletes.

Silver medalists focused more on what they had failed to accomplish (win gold) compared to bronze medalists. They also made more envious comparisons to the gold medalists who finished ahead, wallowing in their relative inadequacy. In contrast, the bronze medalists who finished behind the silver winners focused on what they did accomplish (winning a medal).

The roots of the pursuit of green grass and the surprising sorrows of the 2012 London silver medalists trace back to the work of one of the world's most prominent psychologists, Leon Festinger. In 1954, Festinger proposed that all people have a basic tendency to want to know where they stand. He argued that it is hard for us to evaluate ourselves in isolation. Instead, we must look to others to get a better sense of ourselves across areas of our lives we care about, such as wealth, intelligence, and status. Visible markers of our standing include things we can readily measure—the price of a car, the square footage of an office, the size of a budget, the greenness of a lawn, or even the color of an Olympic medal. A 150-square-foot office is big if most offices are 120 square feet but minuscule if most are 180 square feet. The more measurable the resource, the easier it becomes to compare to others. This idea of measuring up is something called upward social comparisons.

Although sometimes looking up to those of greater accomplishment motivates us, upward social comparisons are dangerous when they focus on the allotment of others' resources, emphasizing what others have and leaving us feeling less than adequate. We might be very satisfied with our group's budget until we learn about another group's larger one. Our 6 percent raise generates delight until we find out that a colleague received 8 percent. By always comparing to others who have more, social comparisons make us less likely to appreciate and recognize the many things we can accomplish by being resourceful.*

The allure of upward social comparisons is that they help answer basic questions about how we are doing. For this reason, they become hard to live without and difficult to avoid. Yet they tie our sense of self to the fortunes of those around us. These comparisons also lead us to overlook asking ourselves: What can we be doing to live constructive and happier lives with what we do have?

Consider the entrepreneur Gary Kremen, founder of Match. com, who gloomily referred to his own situation in Silicon Valley: "You're nobody here at $10 million." When making upward social comparisons about resources, even people like Gary Kremen inevitably become disappointed with what they have. Psychologists use the metaphor of a treadmill to describe these experiences—when we get more resources, our minds increase the pace of the treadmill. To stay on the treadmill, we have to run faster even though we get no farther. We simply replace our comparison with someone who has even more, leaving us perpetually let down. Silver medalists look up to

---

* We also make social comparisons to come out on top. These downward social comparisons relate our resources to those people who we think are worse off than us. For example, if we want to feel important on the job, we can get out of our 120-square-foot office to walk through a row of cubicles on the way to the watercooler, while avoiding the 150-square-foot office. On the other hand, downward social comparison can sometimes motivate people. Organizational psychologist Dave Mayer recently summarized research on benign envy. See www.fastcompany.com/3060994.

gold medalists; gold medalists look up to multiyear gold medalists; millionaires look up to billionaires; and the residents of Woodside, California, can't help but survey their even-better-off neighbors to see who's on top. Whether greener grass or golder medals, upward social comparisons make people feel dissatisfied with their lot and motivate them to go seek out *more*. If they get more, they escalate the set of upward comparisons, running faster on their proverbial treadmill to stay in place.

Although few of us live in lavish neighborhoods, most of us are surrounded by people who, at least on some dimensions, have something we don't have. The spread of social media has also led to twenty-four/seven streams of updates that make upward social comparisons a part of our daily lives. We learn about Facebook friends who climb mountains and buy expensive clothes and gadgets, but we rarely see posts about the mundane details of time spent waiting at the doctor's office, paying bills, typing a report at work, or going for an oil change. In our professional circles, LinkedIn provides a similar list of updates about new jobs, promotions, and gained credentials. Companies of all sizes regularly use social media to boast of their accomplishments. These carefully constructed images designed for public consumption often have unintended (or, in some cases, intended) consequences of triggering comparisons that make people feel bad.

To understand how social media influences chasing, a group of researchers sent text messages to eighty-two participants from diverse cultural backgrounds five times a day for two weeks. Text messages occurred randomly between 10:00 a.m. and midnight. Each text message contained a link to a survey that asked questions such as: "How do you feel right now?" "How worried are you right now?" "How lonely do you feel right now?" "How much have you used Facebook since the last time we asked?" and "How much have you interacted with other people directly since the last time we asked?"

# S T R E T C H

The psychologists measured participants' well-being and life satisfaction and found that the more time people spent using Facebook, the worse they felt, and suggest that the decrease in happiness comes from upward social comparisons.

Why might social media trigger the type of social comparisons that make us less happy? It turns out that while 78 percent of participants used Facebook to share good news, only 36 percent used it to share bad news. People post their gold medal performances, not their last place finishes.

Chasing does more than make us miserable. It also degrades our ability to stretch. It blinds us to seeing resources as more than what they appear on the surface. In contrast, stretching allows us to work with untapped potential, just like one of my childhood heroes.

## WHEN A BAROMETER BECOMES A RULER

Growing up, I frequently watched the television show *MacGyver*. The 1980s program depicted Angus MacGyver as a secret agent who could solve virtually any problem (and save lives) with little more than a pocketknife, duct tape, or the ordinary household goods he found lying around. Despite lacking specialized resources, Mac, as his friends called him, always found a way to use whatever was around to craft clever solutions to the seemingly unsolvable dilemmas he faced. From stopping bombs with paper clips to using motor oil to peer through frosted glass, Mac skipped the regular tactics of action heroes and used science to transform everyday objects into a versatile set of tools to battle crooks and criminals.

We remember Mac for his pocketknife and disarmament skills, but his ability to be resourceful carried over to other walks of life. In one episode, Mac took up coaching a high-school ice hockey team and sprang into action when a star player's tremendous physical skills could not compensate for emotional immaturity. Frequent fights routinely put the star player in the penalty box and even sent an opponent to the hospital. An unscrupulous scout pursued the hockey prodigy to add talent to a struggling team, with the hope that the hotheaded kid would bully opponents and use brute behavior to win at any cost. The episode culminates with Mac embracing the boy as much more than a troubled kid. By helping the young man rethink the meaning of success, Mac transforms him into a better person, on the rink and off.

Whether working with what many consider a difficult situation—limited tools and in this case a troubled child—Mac focused on expanding the value of what he had. People who chase take a very different approach. Caught up in the belief that more resources will deliver better results, they think about resources as having limited uses and are compelled to acquire as much as possible. When obstacles prevent chasers from acquiring new resources—after all, they might not be able to move to a bigger office with a better title or hire an extra person for their project—their projects and goals get put on hold.

The difficulty chasers have in emulating Mac comes from the conventional view of resources as fixed to specific uses: a paper clip holds paper together; a competitor is someone who threatens one's business; a map is something that provides accurate directions. For stretchers like Mac, resources can take on many nonconventional uses: a paper clip can be used to stitch a wound; a competitor's insights can improve the business's product offerings; even a wrong map can be used to navigate to the right destination.

To illustrate the psychological block of chasers who narrow their view of resources, imagine yourself as the protagonist in a parable told by scientist and teacher Alexander Calandra. You are a physics student interacting with your mentor. You worked hard and learned a lot about physics, and your teacher calls you to his office to demonstrate your knowledge of the subject. The teacher's challenge question: Explain how you can measure the height of a tall building using a barometer. The physics teacher has thought very hard about this problem and believes there is only one right answer. Examine barometer readings at the top of the building relative to readings at the bottom of the building.

When asked for your response, you provide several different answers: tie a rope to the barometer, lower it to street level, and measure the length of the rope; walk up the stairs with the barometer, using it as a ruler; and ask the building's superintendent the height of the building in exchange for the barometer.

These nonconventional uses of the barometer reflect someone who expands his thinking in unexpected ways. The teacher, steeped in the conventions of physics, misses the many different ways that barometers can help solve the challenge. In much the same way, chasers tend to treat barometers, or any resource for that matter, at face value.

Psychologists call the rigidity demonstrated by the physics teacher *functional fixedness*—an inability to use a resource beyond the traditional approach. It turns out that as we grow older, we become even more tied to social conventions, making it that much more difficult to envision what we have beyond their common uses.

If there's one group of people least prone to conforming to conventions, it is children who have not yet been fully socialized on how to "properly" use a resource. Researchers Tim German and Greta Defeyter presented children with building blocks, a pencil, an eraser, a ball, a magnet, a toy car, and a wooden box. They told them that Bobo the Bear could not jump and had short legs, yet he wanted his toy lion on a shelf out of his reach. Could the kids help Bobo by using only the tools provided?

As children grow older, their cognitive skills advance in ways that should help them solve difficult problems such as finding a way to get to Bobo's toy. Indeed, the oldest children in the study (six- and seven-year-olds) were able to find a correct solution (i.e., using the wooden box to prop up the building blocks) faster, on average, than the younger participants (five-year-olds).

But in one experimental condition, the younger children actually outperformed their older classmates. Were these children particularly precocious and gifted? Artistic?

None of these factors mattered. What made the difference was that the researchers made a subtle change in how they presented the resources. Instead of laying out all of the resources on the table, the researchers used the wooden box as a container to store the other resources, such as the magnet and pencil. This led older children to see the box as only a container. Yet for younger children, the box remained just as flexible a resource as it was before.

As we grow older and gain more experience with using resources in familiar ways, it becomes more difficult to break free from functional fixedness. At work, at school, and around the neighborhood, strong norms condition us to use resources in customary ways, causing us to too quickly discard what's around and instead seek out more. By adopting a stretching mind-set, which we'll cover in the next chapter, we can we break this pattern.

———————

Organizations also fall prey to functional fixedness. A year before my wife, Randi, started working for the book retailer Borders in 2002, the company signed an agreement to outsource its website so that it could focus on growing its brick-and-mortar sales. The company's primary hope was to steal market share from its chief rival, Barnes and Noble, by opening additional stores.

# STRETCH

The mega-chain took a very narrow view of its positioning. Staff, products, processes, and stores emphasized physical bookselling. Management struggled to view a book buyer as anyone other than a customer who walks into a store and walks out with bound pages— these were the company's "boxes" fixed to conventional uses.

At the time of its outsourcing partnership, the CEO of Borders, Greg Josefowicz said, "While our customers' needs are met online by the people who do it better than anyone else, we will provide them with what we do best: the books, music and movies they love to explore in an engaging shopping atmosphere."

It turned out that Borders' customer needs became met so well online that they stopped shopping in its stores and defected to its online partner. Who was this partner?

Amazon.com.

Jeff Bezos, Amazon's CEO, welcomed Borders' customers with open arms, collecting a massive amount of data on their shopping habits that allowed his company to expand its array of products and eventually acquire those customers. Bezos was so ecstatic at the deal that he even shipped a case of Champagne for the Borders executives to enjoy.

Five years after Borders inked the deal that many think ultimately doomed the company, the company had another shot. Randi was assigned the responsibility of exploring nonphysical book formats. Even though Amazon started dominating online physical-book buying, technology changed so rapidly that she saw an opportunity to leapfrog physical-book distribution and move to an all-digital world. With her team, she had worked to secure an exclusive sale of the Sony Reader, which promised to be the world's first commercially viable digital-reading device—ahead of both Amazon's Kindle and Apple's iPad.

Randi stopped by the office of George Jones, who recently had taken over as CEO, to demo the device. He was impressed, but she thought he was steadfast at focusing on the company's traditional business of physical books in stores. As 2006 came to an end, Borders posted its last annual profit; Randi left the company shortly thereafter, frustrated by its narrow view of bookselling. Five years later, the company liquidated in bankruptcy.

## WHY WE WORK TOO HARD

So far we have considered two main foundations of chasing—social comparisons and functional fixedness. The first depends on sizing up our resources relative to others, which often leaves us disappointed, spurs us to seek out more resources, and makes us overlook the value of what we have. The second leads us to take a fixed view of resources, limiting what we think is possible with what's at hand and therefore prompting us to go get more. Let's now examine a third foundation of chasing—mindless accumulation. When chasing, we rack up as many resources as possible, not because we have a specific goal in mind but rather just to collect more.

In a clever study, University of Chicago professor Christopher Hsee and his colleagues wanted to understand if people accumulated more resources than they needed at the expense of their happiness. He asked participants to listen to music—a leisure activity that people enjoy. Participants could earn bite-size Dove chocolate bars by doing a little work: they had to press a button. Pressing the button also interrupted their leisurely music with the annoying sound of a saw cutting wood.

The researchers randomly assigned some participants as "high earners," meaning that their work pressing the button yielded them more chocolates compared to "low earners." High earners needed to press the button 20 times to earn a Dove bar, while low earners needed to press the button 120 times for the same payout. Importantly, the researchers told participants at the beginning of the study they could not take any leftover chocolate with them. Not surprisingly, high earners acquired on average 10.7 chocolates, compared to low earners' 2.5 chocolates.

After earning, the participants could consume the chocolate. High earners ate an average of 4.3 chocolates, compared with 1.7 for low earners. Both groups acquired more chocolate than they could indulge, but the high earners acquired dramatically more than they could eat. High earners focused on accumulating the most, and not on thinking about whether they would want to, or even would be able to, eat all of the chocolate.

Hsee next wanted to see if he could minimize the tendency of participants to mindlessly accumulate chocolate. In a follow-up study, he randomly told some participants they could earn only up to 12 Dove bars. Participants informed about this cap worked to earn 8.8 chocolates, compared with 14.6 for those not bound by the cap. By placing restrictions on the most they could earn, the researchers successfully got some participants to calibrate better between what they needed and their chocolate-eating desires. Indeed, after the earning phase, the participants in both groups consumed, on average, 6.7 chocolates, leading the capped condition to accumulate chocolate at a level far closer to what they actually consumed.

For chasers, the amount of resources they acquire serves as their primary measuring stick, so having more chocolate = getting better results. Yet, even though mindless accumulation led the uncapped group to get more chocolate, they had lower levels of satisfaction, both while earning the chocolate and eating the chocolate.

It was participants in the capped condition who had higher rates of satisfaction. Chasing might sometimes lead us to get more stuff, but it's stuff we don't often need to pursue our goals, and it frequently burns us out.

The more important question we should ask: What do we really want to accomplish?

---

For years, twenty-seven-year-old Joshua Millburn didn't ask this question. He rose to become the youngest director at Cincinnati Bell, a billion-dollar regional telephone provider, climbing up from retail-salesclerk to director of operations, a position that oversaw 150 retail stores—all without a college degree. As Millburn's professional and apparent personal success increased, his social comparison group escalated quickly. Millburn moved from hanging out with salesclerks to spending time with executives, surrounding himself with colleagues with even more impressive titles and much more money.

When there's a wide gap between the haves and the have-nots, more chasing kicks in as the distance between who we are and what we see in others widens. Millburn made good money, but others made even better money, prompting him to double his efforts.

Times seemed good, and his six-figure salary, multiple luxury cars, and spacious house full of material possessions showed that he had made it. With his eager eye squarely on the c-suite, Millburn thought he was living the American dream. The comic George Carlin humorously said this of the American dream: "The reason they call it the American Dream is because you have to be asleep to believe it." A 2014 survey of 1,821 Americans shows that Carlin's concern is no joking matter. Eighty percent of people believed that the American dream is harder to achieve than it was a decade before, making Millburn's accomplishments that much more impressive.

As Millburn racked up raises and rewards, he never reflected on what he truly wanted from his life, why he kept chasing more, or even what the American dream meant . . . until tragedy struck. His mother died and his wife divorced him, just weeks apart. As sad as these events proved to be, they interrupted his life of chasing. He used his personal tragedies to rescue himself from the possibility of a lifetime of misery from chasing and instead began to pursue lifelong satisfaction through stretching.

Millburn reflected on his life's path for the first time in years, a life where social comparisons dangerously mixed with mindless accumulation. What he came to realize was that the American dream carves out a very narrow path to well-being. It sets expectations and shapes behaviors in ways that convince people to chase after things they might not need or want, while overlooking the costs of this pursuit.

Chasing kept pushing Joshua Millburn to want more, but it eventually left him with less. He had all the trappings of a wildly successful professional and personal life, but he stewed in anxiety and unhappiness, trying to soothe himself by advancing further in his career in order to fund purchases that would purportedly make him feel better. The self-medicating aspect of consumption made matters worse. He amassed a lot of debt because he spent money faster than he earned it. In trying to keep up with others on the job, he clocked in so many hours a week that he undermined his physical and mental health, sacrificing his personal relationships and robbing him of his zest for living and vitality. "I really hadn't focused on the things that were most important. I was working seventy- to-eighty-hour weeks, 362 days a year. I wasn't present, either in the marriage or the rest of my life. I didn't hate the job, but everything else was diminished," he says.

Backing up Millburn's insights, researchers followed working professionals in Europe over a seven-year period after they completed a master's degree. Eight hundred twenty-five women and 1,105 men responded to survey questions about their chasing tendencies, such as "I want to make a lot of money" and "I want to gain high occupational reputation." The researchers checked in with the participants three years and seven years after graduation to measure how much money they made. Although career chasing led to obtaining higher salaries in the short term, it failed to predict a higher salary seven years out. More strikingly, career chasing negatively predicted career  satisfaction seven years later. The researchers concluded that chasing sets such high aspirations that it leaves people perpetually disappointed, especially when compared to the success of someone else. People work hard for the wrong reasons—and are worse off for it.

Organizations also uncontrollably chase for more, and perhaps nowhere is this more apparent than with one of the largest destructions of wealth in history.

## HOW TOO MUCH CAN TURN A BOOM INTO A BUST

At the turn of the twenty-first century, Silicon Valley became home to California's most recent gold rush. The dotcom boom created remarkable prospects for riches and rewarding work. Week after week new companies would complete initial public offerings (IPOs), rewarding their venture capitalist funders and employees with lofty payouts. Start-ups with not much more than an idea, let alone a profit, transformed into publicly traded giants worth hundreds of millions of dollars.

Pets.com was the poster child of the dotcom era. During its first year of operations, the company spent almost $12 million on advertising to generate a whopping $619,000 in sales. In its second and last full year of operations, it spent over a million dollars on a thirty-second Super Bowl commercial to funnel business to its website that sold goods below cost. Its founders and earliest employees were worth millions—at least on paper, and for a little while. The company ultimately squandered its long leash of funding to the tune of $300 million. In a mere 268 days, the company went from an initial public offering (IPO) at $11 per share on the NASDAQ stock exchange to a final closing price of 22 cents before ultimately liquidating what few assets remained.

The dotcom companies had an insatiable appetite for resources, especially capital and engineers. Their mode of operation followed the chasing principle of having more resources = getting better results, leading them to acquire as many resources as they could, expend them, and ask for more.

Using a seemingly limitless supply of resources as fuel, the start-up business model during the boom times involved growing as quickly as possible, whatever the cost, and rewarding overworked employees with perks from massages to foosball tables, along with the promise of big payoffs in the future. New money would refill dwindling cash coffers much the same way that novel employee perks and stock options would reinvigorate spirits. As long as resources kept flowing, life in Silicon Valley flourished for both its companies and its workers . . . until, one day, the resources stopped flowing. Companies that had become addicted to free-flowing resources struggled to adapt and survive.

Professor David Kirsch of the University of Maryland wanted to document and understand this historic time for American businesses and started the Digital Archive of the Birth of the Dot Com Era. The archive captured millions of e-mail messages, memos, presentations, pictures, and databases on thousands of early Internet companies. Although the dotcom bust put many of these companies out of business, Professor Kirsch's data shows that around half of them actually survived.

The survivors' common strategy: ignoring the "get big fast" business model that dominated everything from boardroom discussions to cocktail conversations. They avoided the heady quest for more capital, more engineers, more advertising, and more customers from the onset by building businesses that grew at a more modest and measured pace. The type of slow-and-steady business approach Professor Kirsch found that surviving companies used to navigate the dotcom bust successfully is hard to follow when a mentality of having more resources = getting better results persists, as it does today.

---

If you think the chasing from the dotcom era is long gone, all you need to do is visit an office building in South of Market (SOMA), the former warehouse district—now replete with trendy nightclubs and just minutes from San Francisco's famed Union Square, which attracts hordes of tourists for luxury shopping. At the height of the dotcom boom, commercial rents for the neighborhood's office space, where the likes of Pets.com operated, fetched about sixty bucks a square foot. As the dotcom boom busted, office space fell to about twenty bucks a square foot.

As chasing returned to Silicon Valley with the rise of social media companies, the next generation of post–boom-to-bust start-ups has moved into SOMA, pushing its office rents close to their dotcom peaks. Jeffrey Moeller advises companies seeking commercial real estate in the area. A survivor of the dotcom market crash, he's witnessed firsthand the mistakes that cash-rich start-ups made, from renting excessively large spaces to signing too-long leases. Along with rising rents, companies have outfitted their spaces in extraordinary ways, trying to outdo each other with the latest perks—from onsite music studios to classrooms to host lessons about making Jell-O shots. "When you raise a lot of money," says entrepreneur Justin Kan, "it's easy to try to solve your problems by spending money."

# STRETCH

The same goes even for established companies in Silicon Valley that never kicked the habit of relying on endless resources. When she was at Google, Marissa Mayer was known to post a sign outside of her office that read: "Revenues solve all problems." Dylan Casey, a Yahoo executive, summed up the implication of the slogan at Yahoo: "When you have a fire hose of cash coming in, it's like, 'Problems? Who cares.'"

A focus on trying to one-up each other's business—from the latest perks to the most compelling office space—also creates an unwinnable competition. Companies try to outspend one another in the pursuit of the most talented engineers, plushest offices, and most generous perks—constantly raising the stakes and costs for everyone. Bill Demas, a former boss of mine at Vividence, served as CEO of digital platform advertiser Turn, which raised over $100 million in funding. Demas says he felt incredible pressure to grow, and grow fast. Private markets reward growth metrics, such as customers, while overlooking more traditional measures such as profitability. Employees feel entitled to large salaries and generous option packages that vest on a four-year clock, meaning if companies don't strike it rich during this time frame, employees are likely to jump ship to the next big possibility. Demas observes that everyone's focus on getting more—salary, customers, funding—shifts the mentality away from the resourcefulness that helped get many new enterprises off the ground. "Creativity and discipline gets lost as you simply want to grow so much so quickly," he says.

Perhaps no company wanted to grow as much as Jason Goldberg's Fab.com, founded in 2010. The gleeful CEO boasted that the company was "crushing it" and that "every investor and their mother" lined up to hand him wads of greenbacks. With eleven rounds of funding totaling over $335 million, Goldberg did what chasers so frequently do. He spent it, and spent it fast, adding head count, opening up ninety distribution centers, and at one point burning through $14 million in cash per month.

Every time Goldberg raked in more investor cash, the value of his company magically grew. The more he spent, the more people seemed to reward him, allowing him ultimately to grow the valuation of Fab.com to $1 billion. Goldberg's motto, "Grow now, figure it out later," worked as long as resources kept flowing in, and deep-pocketed investors eagerly forked over money after hearing his simple but compelling pitch: "Look, there are four e-commerce companies in the world that are worth more than $10 billion. Is it possible to have a fifth?"

As his company's value rose on paper, the proud businessman shared with Facebook friends pictures of himself driving his BMW convertible and taking private helicopter rides. He even ranted on social media about another first-class passenger's refusal to accept his offer to switch seats for $100. Apparently, those accustomed to limitless resources may even feel entitled to your warm seat.

Unlike Joshua Millburn, Jason Goldberg didn't get off his escalating chase until it was too late. As soon as his backers stopped feeding his hungry operation, the company crashed hard. It sold at a fire sale price that left investors with substantial losses and the world without another $10 billion e-commerce company.

As Jason Goldberg learned, acquiring resources can prove far easier than using those resources in productive ways. The problem is that chasers become so fixated on acquiring resources that they lose sight of what those resources will do for them, leading to a fourth misstep caused by relentless chasing: resource squandering.

Harvard Business School dean Nitin Nohria and his colleague Ranjay Gulati studied consumer electronics subsidiaries at two multinational companies, one European-based and the other Japanese-based. The researchers sent surveys to 256 department managers to identify how well the businesses improved in key areas such as streamlining work procedures and enhancing products. They then had the department managers quantify the economic impact of each improvement, such as the yearly savings from it or the additional sales it facilitated. Afterward, Nohria and Gulati measured the slack, or additional resources, the companies had in their departments but did not really need.

The researchers found that some extra resources helped drive improvement because it allowed the departments freedom to experiment. They could take risks knowing they wouldn't topple the business. But there was an important twist in their data, an inflection point where the opposite happens. Departments with too many spare resources become less likely to improve—so much so that those departments with the highest amount of extra resources get as equally poor results as those with no spare resources.

Nohria and Gulati reason that when resources—such as people and money—are abundant, they need to be used even if there is no good reason. A careless pursuit of projects and the continuation of poorly performing projects follow—whether hiring people not needed or taking on more expensive and expansive office space. Too much also makes us complacent and unengaged. We pass on important projects because of a lack of urgency. Why worry when a fire hose of cash and other resources is coming in the door?

Another reason we squander resources is that we've already invested them. It's what University of California–Berkeley professor Barry Staw calls escalation of commitment. In one study, Staw asked 240 business school students to play the role of a corporate executive and allocate research and development funds for a fictitious company called Adams & Smith. The large technology firm had seen its profitability decline, and its board reasoned that underinvestment in the firm's research and development was the culprit.

Staw split the participants into two groups. The first half were asked to select one of two divisions to receive the entire sum of $10 million of funds provided by the board, whereas the other half were told that another person had made the choice about which division to fund. Since the first group actively selected which division to fund, they were personally responsible for the decision. The second group simply learned of the decision another person had made, avoiding personal responsibility for the initial decision.

The experiment then fast-forwards five years to when participants learn that the company's board allocated an additional $20 million, but this time both groups of participants would dish out the money, and in any proportion across the two divisions. To aid the decision, the researchers provided information about how each division performed during the previous five years. Within each of the two existing groups (those with personal responsibility for the first funding decision and those without personal responsibility), participants either learned that the division initially allocated the entire $10 million performed better than the other division, or that the division not chosen performed better. If people acted rationally, we'd expect that when performance declined participants would allocate fewer resources.

Yet, Staw found something very different. When participants had personal responsibility for the first five years' funding, they doubled down on their choice in the face of poor performance, allocating about $13 million of the $20 million to the declining division. For participants who didn't have personal responsibility for the choice to fund the poorly performing division, the allocation was much more limited, about $9.5 million.

When people have high personal responsibility for a project, they escalate their commitment to the project by investing additional resources to try to turn things around, even if offered more promising options instead. Having lots of resources only increases the tendency to escalate commitment and squander even more. With so much extra to go around, even bad ideas can look good.

# STRETCH

## THE MYTH OF MORE

The people and organizations we have met in this chapter illustrate the four elements of chasing: upward social comparisons, functional fixedness, mindless accumulation, and resource squandering. Motivated by what others have, and fueled by a lack of appreciation for what they do have, chasing leads to working and living in ways that depend on a constant stream of resources, closing off the possibility of better using what's already at hand.

In the short term, chasing might reap some rewards. But in the longer term, it makes people less satisfied and successful. Chasers blame setbacks on not having enough and miss opportunities to stretch what's already around them. They direct their energy into accumulating more. Ironically, as chasers accumulate more, they frequently squander what they have, resting on their seemingly good fortunes and convincing themselves that the party will never end.

When we chase, the grass is always greener on the other side. Ted Steinberg, a legal and history professor who has studied our quest for the greenest grass, points out an irony to all this. When ogling our neighbors' lawns from a distance, the angle of sight from which we observe their lawns creates an illusion of richer-looking grass. Our own grass is, indeed, often just as lush and green as our neighbors'. Once we realize this, we can change the way we think about pursuing the right things and become resourceful for the better. This starts with shifting our mind-set from chasing to stretching, which we're now ready to tackle in the next chapter.

# THREE

## ALL THINGS RICH AND BEAUTIFUL

### THE BASICS AND BENEFITS OF A

### STRETCHING MIND-SET

n 2010, I visited Chicago to research a company I will call BoutiqueCo, a chain of women's clothing, jewelry, and accessories stores. Three Korean American siblings started the company in 1999 because the family's manufacturing business had extra merchandise it couldn't sell.

The first store had strong sales, with customers finding the displays featuring jewelry, gifts, and accessories a compelling mix. The inviting boutiques—adorned with glowing lamps, scented candles, and floral arrangements—appealed to the senses and catered to eighteen- to thirty-four-year-old women with household incomes of $75,000 or more.

Using profits generated from existing sites, the family opened several more locations. The Chicago-area store I came to observe was part of an expansion that got under way during the throes of the Great Recession of 2008. At a time when a downtrodden economy and poor consumer sentiment led major retailers to cut hours, close stores, or even go out of business, BoutiqueCo dispatched a fifty-two-foot truck full of merchandise to open a new location each week, allowing the company to grow from sixty-five stores in 2007 to more than six hundred stores throughout the United States in 2015. Each store customized its merchandising to retain the charm of an independent, local boutique.

I arrived early one morning to observe the company's expansion efforts in action. I watched a team of four employees from nearby stores start transforming an empty space into a beautiful boutique in less than five days, using thirteen pallets' worth of boxes stuffed with merchandise.

Within minutes of arriving to start my research, the crew's leader asked me to start working hands-on. I ambivalently complied, feeling excited by the new experience but intimidated by my lack of knowledge or experience with women's fashion and boutique shopping.

I started tinkering with a cache of hard, yet bendable, silver-colored loops I had found piled in a shipment box. I could flex, twist, and fold them into a variety of forms. My first instinct was to label them stress relievers (since they made me feel a little less anxious as I worked outside my comfort zone). But what I had actually unpacked was moldable jewelry. I could shape a piece into many different products, elongating it into a necklace, wrapping it around the wrist to make a bracelet, or turning it into a headband. I eventually made a stand out of the product itself, using it to display other moldable jewelry, even though functioning as a stand was not its intended use.

As I traveled from store to store around the country, I observed other employees having similar experiences to mine with the moldable jewelry—moments when they too applied new uses for what they had in hand—with products, processes, or even people.

If the cornerstone of chasing is to seek out as many resources as possible, the foundation of stretching is to focus on what we already have. A stretching mind-set releases us from the anxiety of never having enough and teaches us that we can make more than enough with what's right here.

In this chapter, we'll cover four critical elements of a stretching mind-set. First, we'll start with the importance of psychological ownership. By believing that we control our resources, we allow ourselves to work with them in expansive and inventive ways. Afterward, we'll learn why embracing constraints can counterintuitively liberate us to use resources in different ways. When chasing, we see constraints as something we need to overcome by getting more resources. But when we stretch, we use constraints to spark new uses for what's already around. Next, we'll cover frugality, which signals a lack of status and success for chasers, but when stretching we'll learn why it's a virtue that achieves better results. We'll conclude by observing how stretchers appreciate and see potential in resources that others overlook or dismiss, turning trash into treasure.

## WHY PEOPLE WITH LESS OWN MORE

After helping set up BoutiqueCo's newest Chicago location, I paid a visit to one of its existing stores in the heart of the city. It was bustling with customers hovering over gift tables, while a relaxed sales staff stayed out of their way. The urban vibe differed considerably from some of the suburban stores I had observed earlier in the month, where salesclerks could be found outfitting shoppers or phoning their best customers to inform them of new products or promotions. After passing through racks of clothing, spinners gleaming with costume jewelry, and tables touting clever gifts, I located Ethan Peters, the twentysomething manager, near the back of the store. We headed to a basement storage area, away from the buzz and energy of the sales floor above.

We sat down on a couple of stools, and I asked Ethan to tell me how he had repeatedly led the company's strongest-performing store. He started by contrasting his current job with the one he had left at a nearby mall. Ethan had become frustrated with the traditional retailing model at his former job, where home office staff told him how to approach everything from creating merchandise displays to training new employees to greeting customers. "Things are very regimented. Everything has to be a certain way," he told me. When a former colleague let him know about a chain of boutiques expanding in the Chicago area, he jumped at the opportunity, eager to make a difference at the store by trying out his own ideas.

Ethan told me about a time one summer when his store received a bunch of poorly crafted dresses that fell short of the typical quality of the company's products. The cheaply made item slid off the hangers, and customers showed little interest in purchasing them. Other stores had also struggled to sell the item, but the company had bought deep into the style. In Ethan's view, dresses weren't necessarily dresses, just because that's what they were originally intended to be. He took a pair of scissors and cut off the straps. He rolled them, tied them up with a ribbon, and made a sign labeling them as "beach cover-ups," creating a new and more appealing product that would become a key performer of his swim section.

When the company's head of merchandising called Ethan to find out how his store had managed to sell out of the undesired product, Ethan excitedly told her about his beachwear idea. In other companies, intentionally damaging a product could have gotten him fired. In this case, though, BoutiqueCo highlighted Ethan's resourceful solution to other employees.

My research honed in on understanding what allows people like Ethan Peters to transform resources in unexpectedly valuable ways. How do institutions—businesses, schools, and families—encourage their members to "cut off the straps" so that they, too, can unlock hidden value? The answer lies in one simple word that changes a person's entire outlook on resources: ownership.

An owner might seem like an unusual descriptor for retail store employees whose salaries start at under ten bucks an hour and top out south of fifty grand. Our commonsense understanding considers ownership as an objective fact—it's a legal set of rights. Even toddlers playing with toys clearly recognize the basics of property rights.

The sociologist Amitai Etzioni describes another form of ownership that we frequently overlook. For Etzioni, ownership is just as much an attitude. Building on Etzioni's work, psychologists have come to label this psychological ownership, something material or immaterial that we experience as a part of our self. People with this psychological ownership exhibit a feeling of possessiveness, even if they don't literally own the resource. As Ethan Peters learned, that sense of possessiveness provides a license to transform resources.

The origins of Ethan's psychological ownership go back to the struggles in the company's earliest years. The company's founders lacked the time, money, and skills to provide guidance about many aspects of a store's operations. Without much to go by, Ethan started to experiment with merchandising, customer service, and employee training. As he imprinted the store with his own views, he began to see himself more and more as its owner. Although he lacked actual ownership of the store, he activated what psychologists call self-perception processes. He came to believe he was an owner because he behaved like one, so much so that customers took notice. As he told me, "I have people ask me all the time if I own the store—all the time."

As BoutiqueCo grew and became resource richer, it fought hard to keep fostering the conditions and culture that allowed Ethan Peters and his colleagues to act like they owned their stores. The company avoided the temptation to centralize control and exert authority that would have stripped psychological ownership. Its executives launched a "Year of Ownership" program that encouraged employees to think of themselves and act as owners, sending out "owner's manuals" to employees with tips for embracing this mind-set. The management team also withheld resources typically provided by an operation of its size. Its CEO told me that while they could easily provide these resources, it would be "over [his] dead body" because it would take away employees' sense of ownership.

BoutiqueCo had good reason to keep fostering psychological ownership. Research shows that when people feel a sense of ownership, they are far more satisfied with their jobs. In a sample of diverse professionals ranging from accountants to software engineers, psychological ownership accounted for 16 percent of a person's job satisfaction. It helps them think they can control their circumstances, lets them express their individuality, and offers a sense of place that belongs to them.

Psychological ownership also leads to better financial performance. In a survey of 2,755 employees across thirty-three locations at a retail company, a team of researchers wanted to test how psychological ownership influenced store sales. They sent questionnaires to measure psychological ownership and behaviors typical of actual owners, such as wanting to learn about profitability or trying to cut costs. Afterward, the team examined the sales performance of stores based on their size, sales plan, and actual sales. They found that strong psychological ownership and owner-like behaviors predicted improved financial performance of the stores.

Ethan Peters had a strong sense of psychological ownership, but he still faced some tough constraints—not only a shoddy dress but also the limited experience of his superiors and his tiny staff. When chasing, our first instincts are to acquire resources to overcome these constraints. But there's another, and often better, way to manage.

## THE ART OF CONSTRAINTS

As a talented adolescent, Phil Hansen threw himself into art and couldn't stop drawing. The teenager became obsessed with pointillism, a style that uses small dots to create a larger image when viewed from a distance. After spending his teenage years making thousands of tiny dots, his right hand developed a persistent shake when he was in high school. The more he tried to draw, the less he could do. He attempted to fight the shake by tightening his grip, but these adjustments made matters only worse. Eventually, he couldn't even draw a straight line, leading him reluctantly to put aside his dream of becoming an artist.

Phil Hansen wondered whether he would ever make art again and sought out the advice of a neurologist who provided a devastating diagnosis—permanent nerve damage. Although the news was hard to hear, his doctor provided a life-changing prescription that ultimately was a catalyst for Hansen to adopt a stretching mind-set. The doctor told Hansen to embrace the shake.

Phil Hansen set out to do what he *could* instead of focusing on what he *couldn't*. He found new ways of creating pictures with his wobbly hand. If pointillism involved small dots that aggregated into pictures, why couldn't the squiggly lines from his wavering hand do the same?

Hansen finished school and landed a job that could finally support his ambitions to be a career artist. His immediate instinct was what many of us do after receiving our first paycheck—go out and buy something. Phil Hansen became convinced that his art would substantially improve by replacing his makeshift tools with a more refined kit of brushes and buckets. After stocking up, hours and days went by when the young prodigy couldn't come up with an original idea. The new supplies meant to invigorate his art impaired him much more than his shaky hand.

To overcome his slump, Hansen dropped his focus on his supplies and looked inward to reflect on what he really wanted to create. He wondered, "Could you become more creative . . . by looking for limitations?" Instead of relying on his new tools he sought out to make art by using very little. His first project, transforming fifty Starbucks coffee cups and a dollar's worth of supplies, created a well-regarded portrait of a boy called Daudi. He also turned his own chest into a canvas, rotating several paintings on his body and then photographing them.

The budding artist also continued to find new ways of overcoming his physical limitations. He used his two capable feet, dipped in paint, to make art. Karate chopping a wall with a paint-soaked hand to make a Bruce Lee portrait didn't require precise body movements. Phil Hansen embraced limitations to improve his work, forcing him to learn new ways to do art. These constraints allowed him to stretch his art to new levels, eventually earning him a gig as the commissioned artist for the 51st Grammy Awards.

Phil Hansen's key insight was that constraints—whether his shaky hand or makeshift materials—sparked his ability to be creative with resources. As he put it, realizing that "a limitation could actually drive creativity" provided a new outlook on his work.

———————————

It turns out that Phil Hansen was not the first artist to discover the power of limitations. Columbia psychology professor and former artist Patricia Stokes spent years evaluating what led Claude Monet to produce a constant flow of masterpieces. From pupil to professional, Stokes characterized Monet's art as having one constant: constraints.

In his early years, he eliminated dark/light contrasts, pushing him away from representational painting and allowing him to develop impressionism. In later years, he would impose other constraints that would drive him to be in a constant state of learning. Monet knew how to paint very well, but what separated him from many other artists is that he knew how to paint well in very different ways.

Our common sense tells us that people are born with creativity, but Stokes finds that creativity is as much a part of our mind-set as it is an inborn skill. She finds that embracing constraints helps separate the good artists from the truly exceptional ones, a pattern she also finds in the architecture of Frank Lloyd Wright and the musical compositions of Claude Debussy.

In professional settings where performance also relies heavily on creativity, Stokes uncovers the same, whether illustrated by the fashion designs of Coco Chanel or the advertising campaigns of Leo Burnett, who turned Marlboro cigarettes into a global brand. Yet even for those of us whose main responsibilities don't depend on creative works, Stokes also reaches the same conclusion: from elementary schoolchildren to lab rats, constraints help us use resources in more creative ways to drive performance.

# STRETCH

When one of Stokes's experiments forced rodents to press a bar with *only* their right paw, they eventually learned how to press the bar in more ways compared to a group without the right paw constraint. The rats exhibited what researchers call "little c" creativity—a form of creativity not focused on producing creative works but rather on solving practical problems through new uses and applications of resources. Although we tend to think of creativity as something that produces masterpieces, it's an important part of getting everyday stuff done. It's what allows a programmer to complete her first line of original code, a product manager to identify a new market for an existing product, and an elementary-school teacher to find an entertaining way to teach subtraction.

For decades, the dominant view among psychologists was that constraints served as a barrier to using resources creatively in this manner. One need only spend a short time experiencing a confining bureaucracy, working for a micromanager, or sitting in a classroom that teaches to the test to recognize the appeal of this argument. Constraints can erode the psychological ownership that allowed store manager Ethan Peters and other employees at BoutiqueCo to thrive because they prevent the fulfillment of some basic psychological needs, particularly feeling autonomous and in control of one's work.

Besides stripping away psychological ownership, constraints— especially in the form of limited money—sometimes lead to feeling that our work is not a priority. This viewpoint, rooted in chasing, values our efforts based on the quantity of resources dedicated to pursuing them. The fewer the resources, this reasoning goes, the lower the importance of the effort.

Despite the intuitiveness of this logic about the harm of constraints, recent research has started to cast doubt on it—finding that constraints serve an important purpose.

Ravi Mehta at the University of Illinois and Meng Zhu at Johns Hopkins University examined how thinking about scarcity or abun-

dance influences people's creative use of resources. T'
thought that by making scarcity more apparent to pe
put them into the same type of head space that allo
sen and Claude Monet to produce beautiful art. They'd reduce the
natural tendency to use resources in conventional ways. In contrast,
making abundance more apparent would lead them to use resources
in more traditional ways.

To test their predictions, the researchers ran five experiments. In
one, they started by randomly dividing sixty undergraduate participants into two groups. Mehta and Zhu then instructed the first set
of subjects to write a brief essay about growing up having scarce resources, while the second set wrote about growing up having abundant resources. Afterward, the researchers presented both groups of
subjects with an actual problem their university faced.

With a recent move of its computer lab, the school had 250
bubble-wrap sheets and wanted to find a use for them. The experimenters provided a sample of the material to ensure familiarity
among the participants and then asked them to come up with a plan
for how to use the bubble wrap. Afterward, participants completed a
survey to measure the different ways they approached the challenge.

The professors then hired twenty judges to assess the novelty of
the suggested uses of the bubble wrap. The judges, blind to whether
participants belonged to the scarcity or abundance group, scored
people assigned to the scarcity group as having more creative uses for
the bubble wrap compared to those in the abundance group.

Why might fewer resources lead people to view them more expansively? Diving in deeper, the researchers uncovered a key explanation for their results. With abundance, people treat resources as
what they appear on the surface, utilizing them in traditional ways.
But when people face scarcity, they give themselves freedom to use
resources in less conventional ways.

Our problems, challenges, or opportunities become more manageable with constraints that direct us to make the best out of what we have. Without constraints, research finds that our tendency is to retrieve from memory exemplary uses of resources—we typically sit on a chair, so that's how we think of chairs. It's the functional fixedness we discussed in chapter 2 that drives chasing—seeing resources only as what they appear to be on the surface. We follow a "path of least resistance" model, which allows us to conserve mental energy by instinctively turning to commonplace ways of thinking.

With constraints, things unfold quite differently. We dedicate our mental energy to acting more resourcefully. Research regularly finds that if you ask someone to design or build a product, you might get a handful of good ideas. But if you ask someone to design or build it while sticking within a budget, the chances are you'll get much better results. That's precisely what a team of researchers found when they examined how people design new products, cook meals, and fix broken toys—budgets significantly increased how resourceful people were in responding to these challenges, leading to better results.

By embracing constraints, and not trying to overcome them by chasing after more resources, we not only work through them but we ultimately work better because of them. This is precisely what artist Phil Hansen did with both his body and materials.

But what happens when we have a lot—how do we get into a stretching mind-set? Here's where we'll need to be frugal with our resources to turn them into an even bigger fortune.

## THE FORTUNES OF FRUGALITY

When Bob Kierlin travels for work, he usually goes as cheaply as possible. You'll find him taking road trips to business meetings and staying overnight on the outskirts of town, favoring Red Roof Inns over Ritz-Carltons. He'll avoid the town's fanciest restaurants, preferring the bargain of McDonald's extra-value meals. In the office, chances are he's wearing a secondhand suit.

Kierlin's frugality started at an early age, as he grew up with parents of modest means. The family couldn't afford to eat at restaurants, and instead of taking trips they vacationed at local parks. This humble upbringing taught him about the importance of not wasting stuff, which he says "sticks with you in everything in life."

*Inc.* magazine labeled the founder and former chief executive of an industrial supplies company called Fastenal as the cheapest CEO in America. He might also make a strong showing for the cheapest person in America. In any case, he's for sure one of the most successful people in the country, earning hundreds of millions of dollars by starting and growing a multibillion-dollar business whose stock performed better than just about any other company over the last several decades.

From its 1987 IPO until Bob Kierlin's retirement from the company's board in 2014, Fastenal achieved astonishing returns. Out of more than eighty-four thousand listed securities, the company's performance was second best,* more than three times the return of twelfth-place Microsoft. The 47,782 percent compound return over this time period means that a $2,100 investment on day one of trading would have grown to over a million dollars by Kierlin's retirement.

The key to Bob Kierlin's success, and the way he works and lives, contrasts with most Fortune 1000 executives. His mission, which started when he was a child, has been to promote frugality.

As a seven-year-old hanging out in his father's newly opened auto-parts store in 1946, Kierlin earned a nickel a day sweeping

---

* In case you're wondering, UnitedHealthcare earned the top spot.

floors. He enjoyed being in the shop and by age eleven earned a promotion, working his way up to be a counterman—responsible for finding, selling, and billing customers for the nuts and bolts that kept their cars running.

The precocious boy realized many of the parts his father sold came packaged in cartons about the size of a box of cigarettes. He got an idea. What if he could save money by selling parts through a vending machine? The idea would help reduce labor costs while offering the benefit of expanding to many possible locations without a large outlay of cash.

The childhood dream stuck with Kierlin while he completed engineering and business degrees at the University of Minnesota. After brief stints with the Peace Corps and IBM, he tried to turn his childhood idea into a reality. With four friends, he pooled $31,000 to jury-rig a vending machine, replacing cartons of cigarettes with sleeves of screws. Company personnel would maintain the machines, but day-to-day operations would not need the expense of full-time employees.

It sounded like a good idea, but Bob Kierlin's vending machine flopped. Some of the most popular products couldn't fit into the contraption. Customers' questions about parts required on-site staff, undermining the idea of reduced payroll expense. It was time to go back to the drawing board.

The entrepreneur reformulated his idea of cheaply getting nuts and bolts in customers' hands and in 1967 he opened an outlet in Winona, Minnesota. Instead of turning to experienced salesclerks, he favored inexperienced (and less costly) yet ambitious employees just starting their careers. He quickly transformed these green go-getters into store managers, allowing them to pick products and design marketing plans in ways that minimized centralized overhead.

To stock his stores with parts bought at reasonable wholesale costs, Kierlin needed to buy inventory in bulk. Taking three years to sell down a typical product bought in such large quantities at a single store created inefficiencies and cash-flow problems. Instead of sitting on the dead inventory, he expanded to markets overlooked by his larger competitors and opened them without the need for additional product investments. He sparsely furnished these stores with not much more than a desk, a chair, and some shelving.

By 1987, Fastenal had grown to fifty stores across seven states. It now stood ready to make its public debut as one of the world's leading sellers of industrial supplies. Despite an influx of capital from its IPO, Fastenal kept to the frugal roots of its founder. The company's philosophy on resources reflected psychological ownership and frugality—spend money like it's your own, so you'll have more to take home.

Under Kierlin's leadership, Fastenal did not reimburse employees for meals during travel because they need to eat anyway—a policy that didn't save a lot of money but went a long way toward instilling a culture of avoiding waste. Company guidelines required car travel to meetings within an eight-hour drive. Kierlin drove the entire five-thousand-mile roundtrip from company headquarters to a meeting in California with his CFO, building a camaraderie between the two travelers that is hard to do in short bursts at the office. Secondhand office furniture and equipment adorned the company's modest two-story concrete headquarters, where Kierlin successfully implemented one creative use for vending machines: soda machine proceeds funded the annual holiday party.

Although such measures might create a tough change for employees accustomed to perks, the company performed better—and so did employees. Their paychecks rose with hitting profitability targets and cost-containment goals. By saving on what he considered unnecessary expenses, Kierlin not only created a culture that avoided excessive waste and taught employees to do more with less, but he also had the cash to make investments in the business and his staff.

# S T R E T C H

The company's strong balance sheet allowed it to bolster inventory quickly based on spikes in demand and invest heavily in training employees, allowing them to take on roles of increasing responsibility and pay. The Fastenal School of Business provided classes for thousands of employees at eighteen locations, in addition to hosting an extensive online course offering. Generous bonuses helped keep turnover at an impressive 7 percent.

When Kierlin moved from CEO to chairman of the board in 2002, he turned to company veteran William Oberton as his successor. Oberton had risen from the very bottom of the organization to the very top because he embodied the type of frugality Kierlin values. As Oberton explains, "We're not afraid to spend. We're afraid to waste money on something that won't improve the business."

Decades after experimenting with his first vending machine, Fastenal made good on Kierlin's original ambition. In 2011, the company teamed up with a snack vending manufacturer and used off-the-shelf software to invent a device that provides quick access to industrial products such as gloves, safety glasses, and drill bits at customer facilities. Employees swipe an electronic card to obtain supplies, providing greater accountability for stuff regularly pilfered from storage rooms. Although most companies go to great lengths to get their customers to consume more, Fastenal's vending machines helped customers buy less. The vending machines reduced supply usage by about 30 percent, yet created loyal and satisfied customers. In 2014, the company had roughly forty-seven thousand vending machines at customers' locations, representing almost 40 percent of its sales.

Bob Kierlin's modest upbringing and limited capital to start his business match our common understanding of what leads people to frugality. But as he, and his company, became incredibly wealthy, he doubled down on frugality, not shedding it as an embarrassing necessity but proudly and joyfully wearing it as a badge of honor, bringing its merits to his employees, customers, and investors.

———————

Most people don't have a positive opinion of frugal people or frugal organizations. They're either stingy or poor. Bob Kierlin and his company are neither—they're incredibly generous with other people, from employees to charitable causes,* and also very resource rich. It's precisely their frugality that helped generate their fortunes.

Although Kierlin's commitment to frugality brought tremendous benefits, it raises an important question: Do we need to become as frugal as Bob Kierlin to stretch? The answer turns out to be no—we simply need to think differently.

A team of marketing professors led by John Lastovicka used interviews with frugal consumers, a writing exercise with undergraduate students, and videotaped episodes from Oprah Winfrey's and Montel Williams's shows on frugal spouses to understand their mind-set. Lastovicka found three common patterns among the most frugal of us.

First, frugal people emphasize long-term objectives over short-term pleasures, exhibiting the type of patience Bob Kierlin used to grow his business. With a long game in mind, Bob Kierlin avoided short-term perks to offer long-term (and rewarding) careers to employees, lifetime relationships with customers, and a sustainable business.

Second, frugal people reuse what they have instead of buying

---

* Kierlin's frugality is matched by his generosity to others. He supports several charitable causes, often anonymously. In 2001, he rewarded employees with stock options. Resisting the typical path of diluting existing shareholders, Kierlin gave employees stock options on two thirds of his personal stash of 7.8 million shares.

more. In so many spheres of society—and perhaps most prominently in corporate boardrooms—wasteful spending is a marker of status. The greater the waste, this line of thought goes, the more successful the person must be, because only the well-off can afford waste. That's why just down the road from my office at Rice University in Houston sits the former headquarters of the Stanford Financial Group, a Ponzi scheme that bilked investors out of $8 billion. Its offices—complete with green marble floors, dark wood furniture, and expensive Persian rugs—signaled to its customers that it was so rich it could afford to waste money on these luxuries. Bob Kierlin's office, with its used furniture, lacked the opulence of the Stanford Financial Group, and he wouldn't have had it any other way.

Third, frugal people feel freer from conventions, making them less susceptible to social comparisons that lead to chasing. They avoid fretting over what they don't have and instead carve out a path using what they do have. Bob Kierlin's frugality might have roiled corporate traditionalists, but it forged a culture of stretching where employees learned to find more possibilities from the resources at hand, leaving them proud of their accomplishments (not to mention wealthier).

So far we've examined how psychological ownership, embracing constraints, and frugality help us become resourceful. But there's another critical part of a stretching mind-set we'll now cover. Stretching means constantly realizing potential in resources that other people readily discard, even when looking in the Dumpster.

## FROM TRASH TO TREASURE

The New Covent Garden Market is the largest wholesale fruit, vegetable, and flower market in the United Kingdom. The bustling fifty-seven-acre complex houses hundreds of vendors who supply much of the produce eaten by Londoners. Droves of visitors walk its energized aisles while trying to dodge forklifts moving pallets of food and flowers from all over the world.

On a cold, frosty morning in 2010, Jenny Dawson headed out at 4:00 a.m. with clothes thrown on over her PJs. The twentysomething math and economics grad from the University of Edinburgh and former fashion model worked for a prestigious London-based hedge fund, pulling in a large salary that funded her Notting Hill residence, annual ski trips, and jet-setting travel.

That morning, she hopped on her bicycle and rode over to the New Covent Garden Market to start investigating an issue that deeply troubled her. From the local newspaper, Dawson learned that authorities had arrested some people for what she hardly considered a crime. The perpetrators had rummaged through supermarket Dumpsters in search of their next meal.

Jenny Dawson started reading up about one of the world's most unfortunate ironies. Although almost 800 million people lack enough food for an active, healthy life, tons of food find their way to landfills each day. In her home country alone, people throw out 7.2 million tons every year, costing billions of dollars to manage food waste and accounting for roughly 10 percent of greenhouse gas emissions.

When she arrived at the New Covent Garden Market, Jenny Dawson strode into a bustling bazaar hardly emblematic of a global food crisis. Yet steps away from the trading action, she stumbled upon the traces of a worldwide problem. She opened a box of plastic-wrapped packets of peapods from Kenya, mangoes from the Philippines, and tomatoes from Turkey. The international goods, perfectly edible, would soon be making their way to the trash bin while millions of citizens in these countries would go hungry. As she put it, "I just thought, 'How can we afford to be this wasteful?'"

# S T R E T C H

Raised on a farm in Scotland, Dawson learned at an early age the problems of balancing demand and supply for food. Farmers, leery of running out of food to sell, err on the side of overproduction. They suck up precious natural resources to grow food people will never eat or even buy. Making matters worse, some of the food they grow never has a chance of ending up on a kitchen table. Shoppers, who judge a fruit by its skin, reject tasty and healthy produce with the most minor cosmetic blemishes. In the United States, grocers discard more than a quarter of all produce because of cosmetic issues.

Dawson's mother had come up with a solution for the family's excess produce—turn the potential waste into jams and chutneys, saving them from the trash bin while extending their shelf life. The hedge fund prodigy, wanting to try her mom's recipe on a grander scale, put aside her budding banking career to start a company called Rubies in the Rubble. A play on finding diamonds in the rough, the name fit the company's mantra: "To put to good use the things that are discarded in our society without reason . . . Everything, and everyone, is unique and has value."

Farmers who see their unused and cosmetically abnormal produce as worthless cheaply offload it to her. The chutney maker then uses the blighted and overstock fruits and vegetables as essential ingredients of premium-priced goods. Her chutneys not only delightfully fill bellies but also achieve a laudable goal of minimizing the environmental impact of food waste.

Dawson's transformation of waste into wonders goes beyond food. As she started her company, she looked to women struggling to find work because of homelessness and drug addiction, turning these vagrants into diligent and dedicated employees. She employed a man with brain damage to help label jars of food, and says it is unfortunate that "we judge a person by their looks, in the same way we reject a wonky carrot."

Dawson's growing business now has distribution in more than

150 locations in the United Kingdom, and the start of her company's values statement reads like a manifesto for stretching: "Make use of what you have. Care about your resources."

---

Just northeast from the New Covent Garden Market you'll find one of the world's most influential thinkers housed at one of the world's most prestigious universities. The London School of Economics Professor Anthony Giddens's ideas set the agenda for much of contemporary sociology, and his ideas around what he termed structuration theory also allow us to explain how people like Jenny Dawson turn trash into treasure.

In its simplest terms, structuration theory proposes that you can't understand social behavior by simply zooming in to examine small actions taken by individuals, nor can you understand it by zooming out to grasp the big picture of how collectives such as businesses or societies act.

Instead, Giddens reasoned that both the small and the big work hand in hand, meaning the small actions individuals take produce big structures such as norms, traditions, and regulations that, in turn, shape the smallest of our actions. On this view, we are never fully constrained by big structures because our actions, in part, create these structures. At the same time, we're also never completely free from big structures because they always shape, even in the subtlest ways, what we do.

During my PhD studies at the University of Michigan, organizational theorist Martha Feldman was busy taking some of Giddens's ideas and applying them to the study of resources. Traditional approaches have largely treated resources as fixed objects that we acquire. Our interaction with them doesn't change their meaning—

they have an innate value defined by the big structures of norms, traditions, and regulations. If you want to know the prospects of success for anything—a new hire, a company, a teenager's future— simply examine its stock of resources. Under this view, trash remains trash because that is what it is.

Professor Feldman conceptualized resources quite differently. Instead of focusing on their innate value, she emphasized how people put them to use. Sure, things have natural qualities—a rock is heavier than a pebble—but these qualities only give them potential for use. You'd have to throw a rock to make it a weapon or put it on top of paper to turn it into a paperweight.

Feldman argued that almost anything—tangible and intangible— has potential as a resource, but that to become anything valuable requires action. This helps us realize that resources don't come from outside us—they're not things we go out and get but rather things we create and shape.

Jenny Dawson creates valuable resources through actions that procure, cook, and preserve unwanted produce, and then distributes and markets it as gourmet chutney. By taking these actions, she shapes larger structures such as norms about what to do with unwanted produce and others' beliefs about food waste, leading her to run a growing business, help find a more meaningful career, and contribute to solving a critical social problem.

It isn't just individuals whose actions can add value to resources. Professor Feldman's research, along with her colleagues', discovered that social systems—whether organizations, schools, or families— can also create valuable resources in some of the most unexpected places. My colleague Utpal Dholakia and I wanted to examine these ideas under the difficult conditions of a major organizational change. During typical change efforts, managers regularly consider employees as resisters who don't always cooperate. Does it always have to be this way?

We examined a large retail company we'll call EntertainCo that was combining its mall and big-box-store divisions. In the early 1990s, the company used the mall stores as steady profit-makers to fund expansion of its big-box locations. The mall and big-box divisions operated semiautonomously under different brand names and leadership teams. By the turn of the century, decades of neglecting the mall-based stores and increased competition led to a multiyear decline in performance at the division. Top managers decided to rebrand, remodel, and remerchandise the smaller stores to match their big-box locations.

For Rebecca Rogers, the transformation couldn't have been any worse. Changing the name of the mall-based stores was "confusing" for customers, and it eroded the rich history of the mall division by eliminating its nameplate. She wondered "what's the point?" and considered the entire effort "a waste of time and money." Echoing a typical "resistance to change" story, Rebecca interpreted the company's plans as a negative experience that would destroy precious resources while delivering minimal returns.

Brianna Baldwin, one of Rebecca's colleagues at the same suburban Pittsburgh, Pennsylvania, store, had a similar background to Rebecca's but had a very different assessment of what was unfolding. She thought that while the adjustments created some more work for her, they increased "customer recognition" and provided a "benefit from more marketing and promotions," which helped the company get more out of its existing advertising and branding resources.

How could two women, so similar on paper, working for the same company, at the same location, offer such different assessments of the initiative, and how would these different evaluations shape the prospects for the company?

Using data from 159 employees across forty-five locations, Dholakia and I instructed participants to complete a survey that asked them to write their thoughts and feelings about the project.

# S T R E T C H

Afterward, we measured three psychological resources scholars consider essential for success in change efforts—commitment to the change, self-efficacy (a sense that employees have what it takes to implement a change), and psychological ownership of their store.* We then measured their behaviors that supported the project, everything from following instructions to praising the initiative to others.

We were surprised at how much employees' interpretations about the effort differed. Some of them, like Rebecca, thought the transformation lacked sufficient resources to be successful, believing the organization needed to invest more in marketing or that the change would hurt the company's brand. Other employees, like Brianna, thought that the change enhanced existing resources, such as by making customers more satisfied and offering employees better job security and additional career opportunities. Which reality was right?

It turns out both were, but they had different consequences for employees and the company.

Employees who, like Rebecca, viewed the change as depleting company resources ended up depleting their own psychological resources, such as self-efficacy, commitment, and psychological ownership of their store. Yet employees like Brianna, who viewed the change as enhancing company resources, ended up enhancing their own psychological resources.

Even more important, those employees who saw the change as enhancing company resources, and whose own psychological resources expanded as a result, took significantly more actions to make the change successful. For some employees, what's often a difficult

---

* Technically, we measured a form of unit identity—the extent to which employees identified with their stores. Research finds unit identity to be conceptually close to psychological ownership because strong identification usually implies ownership. For example, we asked employees, "When I talk about the store, I usually say 'we' rather than 'they.'"

experience—a major change—turned into a way for them not only to boost their psychological resources but also to contribute to their organization's success.

## MOVING TO A STRETCHING MIND-SET

Ethan Peters, Phil Hansen, Bob Kierlin, and Jenny Dawson came to stretching from different places, but they all cultivated and spread beliefs about making more out of what they already had. Ethan Peters's psychological ownership allowed him to transform inferior products into bestselling ones. Phil Hansen embraced physical and material constraints to allow him to work more creatively with his body and brushes. Bob Kierlin practiced the penny-pinching instilled by his parents on the grandest of scales. By bringing his family's frugality to employees and customers, he built one of the country's most successful companies and best-performing stocks. Jenny Dawson's treasure hunting proved that even the least valuable things around us have unrecognized potential.

Stretchers find beauty and richness in places where others struggle to see anything of value. Too often, we understand, interact with, and use things at face value, locking ourselves into conventions that limit possibilities. By adopting a stretching mind-set, we can reach extraordinary potential with what we already have. It's a matter of recognizing the untapped value in our resources and directing our energy to nurturing and developing what's in hand. Once we make this shift in mind-set, it's possible to start building some of the skills of stretching—something we're now ready to start.

# FOUR

## GET OUTSIDE

THE VALUE OF KNOWING A LITTLE ABOUT A LOT

T he 2004 film *Napoleon Dynamite* starred Jon Heder playing an alienated teenager who helps his friend successfully run for class president. It became one of the most watched, yet polarizing, films on Netflix because it contains lots of ironic humor—the kind that engenders a cult following as much as it alienates critics.

Netflix collects a trove of data on its users to make recommendations about potential movies they'd like to watch. *Napoleon Dynamite* garnered more than 2 million ratings, providing plenty of information to feed into the complex algorithms that power its suggestions. The problem was that those ratings disproportionally fell at the lowest (1) and highest (5) parts of a five-star scale. Even close friends, who frequently rate movies similarly, passionately disagreed about the delights or disappointments of watching *Napoleon Dynamite.*

Jon Sanders, the company's director of recommendation systems, was responsible for improving its in-house software, Cinematch. The homegrown product that linked customers' viewing preferences to recommended titles facilitated 60 percent of Netflix's movie rentals by 2006. Making the recommendation engine better would improve customer satisfaction and increase retention, keeping subscribers paying for unlimited plans.

Despite their best efforts, Sanders's math and computer experts couldn't improve upon Cinematch. Facing demands to enhance the software, he turned away from hiring more engineers or a professional services company with expertise in the area and instead, at the direction of Netflix CEO Reed Hastings, took inspiration from a move used by a very different Napoleon.

In 1869, Emperor Louis Napoleon III had a problem on his hands. Industrialization in France sparked a mass migration from rural areas into its growing urban cores. City dwellers didn't produce their own food, which contributed to a steep rise in costs, including for one of the most important staples in the French diet: butter. With citizens fed up over the inflationary pressures, the emperor offered a prize to anyone who could come up with a cheaper alternative to butter that would mimic its nutrition, flavor, and texture. The innovation contest would ultimately allow the same nation that brought us pastries loaded with butter to invent margarine and introduce us to asking outsiders to solve some of our stickiest challenges.

Following in the footsteps of Napoleon III, Netflix launched its own innovation contest called the Netflix Prize. It offered a $1 million award to the first team that could improve Cinematch's recommendation accuracy by 10 percent. The company provided contestants with approximately seven years of data and 1.5 million movie ratings. The intellectual challenge, not to mention the large bounty, attracted the brightest minds from some of the world's most prestigious organizations and universities, along with someone by the name of Gavin Potter.

Gavin Potter had recently quit his job after IBM purchased his former practice at PricewaterhouseCoopers, where he worked in operational research and performance improvement. He entered the international competition by declaring his intentions on his little-read blog: "Decided to take the Netflix Prize seriously. Looks kind of fun. Not sure where I will get to as I am not an academic or a mathematician." He called his team "Just a Guy in a Garage," a fitting label for his scrappy operation that consisted of a bedroom in his London home, a math consultant in the form of his teenage daughter Emily, and a vintage Dell desktop computer, which he didn't run overnight to prevent its rattling fan from interrupting the family's sleep.

More than five thousand teams submitted solutions. Compared to many of these teams, "Just a Guy in a Garage" lacked the computing power, training, staff, institutional support, and social connections of his better-equipped rivals. Gavin Potter also didn't know how to build the complex models that experts with far greater resources used to vie for the prize. Instead, he reflected, "What can I do to solve it without mathematical knowledge?" It turned out he could do quite a lot.

During his college years at the University of Oxford, Potter learned about the pioneering work of cognitive psychologist Amos Tversky and the Nobel Prize–winning psychologist Daniel Kahneman. Tversky and Kahneman launched the field of behavioral economics, designing studies that showed the irrationality of human behavior. In one of their most influential experiments, participants spun a wheel of fortune with numbers from 0 to 100 and made a prediction, such as the number of African countries in the United Nations. Where the wheel stopped influenced participants' predictions. For example, the median estimate of the percent of African countries in the United Nations was 25 when the wheel stopped at 10 but rose to 45 when the wheel stopped at 65. Paying subjects to make accurate predictions didn't improve their precision. The researchers labeled this effect anchoring because it involves basing predictions on irrelevant data (in this experiment, the number showing from the spin of a wheel) that people start from when making a subsequent, but completely unrelated, prediction.

For Gavin Potter, the Netflix Prize was as much a puzzle in understanding these types of human irrationalities as it was a show of math and computing prowess. He reasoned that the same principles that led people to base the number of African countries in the United Nations on an anchoring point also would influence their movie ratings. If a Netflix customer watches a movie she really enjoys, followed by one she dislikes, the better-liked movie will artificially inflate the rating of the following movie. Similarly, watching a movie she can't stand will lower her rating, independent of its actual enjoyment, of the next movie she rates.

By accounting for how psychology shapes movie ratings, Gavin Potter improved Cinematch by 9.06 percent over Netflix's experts. His results placed him in contention for the prize (he ultimately finished in seventeenth place out of more than twenty thousand registered teams), and his different perspective would help other teams crack the 10 percent winning threshold.

At a conference while the competition was under way, Potter shared his outsider approach with other players who were treating the prize as a math and computing challenge. The finalists for the prize incorporated Potter's work, with the winning team cracking the 10 percent threshold merely twenty minutes earlier than the runner-up, ending the three-year race.

Gavin Potter's unconventional background not only helped him achieve remarkable results but also elevated the work of the best performers in the contest. His only regret, he told me, was that instead of simply sharing his work, he "should have teamed up with one of the mathematics teams because diversity is what's important."

In this chapter, I will introduce two very different ways of using experiences to find success. The first follows our common sense and conventional wisdom. We're regularly told about the virtues of developing specialized expertise—from picking a college major to plotting out a straight career path. Yet taking such a deep but narrow track comes at a cost. I'll introduce research that shows some substantial blind spots of expertise and then turn to a second, and less intuitive, path to finding success—being an outsider with different experience, knowledge, and resources.

Although we might find it hard to believe, an outsider can regularly outperform experts in solving a problem in their own area of expertise, especially for complex challenges. The key to outsiders' results lies with the diversity of their experience.

Outsiders follow what I call the multi-c, or multi-context rule; simply stated, *breadth* of experiences helps people stretch. With reach into several places, outsiders take resources to new problems and opportunities in ways invisible to experts blinded by the narrowness of their experience. Because there's often good reason to develop expertise, I'll end the chapter by explaining how experts can also cultivate an outsider's approach to stretching.

## WHERE EXPERTS STUMBLE

A stream of psychology research popularized in Malcolm Gladwell's book *Outliers* reasons that obtaining expertise depends on extensive practice—roughly ten thousand hours—and not inborn talent. Along with extensive practice, Gladwell suggests, experts have access to resources such as training and equipment that provide them with a leg up over others. The argument makes a lot of sense but while compellingly reasoned, is ten thousand hours always the key to success?

On a closer look, many of the examples Gladwell provided when formulating the ten-thousand-hour rule involved playing games with strict and largely unchanging rules such as hockey or chess. Lots of practice allows people to become adept at learning the ins and outs of the game. But for fields without stable rules, thousands of hours of practice turn out to be less relevant because the rules constantly shift; it is hard to become an expert at something always changing.

Research by Brooke Macnamara at Princeton University, David Hambrick at Michigan State University, and my Rice colleague Fred Oswald, examined all of the empirical studies evaluating the relationship between the number of hours of practice and performance. Their search yielded eighty-eight studies that involved 11,135 participants.

Looking across this research, they found that for games with infrequent rule changes such chess or Scrabble, practice does predict performance, but perhaps less than we might guess. It accounts for only 26 percent of performance. Music and sports fare a little worse, coming in at 21 and 18 percent of performance, respectively. The research becomes even more eye opening for less rule-bound and rapidly changing fields.

For education—think college students trying to get the best grades—the amount of practice accounted for only 4 percent of performance. For the professions (not including sports or music) such as insurance selling, computer programming, and aircraft piloting, the number was even lower—less than 1 percent.

Why does extensive practice explain so little of a person's performance in certain domains?

To find out, Macnamara and her collaborators regrouped the eighty-eight studies based on the level of predictability—high-predictability areas like running, moderately predictable areas like fencing, and low-predictability areas like aviation emergencies. They found that for areas with the most predictability, practice explains 24 percent of a person's performance, but this number decreases to 12 percent for moderately predictable events and to only 4 percent for low-predictability events. As challenges become less predictable— that is, as they become more like what we regularly face in many of our professional and personal efforts—practice doesn't always make perfect.

---

Despite the limitations of experience, we rightly (for the most part) place tremendous trust in experts, deferring to their judgments for some of our most important decisions about our work, health, finances, and children's education. Even though the researchers show that practice only moderately explains performance, experts still offer useful guidance. But they don't always have the best answers.

Starting from an early age, we place experts on a pedestal. My daughters believe their teachers know everything because they reward (or punish) them for conforming to their ways of viewing the world. Later in life we defer to experts at work—the IT guy, the financial analyst armed with data, and our boss who presumably has more experience (and therefore greater expertise) compared to us.

Experts also rely on symbols to prop them up—doctors wear white coats, professionals hang degrees on the wall, and professors have lots of books in their offices. By displaying their credentials, they signal to us that they know better—but that's not always the case.

The social psychologist Robert Cialdini has spent decades study-

ing the principles that influence people, finding that expertise sometimes sways people too far. He recalls a time when a doctor treated
a patient with an ache in the right ear. The doctor's sloppily written
instructions were to put eardrops in the patient's "R ear." The nurse
promptly put eardrops into the patient's rear end. The patient complied, believing that despite the unusual treatment for an earache,
the experts obviously knew what they were doing.

Although we might rack this up to a sloppy set of mistakes, in
some situations, experts routinely don't provide the best answers.
Psychologist Phil Tetlock spent twenty years examining predictions
for some of the most important political issues facing our time—
transitions to democracy and capitalism, economic growth, inter-
state violence, and nuclear proliferation. He followed experts who
regularly appear on television and in newspapers, and who advise
governments and businesses about these issues. When he tallied
their performance, he found some startling results.

Experts were no better than the average person in forecasting
future events. The professional background and status of experts
barely made a difference. Whether experts were liberals or conser-
vative leaning didn't tip the scales. Optimists and pessimists didn't
differ in their accuracy. It turned out there was only one major difference that separated the high performers from everyone else.

People who knew lots of little things and drew from multiple
perspectives routinely outperformed those who knew one big thing
really well. It was the well rounded who excelled.

## WHY OUTSIDERS OUTSHINE EXPERTS

When faced with complex challenges, knowing lots of different
things helps people regularly prevail over experts deeply focused on

a single thing. To understand why, let's examine some of our most lauded experts: scientists. They turn out to be remarkably successful at solving complex problems, although not the kind of problems you'd imagine.

To understand how scientists approach problems, Lars Bo Jeppesen of Copenhagen Business School and Karim Lakhani of Harvard Business School studied a company called InnoCentive. Formed in 2001 with backing from the giant pharmaceutical company Eli Lilly, InnoCentive applies crowdsourcing to solve some of the world's most vexing problems—from fighting diseases to providing electricity in impoverished African villages. People from all sorts of backgrounds can join InnoCentive's team of 350,000 registered solvers to take their crack at helping others who detail a question, the time frame for solving it, and the prize for the best answer.

Using data from 166 problems posted on the InnoCentive platform that originated from the scientific labs of twenty-six companies across ten countries, the researchers wanted to see whether people with the most expertise for the specific challenge would come out on top. This seems like a fairly straightforward study—we'd expect, for example, those with the most chemistry knowledge to outperform other scientists at solving chemistry problems.

Surprisingly, the researchers found the opposite.

The further the problem was from a person's expertise, the more likely he or she was to solve it. Biologists solved more chemistry problems compared to the chemists. Like Gavin Potter, scientists outside a specific field had different, and ultimately better, ways of approaching a problem than the experts. What might explain this rather remarkable result?

Experts come with a significant liability—they become what my Rice colleague Erik Dane calls cognitively entrenched, blinded to using resources in ways that depart from conventions. As people gain expertise, they fall back on ways they've already learned to do

**79**

things—even in the face of new information or a change in circumstances. It's what researchers discovered over a century ago, but its implications are long forgotten.

As far back as the early 1900s, psychologist Cheves Perky conducted a series of experiments to understand how people's visualization of images shapes their perception of real objects. She asked people to think about objects, such as bananas, and then to mentally envision them on a blank wall. Without their knowledge, she projected a very dim picture of the same object they were asked to visualize on the wall. Those not participating in the experiment could readily see the object when they walked into the room, but Perky's research participants reported they couldn't see the projected image. Instead, they simply incorporated the picture of the projected object into their visualization of that object, blurring the lines between what they truly saw and what they imagined. What became known as the Perky effect holds that having a prior mental image of something alters how we perceive and assimilate new information.

Perky's subjects didn't realize they observed *actual* images of bananas because they were first asked to imagine them. In a similar manner, experts struggle to find new solutions because they're already mentally visualizing how to use their resources—a carpenter visualizes a hammer as a device to put nails into a wall—and becomes less likely to abandon this use ingrained through thousands of hours of practice. My preschool-age daughter, who's never picked up a hammer before, might consider it to be a back scratcher or percussion instrument.

Outsiders exist in all parts of life. An outsider is anyone who lacks resources that experts take for granted: a newcomer to an organization, a professional from another field, or an English major in a psychology class.

For science—although the same holds true for many management teams and professions—there's another group that regularly finds itself on the outside for a very unfortunate reason: women. They regularly are shut out from critical social resources that men typically get, an indefensible situation.

In 2015, the British biochemist Sir Tim Hunt shocked many of his colleagues with his musings about women. During a conference of science journalists in South Korea, the Nobel Prize–winning professor at University College London spoke about three problems with "girls" in the lab: "You fall in love with them, they fall in love with you, and when you criticize them they cry." The uproar in the scientific community and broader population pushed Hunt to resign from his university post, but it didn't resolve an unconscionable truth about women in science: they are outsiders—too often denied access to the connections, mentorship, and training that their male counterparts regularly enjoy.

Jeppesen and Lakhani returned to their InnoCentive data to examine this second type of outsiders—female scientists who typically lack the social resources of their male counterparts. Would these outsiders outperform the better-socialized and connected men?

The women did incredibly well, so well they had a 23.4 percent greater probability of solving a problem compared to men. The same logic that allows non-experts to outperform experts explained why women outperformed men. Women more openly approached problems unaided, but they were also not wedded to the traditions learned in the inner circle. By viewing the problems from a foundation of different experiences, they generated better solutions.

If outsiders contribute so much, why don't we engage them more? The irony is that we're unlikely to put outsiders on our teams simply because they are just that: outsiders. We tend to be attracted to people more like us—insiders, by definition. We also embrace an expertise bias: the more experts around, the better our performance.

Indeed, when tasked with putting together a group to solve our problems, which would you prefer: a group of experts or a random group? If you're like most of us, you'd likely opt for the dream team—who wouldn't pick the team of experts with the most resources? In most cases you'd be wrong.

Experts can be insular, with lots of overlap in their knowledge base. This makes their resources redundant with one another, each contributing very little that's unique to the group. In *The Difference*, political scientist and mathematical modeler Scott Page shows that for everything from democracies to groups of scientists, random teams usually outperform dream teams because random teams more likely have both experts *and* outsiders on them. Diversity in our team's resources turns out to be the most important shaper of performance, making it more likely we'll openly debate and reach a better solution that incorporates multiple perspectives.

Even if they seemingly have less, outsiders bring a very different set of skills gained from spending time in ways unlike experts. To understand why they're so vital to performance, we will focus first on how outsiders pursue a diverse set of experiences and, second, on how they connect resources across different areas.

## THE MULTI-CONTEXT (OR MULTI-C) RULE

In the 1970s, NASA had an ambitious goal—to create the world's greatest telescope capable of peering into the darkest and deepest pockets of outer space. The Hubble telescope promised to provide answers to the most fundamental questions about our world and beyond—the age and size of the universe, the presence of other planets, the birth of galaxies, and the inconceivable discoveries that a huge scientific leap inevitably brings.

The excitement gradually eroded as a series of technical setbacks and budget shortfalls delayed the Hubble's expected 1983 launch. Several years of rethinking and reworking the design finally led NASA scientists to ready its deployment in 1986. And then tragedy struck.

As a fourth-grader, I, like thousands of other schoolchildren, watched the *Challenger* space shuttle blow up on television. The horrible accident eroded the nation's enthusiasm for space exploration, and the Hubble was put on hold while NASA worked to safeguard against future mishaps. Its engineers used the almost three-year delay to test thoroughly and correct any remaining problems with the telescope. Or at least they thought they did.

When the space shuttle *Discovery* lifted off with the Hubble telescope on April 24, 1990, people around the world looked forward to answers to some of their most profound questions about the universe. Within weeks of its deployment, the scientific community had its hands on the telescope's first pictures, and the news was not very good. After almost two decades of waiting, the telescope returned blurry images that fell far short of expectations for the multibillion-dollar project.

An ensuing investigation found imperfections in the telescope's mirror. It was a very small mistake—roughly the thickness of one-fiftieth of a sheet of paper—but it was one with significant consequences. If left unfixed, the Hubble's images would forever remain distorted, and answers to the most pressing astronomical questions would need to wait decades for new equipment.

All hopes for a fix would soon fall on the steady hands of a high-school dropout named Story Musgrave. Born on a dairy farm in Stockbridge, Massachusetts, in 1935, Musgrave always had an adventurous streak, navigating the neighboring forests alone at age three and floating his homemade rafts on nearby rivers a couple of years later. As a teenager, he struggled with the aftermath of his parents' divorce and their alcoholism. When sent off to a boarding high school, he hated it so much that he constantly got in trouble. He found very little compassion and inspiration from his teachers and left without a diploma.

Story Musgrave landed a job as a mechanic for heavy equipment used to build the Massachusetts Turnpike. He had an instinctual knack for fixing things, but when the turnpike gig ended, he had no job, still no diploma, and no obvious prospects.

Seeking an escape from his life's circumstances, Story Musgrave enlisted in the Marines as an aviation electrician and instrument technician, applying the skills he had developed repairing highway equipment to airplanes. The eighteen-year-old loved aviation, and his job kept him close to the aircraft, but without a high school diploma, Story Musgrave would never fly for the military.

To find his way into the cockpit, Musgrave decided to apply to college, but schools rejected the high-school dropout. He trekked over to the dean's office at Syracuse University and talked his way into class. The school reversed its admissions decision, and Musgrave graduated with a degree in mathematics and statistics.

After his first taste of higher education, Story Musgrave couldn't get enough. By the time he had attended his last of almost 160 college courses, he had racked up an MBA from UCLA, a degree in chemistry from Marietta College, an MD from Columbia University, a master's of science degree in physiology and biophysics from the University of Kentucky, and a master of arts in literature from the University of Houston. Along the way, he also obtained his pilot's license and returned to fly for the military.

Story Musgrave had already cycled through several different careers—a corporate mathematician, a computer programmer, a brain researcher, and a pilot—when he came across a NASA posting looking for scientists wanting to travel into outer space, which he thought would be a "job that will challenge me to leverage without exception every single skill I had ever acquired." He began what turned out to be a thirty-plus-year career at NASA, all the while continuing to work as a trauma surgeon three days a month.

His ability to fix everything from a gash in a person's arm to a leak on an airplane would ultimately prepare him for his most important operation. As a mission payload specialist and the lead mechanic to repair the Hubble telescope, Story Musgrave recognized he was both an unusual pick and an obvious choice at the same time, pointing out, "I am not one of the astrophysicists, astronomers, optical physicists, engineers or others that played such an essential and challenging role in this process."

Rather than having a depth of expertise in any one particular area, Story Musgrave had amassed decades of eclectic experiences that prepared him all the more for this vital role. "It is an example," he says, "of the spectacular creativity that accrues from dissecting the details of multiple diverse domains and disciplines and applying the discovered best practices."

The mission to repair the Hubble lasted eleven days and was one of NASA's most complex endeavors, involving a record of five back-to-back spacewalks by a team of rotating crew members. Over his three spacewalks, Musgrave spent twenty-two hours repairing the Hubble's imperfections with the great skill of an experienced surgeon trying to resuscitate a critically ill patient. When asked why he stopped working full-time as a surgeon, Musgrave answered, "So I could operate on the Hubble of course."

Musgrave's ability to solve complex challenges by drawing from his varied background exemplifies the multi-c rule: a diversity of experiences allows people to think more expansively about their resources, leading to more divergent ways of approaching problems. Musgrave saw his mission as an operation, allowing him to use his experience as a physician to repair the flawed telescope.

A rare breed now, jacks-of-all-trades such as Musgrave were not so long ago encouraged and rewarded by our society. Think: Leonardo da Vinci (painter, architect, musician, mathematician, engineer, inventor, and anatomist), Benjamin Franklin (author, printer, political theorist, postmaster, scientist, and diplomat), Mary Somerville (astronomer, mathematician, and geologist), and Paul Robeson (singer, football player, lawyer, social activist, and speaker of twenty languages). Today, a push for deeply specialized expertise leaves us with people who get better and better at narrower and narrower things. Ironically, credit for the shift away from the multi-c rule lies with one of its strongest followers—Adam Smith.

Adam Smith was born on a summer day in 1723 in the town of Kirkcaldy, Scotland, and became one of the world's greatest thinkers. The precocious child started studying moral philosophy at the University of Glasgow at age fourteen and afterward received a graduate scholarship to attend the University of Oxford, where he found the teaching environment too stifling. Taking solace in the library, he spent many hours teaching himself a range of topics that foreshadowed his contributions to philosophy, history, government, language, and astronomy, and ultimately his founding of the field of economics.

In *The Wealth of Nations*, Smith lays out many of the principles that continue to shape economic thought today. Along with his widely acknowledged contribution about the invisible hand—the idea that self-interest unintentionally leads to widespread social benefits—rests a less credited but equally powerful idea: the division of labor.

Smith opens his treatise by describing an industrious pin maker. The craftsman might spend all day working tirelessly but end up with only a single unit. Smith observed what he considered a better way, breaking the job of making pins into specialized tasks performed by different people: drawing out the wire, straightening it, cutting it, pointing it, and so on. As each person repeats his task, he becomes an expert, so proficient that he makes few mistakes and so quick that he's exceptionally productive. Higher output and fewer errors led Smith to reason that ten people with divided responsibilities could produce almost fifty thousand pins a day, a per capita output of nearly five thousand units.

There's no doubt that the division of labor and its popularization during the Industrial Revolution ushered in an era of economic expansion. The challenge, as the sociologist Robin Leidner points out, is that while the division of labor started to split up manufacturing jobs, it soon applied to all sorts of work. Increasing specialization even among knowledge workers led people to know about their responsibilities while remaining ignorant of what unfolded around the corner.

If there's one place in organizations where you'd expect specialization to give way to diverse experiences, it's at the very top, where executives need to understand and connect different areas. But the forces of division of labor make it hard to develop the diverse experiences needed to lead. Yet it turns out that the people who manage to gain this diverse experience get richly rewarded.

In an examination of executive résumés at small, medium, and large publicly traded firms, a research team led by finance professor Cláudia Custódio evaluated the extent to which the executives followed the multi-c rule. They compiled data on forty-five hundred CEOs who held 32,500 past positions and constructed an index of the diversity of experiences comprised of five items: number of positions to account for experience in different areas such as production, marketing, and human resources; number of companies worked at; breadth of industry experience; previous experience with big-picture thinking; and experience working in operationally diverse companies. They also accounted for other potential explanations such as age, tenure, and educational background. The researchers then grouped the executives into those who endorsed the multi-c rule (participants who scored above the median on their experience index) and those who scored below the median.

There was a striking difference in pay. Multi-c executives earned a 19 percent pay premium, translating into roughly $1 million in extra pay per year. The compensation boost applied across a variety of industries, but the research team found one factor that made the pay package even bigger. When the job requirements involved more complex tasks such as a merger, acquisition, or industry shock—the kinds that Professor Macnamara's research shows are most difficult for experts—multi-c executives earned up to 44 percent more.

Like executives who get paid handsomely for embracing the multi-c rule, many of us also find ourselves in complex situations that could benefit from a breadth of experiences. In his book *A Whole New Mind*, Daniel Pink writes, "While detailed knowledge of a single area once guaranteed success, today the top rewards go to those who can operate with equal aplomb in starkly different realms." But for those not at the top, Pink's prescription proves difficult because Adam Smith was right. The division of labor grows organizations' productivity by leaps and bounds by pushing people to pursue increasingly specialized experiences at the expense of diverse experiences. It benefits organizations' ongoing operations— they can build, sell, and service more, just like Adam Smith's pin factory—but it also makes it incredibly difficult for employees to learn what they need to develop personally and to help their organizations with complex challenges.

But here's the good news. Even experts can learn how to take an outsider's position. We'll learn how we can bring a specialized focus on solving narrow types of problems to a larger world. By taking expertise on the road, we expand possibilities for ourselves and others.

## STEP OUTSIDE OF YOUR WORLD

On March 24, 1989, the *Exxon Valdez* ran aground in Prince William Sound, Alaska, spilling more than 10 million gallons of oil into the pristine habitat for salmon, sea otters, seabirds, and seals. The accident was one of the world's largest human-caused environmental catastrophes, and the residue from it would last for decades. In the aftermath of the tragic incident, Congress created the Oil Spill Recovery Institute (OSRI) to figure out the best way to prevent future oil spills from similarly turning into devastating disasters.

As research program manager at OSRI, Scott Pegau's job was to find solutions that would cap future troubles in the area, and the *Valdez* oil spill had taught him that one of the most pressing priorities was dealing with semifrozen oil. In the arctic waters, oil turns into an icy slush mixture, making its safe recovery nearly impossible. Unfortunately, the experts had run out of ideas.

With no solution in sight, Scott Pegau turned to InnoCentive, the same company studied by Jeppesen and Lakhani, to see if its diverse base of problem solvers could come up with an answer. He offered a $20,000 prize for the best proposal and opened the contest up to experts and outsiders.

John Davis, a chemist from Bloomington, Illinois, didn't know much about oil spills or, for that matter, the energy business. But he had worked a summer job pouring concrete, where he had learned about vibrators that restore concrete flow when the material starts to harden and get stuck. Davis wondered whether the same approach could break up the icy oil mixture, allowing it to continue to move in liquid form. As an outsider, he came up with a solution the experts had never even considered.

After evaluating more than twenty submissions, Pegau named Davis the winner. As Pegau acknowledges, if it was "easily solved by the people within the industry, it would have been solved by the people in the industry . . . sometimes you slap your head and go, 'Why didn't I think of that?' I'm glad that we asked someone else."

Scott Pegau did what we too rarely do—he turned to outsiders for help. John Davis was no expert in oil recovery, but he knew something Scott Pegau and other experts in oil recovery didn't. Separated by as many differences in their backgrounds as miles between their homes, the two men came together because of what sociologists call small worlds. We live in self-contained pockets of knowledge, relationships, and other resources, but surprisingly it takes little to step outside and connect across small worlds.

No organization or group of people is more skilled at stepping outside than California-based engineering design firm IDEO. Professor Andrew Hargadon and his colleague Robert Sutton spent several years conducting fieldwork at the company. They interviewed and observed employees to understand how they repeatedly turned out ingenious solutions to difficult problems. The research pointed to a clear answer: IDEO organizes itself around helping employees make the world smaller by bringing overlooked expertise to new areas.

IDEO and its employees routinely borrow stuff meant for one situation and use it to solve very different problems in very different situations. Hargadon and Sutton describe four critical steps to create a culture that allows people to take their resources to new places.

First, explore the world around you. Embrace the multi-c rule to build a mental database of ideas—not to serve a specific goal but rather to satisfy a curiosity. At IDEO, employees visit places such as a hardware store, the Barbie Hall of Fame, and an airplane junkyard. These excursions may appear odd, but that's entirely the point. They're not meant to teach them anything specific but rather complicate the way they think about the world. Outsiders don't operate along the same conventions as experts, so instead of honing in on a traditional body of knowledge about a topic, they cast a wide net, embodying Thomas Edison's advice: "To invent, you need a good imagination and a pile of junk."

Second, make sure resources remain accessible and top of mind. It's easy to forget what we already know and overlook what we already have, preventing us from making connections between resources we've used in one situation with the current problems we have in other situations. At IDEO, the company uses the metaphor of a museum collection. They employ curators to catalog and care for a diverse set of materials from previous projects—prototypes, sketches, equipment, and memos. Some people like to hoard resources for personal gain, but outsiders depend on sharing ideas with others to keep learning.

Third, use analogical reasoning. John Davis viewed the oil-recovery challenge in terms of flowing concrete, opening up the possibility of drawing on an unrelated experience to solve what turned out to be a similar problem.

At IDEO, the company uses an open office space to allow its employees to eavesdrop on one another's problems, inviting them to make analogical links to one another's work. When Hargadon and Sutton were sitting with two engineers designing a razor that also vacuumed loose hair, an IDEO colleague, who had overhead their conversation, came by with ideas from a similar challenge—a way of carrying away fumes from skin cauterized by incisions made with a scalpel. By using analogies to make connections to similar problems that on the surface look different, the organization and its members find that it has already solved many of the new problems it faces.

Finally, regularly test ideas, expecting most to fail. IDEO has lots of failures from past projects, so testing new uses for them turns out to be pretty inexpensive. The problem is that we find it hard to abandon our ideas even in the face of evidence that shows they don't work because of the escalation of commitment we learned about in chapter 2.

By stepping outside, people discover greater richness in what they already have. Our short-term and long-term challenges become more manageable once we break down barriers that limit the movement of resources across areas. Outsiders play this role, but even if we're not outsiders, we can still gain outsider experiences.

## EVEN EXPERTS SHOULD GAIN OUTSIDER EXPERIENCES

A barrier to the outsider path is that many of us have good reason to gain deep experience. It's hard to be a competent physician, accountant, attorney, or architect without clocking in lots of hours. The educational, occupational, and organizational forces of division of labor also push us onto the expertise path. But it's critical for even experts to embrace an outsider's view and for organizations—whether business, governments, or schools—to encourage them in these efforts.

Getting outside of our worlds is a first step, and the most successful experts also follow the multi-c rule, staying close enough to be relevant but far enough to be free from the orthodoxy that steeps people in a narrow, and insular, world. Story Musgrave studied literature, and Nobel Prize–winning scientists tend to be fond of the arts. Indeed, researchers found that these top scientists had a significantly greater likelihood of engaging in the arts compared to either scientists at large or the general public. Google's chairman Eric Schmidt calls for a return to developing multiple interests, declaring, "You need to bring art and science back together" like in times when "the same people wrote poetry and built bridges." A recent survey commissioned by the Association of American Colleges and Universities found that most hiring managers want the broad experiences of outsiders along with the specific expertise from a major.

As intimidating as it might seem to pursue deep *and* diverse experiences, some experts naturally pursue both. One of the big five personality traits—the broad dimensions psychologists use to classify innate differences between people—is called openness to experience. It captures a person's interest in varied experiences for their own sake. To measure openness to experience, researchers ask participants to rate themselves on scales anchored by opposing adjectives, such as simple/complex, narrow interests/broad interests, conforming/independent, and traditional/untraditional. Closed individuals take comfort in the familiar, and resonate toward the first word in each pair. Open individuals more likely gravitate toward the second word and seek out the unfamiliar, leading them to a diversity of experiences beyond their small worlds that enrich their thinking within those small worlds.

Sometimes our circumstances also put us in a variety of small worlds. We need to move or switch jobs. We travel to unfamiliar places and stumble upon new things. In a recent study, researchers catalogued people's cultural experiences—including parental upbringing, language, favorite restaurants and musicians, and the background of closest friends. They then evaluated the degree to which participants came up with new ways of envisioning a gift for an acquaintance. Those with the most diverse cultural backgrounds came up with the least typical gifts, such as poetry, while those with the most homogenous backgrounds opted for typical ways of thinking about gifts, such as by suggesting chocolate. The study shows that whether by choice or circumstance, people who grow up and live in diverse contexts think about resources in less typical ways.

# S T R E T C H

At other times, we need to make a conscious effort to seek out new experiences, but we don't need to earn multiple graduate degrees like Story Musgrave. Temporary departures from our small worlds can come from short bursts of new activities such as reading about another field, finding a hobby, or having conversations with people from different backgrounds. Research shows that these experiences outside of the office give us a leg up at work. In a survey of 179 senior managers at a large insurance company, participants completed questions about the extent to which they used experiences outside of their core expertise, particularly non-work experiences and hobbies, to help with challenges at work. The researchers then followed up with participants and their colleagues, asking about the participant's use of resources. The more diverse the non-work experiences, the more resourceful people were at work.

## EMBRACE OUTSIDERS

In this chapter, we've discussed two very different approaches to using experience to find success. In the first path, we gain experience in a limited set of activities to achieve expertise, whereas in the second path, we emphasize breadth of experiences. Those with the most training, strongest credentials, and best connections don't always prevail, and a diversity of experiences grants us a way to stretch.

Trying simultaneously to gain a depth of experience and follow the multi-c rule is undoubtedly difficult, which is why it's important for us to have outsiders around. Because we favor people like us, it requires both a conscious effort to forge personal and professional relationships with people of diverse experiences and a mental leap to recognize that sometimes those who know the least contribute the most to our teams.

Indeed, it's hard to find the Gavin Potters of the world and even harder to include them in our work, but the returns make it worth it.

When computer scientist Yehuda Koren and statisticians Robert Bell and Chris Volinsky used Gavin Potter's behavioral approach to reignite their progress on the Netflix Prize, their effort still fell short of the contest's ultimate objective. The trio merged with other teams to diversify even more. "While it might seem obvious to combine with a team that was already doing well," they reasoned, "there would be no gain if both teams were simply duplicating one another's methods." They embraced additional outsiders to get over the finish line first, and offer an important lesson for us. The value of our resources dramatically increases when we join forces with outsiders.

# FIVE

## TIME TO ACT

WHY WE SOMETIMES PERFORM BETTER WITHOUT

A SCRIPT (AND ALL THE TIME AND MONEY IN THE

WORLD)

A healthy twenty-three-year-old aspiring filmmaker named Robert Rodriguez nervously waited for his test results at a hospital on a spring day in 1991. He hoped to be selected to participate in a pharmaceutical study where he would be confined to a hospital for a month and take experimental drugs so he could earn money to fund making a movie. The payoff wouldn't be great—roughly $3,000—but he says, "If you bleed for your money, I mean really bleed for it, you're very careful on how you spend that money." After passing the medical screenings, he changed into his uniform for the monthlong study—green scrubs and a red T-shirt. He became known simply as Red 11.

The study administrators assigned participants to a color group. Although all subjects were physically confined, the red-shirted participants received some special privileges. The most valuable and coveted of these was outdoor recreation. The diet of the red-shirted participants, far from gourmet, also caught the attention of the teal-shirted research subjects, whose low-calorie restrictions led them to raid pantries and bargain with one another for potato chips. In between daily blood draws and regimented bathroom breaks, Rodriguez penned the lines for *El Mariachi*, a Spanish-language film about a traveling musician who gets mistaken for a crook named Azul who is known for toting around guns in a guitar case.

When the drug study ended and he collected his check, Rodriguez went right to work filming, adopting a unique approach that came to epitomize a very different moviemaking style. Hollywood is known for getting caught up in the chase for more. Film producers approach their financial backers for expensive casts, props, special effects, elaborate sets, and a large crew, regarding these resources as a requirement to get good results. If he followed the conventional route to moviemaking, he reasoned, he'd need at least a hundred grand, lots of industry contacts, and more experience.

Rodriguez took a very different approach. He made a list of what he had readily available—a friend's ranch, a pit bull, condoms he could fill with fake blood, desk lamps in lieu of professional lighting, a wheelchair he sat on while holding the camera instead of moving the camera with a dolly, and a guy he met at the hospital whom he could cast in a key role.

Rodriguez did just about everything but star in the film, serving as its writer, cameraman, editor, sound artist, and production assistant. "Even if I didn't know what to do, [I] just had to begin," he recalls, "you'll only get the idea once you start . . . you have to act first before inspiration will hit, you don't wait for inspiration and then act, or you're never going to act." Robert Rodriguez dove in and found his inspiration. Waiting for the supposed "right" resources would have only delayed, or even compromised, his progress.

As Rodriguez started filming the movie, he would often go off script. For some filmmakers off-the-cuff changes might delay production, but Rodriguez turned them into positive adjustments that made the film even better. As he put it, stretching allowed him to "get something much better than if I had all the time and money in the world."

In one scene, Rodriguez borrowed a machine gun from the local police at the Mexican border town where he produced the flick. He filled the firearm with blanks and imagined Azul spraying bullets. But the weapon kept jamming without live ammunition. To avoid the expense of purchasing guns that would actually work, he changed the way he pointed his camera. After filming a frame of Azul firing a shot, he quickly panned to capture the casualties and later added sound effects to mimic a rapidly firing weapon. The cost of the film itself was his biggest expense, so he used editing to stitch together whatever his camera captured, turning mistakes into storyline modifications while giving his movie a fast-paced tempo that delighted the critics. As he puts it, "You end up just working with what you got."

By constantly observing and engaging his surroundings, Rodriguez capitalized on resources that popped up around him. Returning from filming one day, he passed a stand selling coconuts with straws in them to sip out their milk. He thought it would make a good scene but had not planned on it before. That didn't stop him. Opportunistically, he filmed his lead character Mariachi buying a cold drink to quench his thirst as the musician first set foot in town. The scene worked, but Rodriguez made a critical mistake. He forgot to film Mariachi paying for the beverage. Instead of redoing the scene, Rodriguez changed the storyline—all visitors to the town would receive a free drink.

After completing production, he pitched the film to the Spanish video market, eventually receiving a $25,000 verbal offer for its distribution. It wasn't a humongous payday, but it would help fund his next film, where he'd be able to build on what he learned and take another step toward his goal of being a career filmmaker.

Waiting in Los Angeles to formalize the deal, he thumbed through the phone book. Rodriguez's lack of professional connections, reputation, and experience didn't stop him from trying to capture the attention of one of the world's most prestigious talent agencies. He cold-called entertainment agent Robert Newman's office. After pitching the idea to Newman's assistant, Rodriguez dropped off a trailer for *El Mariachi*, hoping for some good news.

Three days passed before his phone rang with exciting news. Newman loved the trailer and wanted to know how much it cost to make. When Rodriguez answered about seven grand, Newman was impressed with the young prodigy, telling him that most trailers cost between $20,000 and $30,000—not realizing that Rodriguez was referring to seven grand for the *entire* movie.

It turned out to be a good thing that the Spanish video distributor never delivered its promised payment for the film. Newman quickly signed the unknown filmmaker as a client, and soon *El Mariachi* was in the hands of all the major film studios. Columbia Pictures outmaneuvered its competitors to purchase the film for roughly half a million dollars. The stunning results surprised Rodriguez and convinced him that successful filmmaking can be done through stretching and without the typical chase.

Columbia first considered remaking *El Mariachi* with better equipment, more experienced actors, and a larger crew. The original film's crew was so sparse that Rodriguez had added fictitious names to the ending credits to give the movie the legitimacy of a larger production. Executives at Columbia had the bias that Hollywood films need plentiful resources, but they also realized that the mastery of Rodriguez's moviemaking came from how he skillfully put to use whatever he could, creating a differentiated, authentic style that big bucks couldn't buy.

Box office sales topped $2 million. It was by no means a blockbuster, but its success helped Rodriguez advance his Hollywood career and sign up to write, direct, and edit a sequel to *El Mariachi*, *Desperado*, starring Antonio Banderas. Rodriguez went on to deliver more critically acclaimed (and profitable) movies, which allowed him to have his pick of projects; perhaps even more important, he was able to turn down offers to make blockbusters such as *X-Men* and *Planet of the Apes* because, to his way of thinking, they wouldn't have been fun to make. Their outsize budgets would take away his inherent satisfaction from making movies resourcefully. As he put it: "The creative person with limitless imagination and no money can make a better film than the talentless mogul with the limitless checkbook every time. . . . Take advantage of your disadvantages, feature the few assets you may have, and work harder than anyone else around you."

Rodriguez's resourceful approach to making movies didn't mean he needed to always turn down ambitious projects. It just meant he needed to take on these projects on his own terms. Drawing inspiration from his childhood, he wrote, directed, edited, and helped film the Spy Kids trilogy, which grossed over $300 million. The budgets for these films topped any of his other productions, but their expenses paled in comparison to typical movies in this genre. "It looks like an expensive movie, but it's all magic tricks. I edited it in my garage," he says. When he wanted George Clooney to make a cameo as president in the last film of the series, Rodriguez showed up on his doorstep with a video camera and filmed the scene in the actor's living room.

By putting to use all available resources, including resources that don't, at first blush, appear to be resources at all, Rodriguez made critically acclaimed and commercially successful films—while also having a blast. By his own estimate, Rodriguez is "the only guy who really enjoys being in the business."

In this chapter, I'll reveal how Robert Rodriguez's moviemaking approach provides a useful guide for our own professional and personal projects, empowering us to act with whatever we have to move closer to meeting our goals—and to have a better time along the way. As straightforward as it sounds—to act with the resources we have versus the resources we think we need—we still have a hard time doing it. Why? Our penchant for planning: one of the most important, but also most limiting, tools of modern life. There's no doubt that planning has tremendous utility, but we'll also learn when it slows us down or even forces us to veer us off course.

We often credit great planning for our successes, forgetting that the biggest determination of our performance is *what we do* and not what we plan to do. Some of us naturally like to jump in and get going, while others are more hesitant and dependent on meticulous planning. We'll examine the underlying psychology that controls our acting or planning orientations and understand how to change them.

Next, we'll learn why planning prevents us from listening to and observing our surroundings, making it difficult to stretch. A shift to acting helps us notice untapped potential we can put right to work.

We'll end the chapter by unpacking an alternative to planning: improvisation. By becoming more comfortable with this technique, we free ourselves to stretch, handling the inevitable changes we regularly face.

## THE PERILS OF PLANNING

On September 17, 1862, in Sharpsburg, Maryland, the first major battle of the Civil War on Union turf also became the bloodiest single-day fight in American history, resulting in more than 22,000 people dead, wounded, or missing. The Battle of Antietam pitted the 55,000-man army of Robert E. Lee against the 75,500-man army led by George McClellan. As Lee marched north to invade Maryland, he soon encountered McClellan, a brilliant military mind, salutatorian at West Point, and methodical planner.

When McClellan's army positioned itself to intercept the Confederacy's northward trek, two of his soldiers made a potentially battle-changing discovery: a copy of Lee's detailed battle plans—Special Order 191—wrapped around three cigars. The order indicated that Lee had geographically divided his army, making each part vulnerable to a fast attack by McClellan's larger forces. Here was the North's chance to deliver a decisive victory that could end the war . . . if only General McClellan could act quickly.

The problem was that General McClellan always seemed to have an excuse for delaying movement and spent far more time planning to fight than actually fighting. Earlier in the year, President Lincoln became so frustrated by his general's inaction that he sent him a telegram warning, "If General McClellan does not want to use the Army, I would like to borrow it for a time."

At Antietam, McClellan retreated to planning how to capitalize on this intelligence gold mine. But when reports surfaced that put some enemy troops in areas not included in Lee's Special Order 191, McClellan appeared stumped that his opponents wouldn't follow their plans. Eighteen critical hours would go by before McClellan felt he had his own battle plan ready. In the interim, Lee ordered his soldiers to consolidate, an about-face that erased the advantage McClellan had enjoyed the previous day.

The Battle of Antietam weakened Lee's army, but it managed to escape back to Virginia due to the slow movement of McClellan's forces. The crushing blow President Lincoln had hoped for didn't happen, so he urged McClellan to pursue Lee into Virginia to deliver a final knockout. The president paid the general a visit, hoping to prod him to start moving. During his visit, the two men were to be photographed, and Lincoln jokingly wrote to his wife, "General McClellan and myself are to be photographed tomorrow A.M . . . if we can sit still long enough. I feel Gen. M. should have no problem."

For six weeks, McClellan refused to pursue Lee's vulnerable army, offering a bunch of excuses: tired troops, unknown terrain, a river that was both too deep to cross but not deep enough to hold back Lee's army from marching forward, with broken weapons and too few boots, blankets, and wagons. Lincoln wryly questioned his general's ability to act. The "General is a good engineer," he observed. "But he seems to have a special talent for developing a 'stationary' engine." He would go on to ask McClellan: "Are you not over-cautious when you assume that you cannot do what the enemy is constantly doing? Should you not claim to be at least his equal in prowess, and act upon the claim?" Lincoln soon fired the general.

Common wisdom suggests that you can never be too prepared. Planning provides a well-thought-out road map everyone can follow and signals legitimacy by showing that, yes, we sweated the details. Yet as General McClellan's experiences show, danger lurks in planning; indeed, too much planning prevents us from acting.

We like to plan because it's comfortably familiar. We learn about it as early as kindergarten, and it gets reinforced and practiced throughout adulthood. People plan everything from how to spend their weekends to how to retire. Organizations also love to plan, spanning near-term objectives to long-term road maps. Whether you're an executive devising a new strategy, a middle manager leading a change, or even a family considering a vacation, we tend to believe that the best results come from careful planning.

When we have plentiful resources, including time and information, planning can do wonders. Yet, even the most resource-rich organizations and people often need to make questionable assumptions about a lot of unknown variables in their plans: the moves our competitors will make, the percentage of customers who will buy a new product, or the likelihood we'll connect with new coworkers if we switch jobs. We then rely on these assumptions to plan the future, quickly forgetting about the shaky assumptions that led to our conclusion. And if we don't like the conclusion we came up with, we go back and tweak our assumptions until we get the answer we wanted in the first place—allowing us, for example, to turn an unprofitable new product magically into a blockbuster by simply adjusting how many units we think people will buy.

To overcome any potential shortcomings in our plans, we spend even more time seeking out answers to the unknowns that inform our plans. But our desire for thoroughness just causes a greater delay in our actions. As we delay our actions, our circumstances might have already dramatically changed. We end up spending a lot of time planning for a world that no longer exists, while tricking ourselves into believing that it does exist because that's what we planned for.

# S T R E T C H

Our desire for planning comes from a critical trade-off we regularly think we need to make: speed versus accuracy. When we need quick action, we are willing to overlook some possible alternatives, limit the information we consider, and hasten our analysis about the optimal path. We might not arrive at the best answer, but no one will second-guess us for a makeshift sales pitch when coincidentally sharing an elevator with a potential client or whipping together a meal from leftovers after getting home late.

Alternatively, when we want to address our most critical questions, we tend to favor accuracy over speed, and this is where we easily get lured into overplanning. We'll take our time planning our company's five-year budget, making large investment decisions for new products, or deciding which house to buy. Inside many organizations, entire departments rely on sophisticated planning tools to make the crucial decisions that will supposedly lead to better results. The only problem is that they often don't. In an analysis that incorporates 2,496 organizations, researchers found only a modest correlation between planning and organizational performance.

Why do professional planners, with some of the highest stakes, utilizing lots of resources, come up short? Blame it on the speed-versus-accuracy trade-off.

Stanford University professor Kathy Eisenhardt wondered about how businesses navigated these trade-offs when she conducted in-depth qualitative and quantitative research at eight computer companies. She interviewed chief executives and top managers, collected survey data, and analyzed industry reports and company archives, and she found something rather surprising. Instead of relying on less information and considering fewer alternatives, Eisenhardt found that executive teams who made quicker decisions relied on *more* information and a *greater* number of alternatives—the exact opposite of what we're led to believe by the speed-versus-accuracy trade-off.

To unlock this mystery, Eisenhardt returned to her data and found differences in the kind of information the quicker-acting executive teams used. They focused on the present, relying on real-time information about their operations and competitors. In contrast, the slower teams spent a significant amount of time and energy trying to imagine what the future would look like, generating forecasts about hard-to-predict events. When it came time to tally performance, the quicker firms outperformed their slower competitors in terms of sales, return on sales (profits divided by sales), and the perception of executives and their competitors.

For those who endorse meticulous planning, these results are truly puzzling. How could circumventing these tools lead to better performance? The answer turns out to be quite simple.

We learn from doing. When we plan, we're not acting but delaying our actions and speculating about a future that may or may not exist. Eisenhardt's highest performers remained in the present and developed the ability to adapt quickly. Because the organizations and people she studied operated in turbulent environments, their futures were less certain, which renders planning less useful. With the rules of the game rapidly changing, it became much more important to act constantly and learn in the present.

Another unexpected benefit for the quicker responders? There's less politically, psychologically, and economically invested when not following a plan, enabling us to be responsive to whatever up-to-date information we have instead of overly committed to staying the course. We may trick ourselves into thinking our plans are foolproof, intimidating others (and ourselves) into following them. Yet, even the best-laid plans are naturally incomplete, a fact that can be masked if we believe, often wrongly, that we've figured out everything beforehand. By allowing for multiple possibilities, we avoid the type of escalation of commitment we learned about in chapter 2, where people irrationally stick with the plan, and even invest more in it, when it's clearly not working. Instead of unquestionably reaching for planning, we sometimes need to act and just do it.

## JUST DO IT

The Czech poet and immunologist Miroslav Holub documented a remarkable tale of a group of Hungarian soldiers on a reconnaissance mission who became lost in the Alps. As Holub tells it, the cold and snowy weather made navigating back to safety difficult. Two days passed with no word from the troops, and their lieutenant worried he had deployed the men to their graveyards. Then, miraculously, on day three the men returned unharmed. Relieved but puzzled by their appearance, the grateful leader asked how they made their way back. One of the soldiers had found a map in his pocket. When the weather improved, they used it to navigate home. The lieutenant asked to examine the map. He took a look at it and was baffled. It was a map of a different set of mountains—the Pyrenees.

The management scholar Karl Weick concludes from this tale that when our bearings are lost, "any old map will do." Even though the soldiers used a map covering a different territory, it prevented them from panicking about what they lacked and got them moving. By moving, they learned about their surroundings and kept talking about their shared goal—getting back to camp safely. The map's value rested not in its accuracy but rather in its ability to be a catalyst for action. Even though we often give credit for our success to our professional and personal maps—our plans—it's our actions that usually explain our results. The problem is that many of us like to stay put, getting lost in the excesses of planning or, especially for chasers, waiting for the right resources to fall into place before acting.

Fighting a tendency for inertia was something that advertising executive Dan Wieden tapped into in 1988. Working at his floundering agency that started in the basement of a Portland labor union hall, stocked with little more than a borrowed typewriter and a pay phone, Wieden struggled to find a tagline to unify a bunch of television spots for a small sportswear brand.

After toiling through the night, Wieden finally thought he was onto something when he remembered the decade-old death of fellow Oregonian Gary Gilmore.

By his thirty-fifth birthday, Gilmore had already spent half of his life in prison, with a rap sheet that included theft, armed robbery, and assault. A year later, he committed his last crimes, brutally murdering a gas station employee and motel clerk. A court handed down his final sentence—the death penalty.

Unlike most death row inmates, Gary Gilmore didn't want to appeal. His attorneys tried to overturn his sentence, but he resisted their help. When his mother wrote a letter requesting leniency, Gilmore replied with a public plea for her to get out of the way of his death. He called the governor a "moral coward" for staying this execution and asked "the rabbis, the priests, the A.C.L.U. . . . to butt out."

In 1977, Gary Gilmore became the first person in the United States to be executed in a decade. The last words he spoke—"Let's do it"—would provide Wieden with what he needed to finish his work.

Wieden pitched a potential slogan to his client's cofounder, Phil Knight, who immediately responded with, "We don't need that shit." Wieden's counterpoint: "Just trust me."

It's a good thing Knight relented, because Dan Wieden had just created one of the world's most successful advertising lines ever. The "Just Do It" campaign propelled Nike to the top of the athletic business and forged a global brand recognized as much for its superstar endorsers as for its call to action.

# STRETCH

Dan Wieden didn't fully realize it, but his marketing campaign had tapped into a critical part of our psychology—our regulatory modes. These are the beliefs and states that control how we think about and use resources to achieve goals. When operating from a planning regulatory mode, people feel a strong drive to evaluate potential uses for their resources comprehensively. They seek out as much information as possible about different choices to help pick the best option. When people follow this mode, they are never satisfied with a good choice; they want the very best choice, even if it takes tremendous resources to make it. And when they act, they'll often second-guess what they're doing, regret their choices, and wonder if there's a better way. They'll also speculate about how their paths stack up against others, invoking the dangerous social comparison instinct favored by chasers that upends personal satisfaction.

Now if you tend to jump right in, you're following an acting regulatory mode. When in this mode, we do anything to move away from the status quo and closer to our goals, even if there's a potentially better way we haven't figured out yet.

In a world where we hold planning on a pedestal, our common-sense notion of a person using the acting mode is that he acts recklessly without much thought. People who plan, on the other hand, conjure up more positive images—the careful person pursuing goals with reflection and great success. Our cultural expectation is that planning provides the best, if not only, pathway to prosperity—but that's not the case.

In a study of seventy employees of an Italian computer company, researchers collected two waves of data separated by three months. In the first phase, participants completed a survey to classify their regulatory mode and the extent to which they're intrinsically (focused on the joys of work) or extrinsically (focused on the rewards of work) motivated. In the second phase, participants completed scales about their effort (such as how hard they worked to pursue a goal) and whether they successfully completed their goal.

It was people using the acting mode who were highly stimulated by their work, paying less attention to rewards. They simply enjoyed their work, unburdened by having to figure out the absolute best way forward. Their intrinsic motivation propelled them to put in more effort toward their goals and also made them more likely to accomplish those goals.

The planning group, on the other hand, was more calculated and reward focused. The quest for the best choice sucked the joy out of doing their work, which led them to put in less effort and made them less likely to achieve their goals.* Planning bred anxiety from always worrying about following the plan, and then second-guessing whether it was even the best plan.

Too often planning stifles our action because we're trying to put together a perfect plan, even when an adequate one will serve us well. When he tried to launch his film career, Robert Rodriguez knew he didn't need a perfect debut movie to break into Hollywood; he just wanted to inch a little closer to his dream of becoming a career filmmaker. Instead of waiting for more resources—a crucial connection, additional money, or a better camera—he just made his movie. We'd be wise to follow his lead and start "directing" our own projects.

---

In a world where planning dominates so many areas of life, it's often hard to just dive in. I find this reluctance in the classroom all the

---

* Although the acting orientation helped participants obtain better satisfaction and success, the research still finds a role for a planning orientation, but only if coupled with an acting one. In the study, goal attainment was even higher for people using acting if they also had a planning orientation.

STRETCH

time—whether teaching people with little work experience or senior executives with decades behind them.

It's no wonder, then, that when I ask students to imagine that they are the captain of a large cargo vessel several hundred years ago and need to sail across the ocean, they immediately turn to planning. Lacking modern-day tools such as a GPS device, satellite telephone, and other electronic aids, I ask them to describe how they might go about their jobs. Most of them come up with a similar answer. They'd study a bunch of maps, look for the optimal route by predicting the winds and currents, and then chart a course. I point out that navigating the seas, much like many work and non-work situations, regularly brings uncertain events and unexpected developments. The current may change or a storm might develop.

When faced with these questions, my students usually respond that they will modify their original plan and then stay the new, revised course. They unknowingly articulate the same principles endorsed by European navigators for centuries. Under the European navigational approach, high performance comes from formulating a carefully created plan, accumulating the necessary resources for the plan, implementing the plan, tracking progress to the plan, and reformulating the plan as needed. These approaches serve us well when we have reasonably good information and sufficient time. But what if we lack information about the future? Or what if evaluating that information becomes too cumbersome? Or what if the future is always changing? That's when we need another way of sailing.

There's a very different way of solving such a navigational challenge, including the one I pose in my classroom. Far from Europe live the Trukese, native inhabitants of the tiny island of Chuuk in the Caroline Islands of Micronesia. The Trukese have a very different means of navigating the seas compared with their European counterparts. They do not make a detailed plan or even chart a course. The Trukese start with a goal (such as sail to an island) and

112

then simply sail, inching closer to their objective. When sailing, they see how their movements interact with their surroundings and make adjustments along the way, carefully responding to the currents and winds. If you were to ask a Trukese captain how he planned to travel the high seas, he would have difficulty answering this question because he doesn't know until he does it.

Underlying the navigational styles of the Trukese rests the same drive that advertising ace Dan Wieden tapped into: an acting regulatory mode. They just do it.

Even if your natural tendency is to favor planning, it's relatively straightforward to adopt an action-oriented orientation. I do this with my students by introducing the Trukese sailors and asking the class to think about how they have previously followed comparable approaches in other parts of their lives. Science also backs up the idea that we can readily move between planning and acting.

In one study, researchers were able to shift people's regulatory modes by merely having them recall times when they adopted either a planning or an acting mode. The experimenter instructed participants to write about three different behaviors they successfully used in the past. Based on chance, the researchers put some people into the acting group and had them respond to three statements: think back to the times when you acted like a "doer"; think back to the times when you finished one project and did not wait long before you started a new one; and think back to the times when you decided to do something and you could not wait to get started. Also based on chance, people in the planning mode responded to a different set of statements: think back to the times when you compared yourself with other people; think back to the times when you thought about your positive and negative characteristics; and think back to the times when you critiqued work done by others or yourself. The simple exercise of responding to the three statements effectively put people into their respective modes, showing that, despite our innate preference for one mode, we can easily shift modes by reflecting on times when we approached situations using another mode.

We will no doubt need to use both the European and Trukese approaches when pursuing our goals. But an overreliance on the planning approach favored by the European sailors creates problems. It's time to get more comfortable with the Trukese approach. A good place to start is to carefully feel out the currents and winds in our own situations. We need to become better listeners and observers.

## WHY WE OVERLOOK RESOURCES RIGHT IN FRONT OF US

The first time I ever taught a college course something really puzzled me. The more hands that went up, the greater the chances that the person I called on would repeat the comment of someone who had just spoken. I couldn't help but wonder (usually to myself), "Weren't you listening to the person who just spoke?"

With a few more classes under my belt, I figured out that I was to blame. I wasn't giving my students a chance to really listen. In an effort to manage the multiple hands that would pop up, I would call on a student to speak while also letting several students know they'd be up next. I thought this would help manage the constant stream of eager students, but instead I was setting a speaking order—imposing a plan on how the conversation would unfold before it unfolded. At meetings, a speaking order might come from the rank of people in the room or even the random place you decide to sit down.

By structuring conversations in these ways, we prevent people with the most relevant information from talking at the most appropriate times, limiting our abilities to make the most out of the resources in the room—whether information, talents, experiences, relationships, and so on.

When we set a speaking order, we also encourage people to focus on preparing to speak during their set time, making it difficult for them to listen to others in ways that gather the type of real-time information critical to the most successful organizations and teams in Professor Eisenhardt's study of computer companies.

During his graduate studies in psychology, former National Transportation Safety Board investigator Malcolm Brenner conducted an experiment where he also set a speaking order. He arranged a square table with chairs. On the table in front of each chair, he also placed six unique word cards, facedown, drawn from the five hundred most common printed words in English.

Participants turned over one of their cards and read it aloud, moving around the table in a predetermined way. After cycling through twenty-five words, the readings stopped and they had ninety seconds to write down as many words as they could recall.

Most people easily recalled the words they personally spoke. They also did reasonably well recalling the words spoken by people across the table. But there was one crucial place where participants' listening skills had major lapses. Participants struggled to remember anything said by their neighbors—the three people who spoke immediately before them and the three who spoke immediately after them.

Participants in Brenner's experiments, students in my class, and people sitting around a table at a meeting need to perform two roles simultaneously: speaking and listening. It turns out that performing both roles takes up a lot of mental energy. As we approach our turn to speak, we shift from listening to preparing to speak as much as nine seconds before, unknowingly blocking out what's being said just prior to our turn. When we direct our mental energy to planning our performance—making a terrific class comment, raising a clever point at a meeting, or arguing with our partner—we stop processing real-time information prior to our performance. By the time we finish our planning and speak our words, those points, just like some of my students' comments, may be irrelevant.

Brenner's study also finds that we need a similar amount of time after speaking to shift back to listening mode. This cool-down phase allows us to reflect on our performance—was it well received, did it have an impact on the conversation, what next might I say? During recovery, we miss how people react to what we say, robbing us of vital information that helps us not only evaluate our contribution but also understand how that contribution could help meet our objectives.

It's hard to listen to others or, for that matter, to observe our surroundings, when we're following a plan, especially as our surroundings change. The way forward is to become better listeners, which is unexpectedly easier if we force ourselves to act on the spot without thorough planning.

Viola Spolin, born in 1906, is considered the contemporary mother of improvisational theater first practiced by the Romans around 391 BC. Spolin started working with inner-city children as part of the Chicago branch of the Works Progress Administration's Recreation Project in 1939. The "Theater Games" she developed are used to teach acting skills virtually everywhere in the world. But her initial hope for her work was to teach children who came from impoverished households to be resourceful. By coaching them how to listen to what was happening around them and then act quickly, Spolin taught even those with very little to have the confidence and skills to act with what they had.

Spolin's son, Paul Sills, went on to cofound the Second City, one of the most respected comedy troupes in the world that has been home to some of America's greatest comics, including Bill Murray,

John Belushi, Gilda Radner, Mike Myers, and Tina Fey. Spolin's techniques now gained a larger audience with some of America's best entertainers as its ambassadors.

The hilarious comics all shared one important thing in common. They were all mentored by Del Close, a largely unknown teacher of improv comedy, former resident coach on *Saturday Night Live* and disciple of Viola Spolin.

Del Close picked up on Spolin's work to help turn improv comedy into a more constructive art. Instead of encouraging cheap laughs, he advocated that performers listen carefully to each other and make positive connections between characters and themes. He wanted to have his students keep the action going by building on each other's stories. To discipline his students to listen carefully and work with the stories already verbalized, he taught them to say "Yes, and" to anything a fellow actor said.

When I teach my students to be resourceful, I follow the pathbreaking work of Viola Spolin, its refinements by Del Close, and its current practice featured in a recent book by former Second City leaders Kelly Leonard and Tom Yorton. I invite five students to form a circle and play the "Yes, and" game. In this game, a player starts by speaking a sentence about anything. The other players then take turns trying to keep the story going by responding "Yes, and." The objective of the game is to continue to build on the story by affirming and taking at face value what the person just before has said. Sometimes a player will stump the group by speaking a line that takes the story in a completely different direction. This can cause the group to break down and lose cohesion. In contrast, when players can keep the story flowing by affirming one another, it makes each player feel as if he or she has made important contributions to the story, helping build trust.

But there's another reason why I like to play the "Yes, and" game. Observers often comment at how thoughtful and clever the players' spoken words are, but the players themselves recognize that the key to success is not speaking but listening. This is the often-unnoticed ingenuity behind what both Viola Spolin and Del Close accomplished. Without knowing what will happen immediately before (or after), players need to listen carefully and remain engaged in the present. They're not entirely sure when they will jump in until they jump in, nor do they know what they'll be saying until they say it. By listening, and reacting to one another without a plan, they allow themselves to create something new and potentially more interesting.

Unlike improv, traditional theater works well when actors use scripts and constantly practice their lines. Actors prepare their performances and know what words their colleagues will speak. There's more predictability, but there's little chance for embellishing what's already out there. The best we can hope for is good execution of the plan.

Beyond traditional theater, few places in life are so scripted, although many places are scripted just enough to limit listening and, in turn, the possibilities for what can be achieved. Rank, position, education, status, and personality frequently divide people into speakers and listeners. When I taught the first time, I stuck too rigidly to my lesson plan, missing opportunities to let the class lead itself to unexpected discoveries. I divided the room into speaker (me) and listeners (the students). In my first teaching evaluation, one student commented that my classes were performed like a Shakespearean play. I initially took this as a compliment. I had meticulously executed my well-rehearsed and scripted plan. But I had also overlooked listening to the valuable contributions my students had brought with them to the classroom—their work experiences, unique points of view, and cultural heritage.

It's not just listening for the sake of listening, but recognizing that these voices and perspectives are resources that can be tapped into, and that in building on them we can transform uncertainty into new knowledge and opportunities. That's the heart of the "just do it" mentality and the heart of improvisation.

## THE INGENUITY OF IMPROVISING

Before her flight from Hong Kong to London in 1995, then thirty-nine-year-old Paula Dickson had fallen off her motorcycle on the way to the airport. She shrugged off the accident and continued with her trip. But after boarding, Dickson became concerned about swelling in her forearm. Two doctors on board, Angus Wallace and Tom Wong, diagnosed her with a broken arm. The doctors used the airplane's emergency medical kit to treat the condition with a splint. Satisfied with their work, and with a much more comfortable patient, the doctors returned to their seats.

An hour into the flight onboard the 747 jumbo jetliner, Dickson started experiencing severe chest pain and had trouble breathing. Alarmed by these new symptoms, Dr. Wallace reexamined Dickson and the situation was far worse than his initial evaluation. Dickson's ribs had punctured her lung, and she was in need of immediate surgery.

Landing the plane at the nearest airport might take too long to save Dickson. Making matters worse, the change in cabin pressure that would accompany the plane's descent could prove fatal. What could Dr. Wallace do?

With time ticking, Dr. Wallace didn't have the luxury of doing anything but getting right to work. He created a makeshift operating room at the back of the airplane. His improvised space not only provided a physical place for Dickson's surgery, but also set into motion subsequent actions that made the unusual surgery with atypical tools rather routine. High-end brandy acted as a sterilizer. Dr. Wallace used a pair of scissors to make an incision in Dickson's chest and a coat hanger to insert tubing. A bottle of Evian mineral water drained trapped air inside Dickson's lung. Heated hand towels from the first-class cabin became sterile wound dressings for the critically ill patient.

Fortunately, Dickson survived her harrowing in-flight surgery.

Even though the professional and personal challenges we face differ from Dr. Wallace's, the lessons from his story apply to many situations: when unexpected things arise, getting moving helps us both understand our circumstances and, just as important, change them. As Dr. Wallace took each action, he gradually transformed the airplane into a hospital by improvising.

Because he was well versed in performing surgeries in hospitals, Dr. Wallace faced a situation that was both quite familiar and radically different. The basic steps used to conduct the surgery followed a pattern similar to the way a surgical procedure might happen on land—sterilizing, cutting open the patient, releasing trapped air, and bandaging. Yet the sky-high location and the absence of proper equipment were anything but routine. Improvising allowed Dr. Wallace to bridge the ordinary nature of his task with the unusual way he had to do it.

Like Dr. Wallace, each of us regularly faces situations that can benefit from improvising. New competitors emerge, our customers' tastes change, bestselling products flounder, regulatory shifts change the rules of the game, and we sustain professional and personal setbacks. The way to approach these situations is to recognize that by acting, we allow ourselves to change those situations for the better.

Think, for instance, about the difference between two genres of music: symphony and jazz. They both depend on talented musicians to make great music, but how their musicians go about their work couldn't be more different, with one based on planning and the other on improvising.

The symphony best approximates the planning approach. A formal leader (the conductor) coordinates the work of highly specialized musicians. Sheet music supplies the detailed plans for how the organization executes its performance, something laid out and rehearsed well before showtime. The perfect performance comes from flawlessly executed plans, playing the precise notes on the sheet music, at the exact time.

When we were largely a production-based society, it seemed quite reasonable to orient our work around following a symphony metaphor. Our goal was to eliminate inconsistencies. But as we increasingly move to a society based on individual expression, adaptability, and creativity—and one full of surprises—we need to learn a new tune.

In a jazz ensemble, there's no sheet music to lay out the group's plan, so it's not completely clear how the session will unfold. The musicians aren't entirely sure what notes each will play, so they need to respond quickly to what others end up playing. Instead of planning, they simply want to keep the music playing—avoiding an embarrassing silence. A perfect performance will differ each time, and group members take turns leading the performance.

Too many organizations and people tend to be better at, and place more value on, making symphonic music rather than jazz music. At work and at home, we follow our well-rehearsed sheet music because, no doubt, we keep getting better at playing it over time. We develop a comfortable familiarity with practicing and repeating what we do well rather than risk failing at something we haven't tried yet. The risk is that audience tastes might change—they might grow bored with the usual fare—and yet here we are again, performing the same song, the same way.

To help his band boost its improvisation skills, the jazz musician

# S T R E T C H

Miles Davis would call tunes in different keys during performances. As he told his group, you get paid to practice in front of audiences. The freedom of recognizing that performances were practices, and that there wasn't a single right answer, helped them make beautiful music but also make *different* music—novel, original, exciting, and surprising pieces. Davis's approach follows the same philosophy Robert Rodriguez took when making *El Mariachi*. He never intended the movie to sell to Hollywood and simply considered it a more practical (and less-expensive) film school. The results tend to hold audiences in thrall, but provide the performers and creators with a lasting thrill as well.

When we put this approach to work with our own projects—metaphorically making jazz music with our ensemble—we are also disrupting the ways we use resources. By shaking things up, we grant ourselves and others the freedom to act with what we have and see what happens, learn something, interact with people in unpredictable ways, adjust how we do things—and then do it all over again. Whatever our pursuits, we all benefit from sometimes replacing the best-laid plans with spontaneous action.


## ACTION!

For our biggest ambitions, we cling to the commonsense appeal of planning. It serves us well when the future is predictable, but it also leads us astray at times. By shifting to acting and becoming better observers of our surroundings, we develop skills to improvise with what we have at hand. We don't always need a complete script . . . or even one at all. Instead, we just need to call, "Action!"

# SIX

## WE ARE WHAT WE EXPECT

HOW BELIEFS MAKE US AND THE PEOPLE WE CARE

ABOUT BETTER (OR WORSE)

n 1891, a horse named Hans started wowing large crowds throughout Europe with his extraordinary abilities. His master, a German mathematics teacher named William von Osten, would pose problem after problem to Hans, and the wise horse would regularly come up with the right answer. Hans's specialty was math, but he could also tell time, read, and spell. When asked how many 3's are in the number 7, Hans would stomp his hoof twice, as well as an additional time for the remainder. If von Osten wrote

# STRETCH

the numbers 5 and 9 on a blackboard and asked Hans to sum them, the horse would tap fourteen times. Through years of training and practice—with many of the same techniques von Osten used on his students—the horse appeared to be one gifted animal.

Skeptics wondered if von Osten was secretly signaling answers to the animal or using some other form of deception. Drawing from a group of circus professionals, zookeepers, psychologists, and veterinarians, a commission came together in 1904 to investigate. Despite rigorous analysis, the group couldn't find any evidence of trickery. Indeed, the researchers found that Hans performed almost as well without his master posing the questions. One prominent zoologist concluded Hans "possesses the ability to see sharply, to distinguish mental impressions from each other, to retain them in his memory, and to utter them by his hoof language." The horse earned the German nickname Kluge Hans (Clever Hans). But was he really so clever?

Another three years would pass before a biologist and psychologist named Oskar Pfungst finally revealed Hans's method. Indeed, Hans was quite clever but for very different reasons than the crowds of spectators (and even von Osten) thought. Pfungst observed that when von Osten (or anyone else asking questions) didn't know the correct answer, the horse stumbled. When the physical distance between Hans and the questioner increased, the horse's performance also suffered. Using blinders to obstruct the horse's eyesight turned the prodigy into an ordinary horse.

Pfungst realized that Hans was responding to subtle changes in body language that signaled what the questioner expected him to do. When Hans tapped his hoof the correct number of times, von Osten (or others) would lean slightly forward or make an unconscious change in facial expressions, both which inadvertently led Hans to stop tapping because he had arrived at the answer his master wanted. Providing a carrot or a piece of sugar to reward the horse for solving the problem reinforced his attentiveness to the cues of others.

Like Clever Hans, we too react to subtle (and not so subtle) cues laden with expectations. It turns out that the expectations we set, and that others set for us, are critical for our prospects. Even when based on a false belief, they have a substantial impact on our professional achievements and personal well-being, and in this chapter we'll understand why.

After reviewing some foundational research on expectations, we'll examine how stretchers use expectations to enrich some of the most important areas of their lives: performing at high levels, forming relationships, pursuing opportunities, and meeting life goals. With expectations so vital for success, it's helpful to reflect not just on the expectations we set for ourselves but also the expectations we set for others.

## HOW EXPECTATIONS TURN FICTION INTO FACT

After the end of World War I, the Roaring Twenties ushered in a time of excitement and prosperity. Americans migrated to urban areas and developed a newfound sense of optimism. With economic possibilities appearing limitless, many Americans sought greater fortunes, turning to stocks to expand their wealth. For years, they were handsomely rewarded as stock prices only went up.

Near the turn of the decade, the good times quickly ended. In late October 1929, the stock market lost about a fourth of its value in two days, and a once-upbeat American public lost its confidence in financial institutions.

It was with the backdrop of a free-falling stock market that a businessman in the Bronx went to his local bank to cash out some stock. Founded in 1913 by a New York garment manufacturer and financier, the Bank of the United States had grown to sixty-two branches throughout New York City, with almost $3 billion (in today's dollars) in deposits by 1930. When the businessman asked employees at the Bank of the United States to cash out his stock in the bank, they advised him against the sale, reasoning that the bank remained a sound investment.

Upon leaving with his shares still in hand, the man started spreading a rumor that the bank had refused to let him sell his stake. Within hours, a line of worried depositors formed at the bank's Bronx outpost. One client waited two hours to cash out his $2 savings account. Because banks don't keep all of their customers' deposits in cash, the overwhelming withdrawal requests put a real strain on the bank's liquid assets.

As customers lined up to withdraw their money, other customers saw the swelling crowds and developed their own false beliefs about the vitality of the institution, leading even more to withdraw their money. Onlookers added to the pandemonium at the scene. An estimated twenty to twenty-five thousand people crowded the street by the bank's entrance, leading thousands of customers to withdraw cash representing about 10 percent of the bank's deposits. As news of the bank's "troubles" spread, its other branches also saw increased withdrawals.

A day after the merchant started the rumor, the Bank of the United States closed for good. At the time, its four hundred thousand depositors topped those of any other bank in the country, making its failure the biggest one ever to plague the nation.*

---

* In the aftermath of the bank runs that plagued not only the Bank of the United States but also hundreds of others, the government created the Federal Deposit Insurance Corporation (FDIC) to protect against the dangers of the self-fulfilling prophecy. By insuring customer deposits in the event of a failure, the FDIC makes a bank's potential failure immaterial for the value of a customer's savings account. Nonethe-

The expectation that the Bank of the United States would become insolvent, which was based on a false rumor, drove behavior that eventually *made* the bank insolvent. Sociologist Robert Merton labeled what happened to the bank, along with so many other financial institutions at the time, a self-fulfilling prophecy—meaning that if people think situations are real, they start acting on them, leading to real consequences that change the future.

## THE POWER OF POSITIVE PROPHECIES

Merton's observations about the Great Depression bank runs sowed the seeds for a revolution in the way that social scientists approach how they think about expectations. The forefront of this research started in the 1960s when Harvard psychologist Robert Rosenthal challenged the objectivity of scientific research and wondered whether it was every bit the illusion that Clever Hans's math skills had been. Rosenthal had the suspicion that a researcher's expectations during experiments might unduly tip off his subjects. He found, for example, that rats learned better when their human experimenters believed their animals were bright, while rats learned worse when their experimenters believed their animals were dumb. Echoing the self-fulfilling dynamics Merton observed with banks, Rosenthal's work revealed that the rats' perceived level of intelligence depended on the experimenter's positive or negative expectations.

---

less, some might consider the 2008 financial crisis to be a modern-day bank run. Counterparties to trades at Lehman Brothers, which filed for bankruptcy during the financial crisis, lost confidence that the firm had enough liquidity to meet its trading obligations. As a result, firms stopped trading with Lehman Brothers, which helped accelerate its liquidity crisis. The assets at risk at Lehman Brothers were not FDIC insured.

# STRETCH

Although his results were intriguing, Rosenthal struggled to get his early work published. With no outlet to accept his research, he turned to the interdisciplinary science magazine *The American Scientist*, where he wrote up his results for a generalist readership.

San Francisco elementary-school principal Lenore Jacobson was an outsider to this type of research and had read Rosenthal's article. She wondered if the same dynamics observed in rats unfolded in her classrooms. Jacobson invited Rosenthal to run a similar study at her school. Their findings would go on to change education forever.

The Oak School, where Jacobson worked, had eighteen classrooms, three per grade, from first through sixth. For each grade level students had been grouped into one of three categories: above average, average, and below average.

At the end of the academic year, students at the school took an IQ test. Jacobson told their next year's teachers which of the approximately 20 percent of the children had performed exceptionally well on the IQ test and were therefore the most likely to bloom intellectually in the upcoming year. The teachers then taught the students, with expectations that some of their pupils had higher potential than the rest of the class.

Eight months later, the students retook the IQ test. In the earliest grades, students identified as having high academic potential saw dramatic improvements in their IQ tests compared to the rest of the class. First-grade gifted students' IQ scores increased 27.4 points, compared to a 12.0-point rise for other students. For second grade, scores increased 16.5 points, compared to 7.0 points.[*]

Here's the twist. The students Rosenthal and Jacobson identified

---

[*] Interestingly, the differences in IQ between bloomers and the control group did not occur for children in grades three through six. Rosenthal and Jacobson suggest several explanations, including that younger children are more open to change and social influence and have less-formed reputations than older children, making teachers' expectations about older children less influential.

as "gifted" students were chosen at random, and not based on their test scores. They were no more likely to bloom intellectually than their classmates, but the researchers had changed the teachers' expectations about their students' potential, and that had made all the difference. The false premise of academic potential had nonetheless become true, causing students to work harder based on their teachers' belief in their potential; the teachers, in turn, provided more attention to their supposed star students. The researchers had sparked a positive prophecy—a self-fulfilling prophecy that enhances the value of something.

George Bernard Shaw's play *Pygmalion* takes its name from the mythical statue so beautiful its sculptor wished to marry it, and actually does after it comes to life. The play, a lesson in the power of the self-fulfilling prophecy, unfolds around a bet between phonetics professor Henry Higgins and phonetics enthusiast Colonel Pickering. The gentlemen wager over whether Pickering can train a poor salesgirl, Eliza Doolittle, to pass as a duchess through changing the way she talks. Higgins prevails in transforming the girl's speech but treats Doolittle as his possession because he created her out of nothing. Doolittle shrewdly recognizes Higgins's poor treatment and remarks that she'll always remain a lowly salesgirl with Higgins because that's how he treats her. It is Pickering, she then continues, who has always treated her as a proper lady, and she concludes that it's not how a person speaks or behaves that makes her classy, but rather how she is perceived and treated by others. As Eliza Doolittle so astutely pointed out, people are often exactly what we expect of them.

Like Colonel Pickering's treatment of Eliza Doolittle, a manager's expectations can change an employee's performance because people tend to be even cleverer than horses at reading signals. These expectations are set in implicit, or even explicit, ways: providing more interesting assignments, less oversight and micromanaging, and more frequent discussions of the "big picture."

What's become known as the Pygmalion effect holds that establishing high expectations for others enhances their performance. Management professor Dov Eden has spent most of his career working in this area, primarily through research in the Israeli army. In one study, he randomly told military commanders that some soldiers were either high performers or regular performers. The soldiers designated as "high performers" objectively performed better than the others—learning combat tactics, picking up knowledge of topography, or acquiring greater combat skills such as firing a weapon—even though they had no actual promise exceeding any of the others.*

A manager's expectations shape performance because they alter the expectations of her employees. When employees detect that their manager sets high expectations, they raise their own expectations, which makes them work harder and think more highly of themselves. As soon as employees begin to perform at higher levels, their beliefs of positive expectations become further reinforced, leading to a virtuous circle. Meanwhile, their manager observes the higher performance, confirming and strengthening her initial expectations. Over time, she'll provide better coaching and more helpful feedback to her superstar employees, which continues to give those employees a performance edge.

We also set life-changing expectations at home: beliefs about

---

* Analyses of the studies on positive prophecies at work show that its effects are strongest in military and educational settings. This may have something to do with the more hierarchical structure of these organizations. Additionally, research shows that positive prophecies work best when the initial performance of a person is low.

how satisfying our marriages will be or how long our kids will be in school predict stronger marriages[*] and higher test scores of children, respectively. Our personal relationships, too, are ripe with opportunities to signal what we want from others—and people usually live up to (or down to) those expectations.

## BLIND DATES (AND OTHER FIRST INTERACTIONS) ARE NEVER REALLY BLIND

Much of the ground we've covered so far involves expectations in ongoing relationships—employee and manager, student and teacher, or even horse and master. Other times expectations shape relationships before they even begin, following the old adage that first impressions matter. But what if I told you that first impressions are shaped by the expectations we have even *before* we lay eyes on another person?

In the 1970s, a team of psychologists wanted to understand how expectations shape newly forming relationships. What better setting than to ask a group of college students to go on a "blind" date? Researchers provided a male participant (let's call him Jack) with a picture of a female participant (let's call her Dianne). During the experiment, Jack and Dianne never met but spoke over the phone. Independent raters evaluated the phone conversations to understand the emerging relationship between Jack and Dianne.

In some experimental conditions, the researchers provided Jack

---

[*] It's important that the positive expectations of a marital relationship be coupled with behaving constructively in interactions and coming up with charitable explanations for a partner's behavior.

with a photo of the woman he was told was Dianne. (Dianne was never told that Jack received a picture of her or anyone else.) But it was actually a picture of another woman—an especially stunning one. The photo made Jack think that Dianne was very pretty, but even more surprisingly, women in the role of Dianne started to behave in more attractive ways—such as by being friendly, likable, and sociable—compared to those whose male blind dates had not received a picture.

What would make Dianne behave in more attractive ways? The researchers conclude that due to Jack's false but positive expectation of Dianne's physical beauty (prompted by the picture of the especially stunning woman), Jack interacted more positively with Dianne, which made Dianne feel more attractive. Like Colonel Pickering's treatment of Eliza Doolittle, Jack expected Dianne to be a certain way, and Dianne lived up to those expectations.

Expectations also shape our first meetings with people in the office. What we've heard—good or bad—influences those interactions. When we believe our new officemate is a jerk, we're likely to act very differently upon meeting him than if we've heard he's a great guy—and through the signals we send (how we greet him, what questions we ask, and the way we smile), we push him closer to being either that jerk or that great guy.

One of the most important "blind dates" we go on is with potential employers. Before an interviewer and job candidate meet, both are likely to experience first-date jitters. They know enough about each other to generate some expectations but not enough to make an informed decision about the relationship. They want it to work out but remain uncertain whether they'll be a good match. It turns out that whether they'll be a good match is often decided before they ever even shake hands.

In a comprehensive study, researchers Thomas Dougherty, Daniel Turban, and John Callender compiled data from a large energy company's recruiting department. They evaluated all prospective employees who applied for a wide variety of jobs, from secretary to computer operator. Prior to their interview, the candidates completed a battery of tests relevant to the position, in addition to an application that included their work history and education. Based on this information, and without having met the candidates, recruiters at the company rated the candidates on a 9-point scale, with 1 indicating very low qualifications and 9 indicating very high qualifications. The recruiters then randomly received job applicants to interview and were not given any instructions about how to use the application materials and test scores.

Over an eight-month period of recruiting employees, the researchers tape-recorded interviews between recruiters and prospective employees. They then had three independent assistants listen to the tapes and design a consistent way of assessing the interviews across a variety of dimensions: positive regard (such as interviewers asking supportive questions, agreeing with the candidate, laughing, or speaking encouragingly), positive style (such as interviewers acting friendly), and questioning approach (such as the number of open-ended, close-ended, follow-up, and probing questions asked). They also assessed the likelihood of the recruiter making a job offer.

In addition to evaluating the recruiters, the assistants also gauged the job applicants' performance during the interview.

When the researchers tabulated the results, they found that the impressions formed before the recruiter even met the candidate had a substantial effect on the candidate's prospects. These expectations predicted the interviewers' use of a positive style, creating a warmer and friendlier environment that helped make the interviewee feel more comfortable. The interviewers who had positive expectations before meeting the candidate also spent more time selling the company and job, and less time vetting the qualifications of the candidate. Similar to Jack and Dianne's blind date, the recruiters' expectations led the job candidate to perform better during the interview, building stronger bonds with the recruiter. The job applicants turned out to be everything the recruiter expected (or didn't expect), ultimately shaping the recruiter's intention to extend a job offer.

We've now learned that we typically perform to the level of expectations of people who are authority figures over us—whether our teachers, managers, commanders, or recruiters. Likewise, when we're in positions of formal power, we can help stretch others through setting high expectations. But we also play an important role in setting expectations for ourselves. It's time to consider how our own thoughts can spark positive prophecies that help us accomplish great things.

## HOW OUR OWN EXPECTATIONS ELEVATE US

In 1867, two days before Christmas, Sarah Breedlove Walker was born on a Louisiana plantation to formerly enslaved parents. Orphaned at seven, married at fourteen, child-rearing at eighteen, and widowed at twenty, Walker's life was, to say the least, not easy. Left to raise her little girl on her own, she barely made a living washing clothes, earning, at best, $1.50 a day. As difficult as her life was, it was pretty typical for black women to struggle under an oppressive society that presented few opportunities for advancement and meager hope for a brighter future.

Walker wanted to break free from what she saw as a cycle of

limited opportunities for black women, but like so many people suffering from economic and social disadvantage, she struggled with overcoming low expectations. As she recalled, "I couldn't see how I, a poor washerwoman, was going to better my condition."

To add to Walker's burdens, the daily stress of her life, a poor diet, and hygiene problems due to a lack of indoor plumbing left her with scalp disease and a balding head, a common affliction for women in her circumstances. In a society that offered Walker so little under the Jim Crow laws, the indignity of hair loss was painful. Restoring that dignity—both physically and psychologically—became Walker's avenue for changing herself and so many other people facing the same obstacles.

Starting with a $1.25 in hand, she launched a hair-care business that sold products to help balding women grow back their hair and became known as Madame C. J. Walker. She worked tirelessly to get her business off the ground and spent many hours on the road marketing her products across the South. Yet even as her business gained traction, the budding entrepreneur's successes couldn't change the discrimination she faced due to her dark complexion. With hotels off limits, she roomed with local black leaders who helped her build closer connections with the communities she visited. In these communities, she gained access to a network of product advocates and potential customers.

As much as Walker used beautification to change her customers' looks and outlooks, she made the biggest difference with her employees. She trained sales agents and deployed a multilevel marketing approach that handsomely rewarded them, teaching them that they, too, could elevate themselves and be more than they thought possible. At the time, white unskilled workers earned about $11 a week. Walker's black female sales force, which exceeded a thousand people, made $5 to $15 a *day* while avoiding grueling factory work or taxing domestic labor. As they gained financial independence, Walker's saleswomen educated their children, purchased homes, and contributed to charity—all of which helped promote expectations for betterment in future generations.

For her part, Madame C. J. Walker became America's first black woman millionaire and left an estate worth about $8 million (in today's dollars). She also became a figure on the social scene, actively involved in politics and the philanthropic community. Reflecting on her remarkable ability to create opportunities, Harvard historian Henry Louis Gates observed, "More than any other single business-person, Walker unveiled the vast economic potential of an African-American economy, even one stifled and suffocating."

What made Walker elevate her expectations within the rigid confines of social norms and laws meant to hold her back when so many others could not? It turns out she had a very different way of thinking about opportunities.

Many people expect to discover opportunities—they spend their lives searching or even passively waiting for them to come their way. Whether through skill or luck, opportunities—new products, ways of working, or knowing the right people—are out there, if only they can find them.

Madame C. J. Walker teaches us about a very different pathway to opportunities. She focused on creating opportunities through changing her own expectations—overcoming what little others thought of her and replacing it with a belief that she could, in her words, "make my own living and my own opportunity." The difficulty, as Walker admits, is that many people "sit down and wait for the opportunities to come" when instead they should "get up and make them!" But when others expect so little from us, it's hard to muster the confidence and motivation to get up. Harvard business historian Nancy Koehn observes, "Much of Walker's business model and her animating vision is a product of the constraints that she faced. She had an indomitable spirit that prevailed through the difficulties of finding capital, and through the difficulties of her own very limited social position. In a market in which there weren't many realms where women could play, she found a way."

───────────────

Although not as severe as what Walker confronted, we often face challenges that we can either expect to be opportunities or threats. The labels people, teams, and organizations attach to these challenges have important implications. A "threat" label for our difficult times—whether failed projects, tough competitive challenges, and personal setbacks—leads us to what management scholars Barry Staw, Lance Sandelands, and Jane Dutton call threat rigidity. A threat label has a tendency to restrict resources to traditional uses, limit creativity, and obstruct problem solving. If labeled a threat, Walker's exclusion from hotels would have thwarted her business trips and positioned her as a person with lower self-worth. Similarly, she would have considered her target employees—poor, uneducated African American women—incapable of running their own sales organizations, reinforcing their own low self-expectations.

Making matters even more difficult, threats restrict how we process information, defaulting us to prior expectations about how things have been and preventing us from seeing how things might be. When we're hampered by the lack of the supposedly best resources, a well-crafted plan, or perfect information, we regularly choose to do nothing, fearful of what might happen. We narrow the way we see our resources at precisely the time we most need to mobilize them to make something different happen.

In contrast, when we label the same challenges as an opportunity, we approach them very differently. Walker saw her physical ailment and economic plight as opportunities that allowed her to envision a new and better future. She turned destitute women into an eager sales force and used her exclusion from hotels to build better engagement with customers' communities. This helped her feel in greater control of her fate—encouraging her to do more with what she had at hand.

## LIVE UP TO THE RIGHT EXPECTATIONS

Alex Turnbull picked up his phone to make one of the most important calls of his life. He quickly put it down, only to pick it up, then put it down again. After going through this ritual several times, he headed outdoors for a walk. The stroll calmed his nerves, and he returned inside to try again. When he next lifted the phone, his fingers finally dialed the number that would shape his life's trajectory . . . only to have the phone ring several times before sending the call to voicemail.

An hour later, his phone rang, and he finally delivered news of his decision, confidently stating, "I can't tell you how much I appreciate the offer, but it's not the right move for us right now."

With that utterance, Alex Turnbull had walked away from $12 million. A large software company had been courting him to sell Groove, the customer service software company he founded in 2011. This was not the first time Turnbull had declined a seven-figure check, or a lofty premium offered for his company—whose revenues topped out at a modest $70,000 a month at the time—but it would be the richest so far. The deal also would have provided Groove with substantial resources to continue improving its products, hire the most talented engineers, and build the necessary infrastructure to try to grow into a billion-dollar business.

When mulling over his offer for Groove, Turnbull had asked himself an obvious but rarely asked question: What were his life's expectations? Having high expectations is valuable, but without being anchored to a purpose—what author Simon Sinek calls a "why"—they're of little value.

Turnbull recognized that meeting his life goals didn't require a blockbuster payout or building a billion-dollar business. In fact, they might derail him from pursing what he did care about—building a long-term, sustainable, and profitable business and following his passions outside of work, especially surfing the nearby waves off the coast of Rhode Island and spending time with his family. Instead of seeing Groove as a stepping-stone to the next big thing for himself and his employees, Turnbull saw the company as an enduring place for satisfying and meaningful work.

Turnbull had been down this road before and recognized the rarely anticipated dangers of taking the check. Before starting Groove, he cofounded an online business collaboration service called Bantam Live, taking in about $3.5 million in venture funding. His financial backers pushed him to grow too fast and sell the company to publicly traded Constant Contact. Turnbull's experience from Bantam Live taught him that big investors come with even bigger expectations—expectations that didn't match his.

This isn't to say that Turnbull's decision was easy. Turning down the money imposed some serious resource constraints on the entrepreneur. Without deep pockets, hiring high-quality engineers proved especially challenging. Large tech giants such as Google regularly seduced employees with high status and even higher compensation. Turnbull tried to make sure that his expectations matched those of his employees. Selling prospective employees on more visible impact, greater autonomy, an energetic culture, and remote and flexible work, Turnbull hired his staff in ways that resembled the way he sought out his best customers. Cost-focused customers ex-

**139**

hibit less loyalty and dart off quickly for lower-priced options. If he recruited employees based on price, Turnbull reasoned, that's what he'd get—employees who might quickly change companies for a little more money.

Alex Turnbull's business grew, with monthly sales increasing about 4.5-fold since he turned down the money. But more important, his life was enriched. He became a new parent and loved his work. "The fact that there's nobody breathing down my neck about profits, and no investors to answer to if we don't hit our numbers, gives me the luxury of taking as much time as I want to enjoy this," he told me. "It's a luxury that a lot of my founder friends—whose start-ups may be far outpacing our growth with their fat venture-funded war chests—don't really have."

Making sure we're living up to expectations we value ensures that we end up in a good place. Other people might have their own (and very different) expectations that are inconsistent with our goals. That's one potential pitfall with expectations, but there's another one that pops up when setting expectations for others. The unfortunate reality is that in some settings, we're more prone to expect the worst, especially from other people. And when we expect the worst, that's what we usually get.

## THE DANGERS OF THE DUNCE CAP

John Duns Scotus was widely regarded as one of the most important thinkers of the thirteenth century. His background included studies of philosophy, linguistics, theology, and metaphysics. Known for his sharp mind and ability to detect very subtle differences in thinking, he also believed that wearing cone-shaped hats facilitated learning. Knowledge would enter through the hat's tip and funnel to its wearer. Wizards wore similarly shaped hats, and so did John Duns Scotus's followers, who came to be called Dunces.

The scholar had a profound impact on intellectual thought until the sixteenth century, when his work came under attack for its unnecessary complexity. With his disciples accused of splitting hairs and being too complex in thought, opponents of his teachings hijacked the label "dunce" and made it synonymous with "idiot."

During the Victorian era, the combination of the word dunce as a stand-in for idiot and the cone-shaped hat John Duns Scotus believed held the secret to receiving knowledge led to one of the worst inventions ever—the dunce cap. The pointy hat embellished with a big "D" as a symbol of idiocy took off in both North America and Europe.

The cap was placed on the heads of misbehaving students to publicly shame them for bad behavior. The idea was that their bad behavior was controllable—attributable to internal factors—even if external factors were at play: the child was being teased by others, was raised by parents who didn't value education, or skipped meals because of poverty. The hope was that by stigmatizing a student—i.e., making him wear a dunce cap—he would be induced to work harder and behave better. As draconian as this approach is, some schools still use punishment inspired by it. At Forest Fields in Nottingham, England, teachers recently required that eight-year-old Abdullah al-Ameen wear a fluorescent yellow jacket for throwing leaves at children he said were bullying him. The school's head teacher, Sue Hoyland, defended the decision, saying, "When children's behavior falls below standards, we are keen to see this change by rewarding children when they make the right decision. With the jackets, the teachers know who to give praise to and reward more."

Putting aside the horrific issue of humiliating children, the problem with the dunce cap comes from the same forces that made Hans so clever and Rosenthal and Jacobson's "gifted" students so smart. The cap just works in the opposite direction of these positive prophecies. Since we live up to the expectations that others set for us— including low ones—the dunce cap led to self-fulfilling prophecies that made the students only want to misbehave even more.

Although usually not as visible as a large, pointy hat, we regularly, at least analogously, put dunce caps on others when we expect the worst of them. Our low expectations come from our tendency to attribute their failures to things they control. If a stranger slips on the floor, we consider him clumsy; a new employee who shows up late for work is irresponsible; when an acquaintance loses his job, we question his talents or work ethic. We reach conclusions about other people's results even though we have limited information about their actual situations. If we found ourselves with similar results, we'd have all of the detail about our circumstances: the floor was wet, an unusually large traffic jam clogged the roads, or the company dismissed the entire team. But when we lack this information about others, we typically project the worst onto them.

When it comes to successes, we take a very different approach. We credit others' accomplishments to things outside of their control. If someone beats us out for a job, they must have had an inside connection, or if a colleague lands a client we couldn't, she must have gotten lucky. Now if we were the person who got the job or landed the client, it would be because of internal reasons—our intelligence or our skills. The self-serving way we evaluate our successes and failures, relative to others, protects our ego but sacrifices the expectations we have for others. We feel better about ourselves but think less of those around us.

There's another place where our negative expectations especially undermine our objectives: organization change. It is one of the most common and critical elements of work but something we're pretty terrible at doing. Recent research by the consulting company McKinsey pegs the failure rate of organization change initiatives at almost 70 percent. Why we frequently fumble change has everything to do with our expectations.

Eric Dent and Susan Goldberg of George Washington University analyzed popular management textbooks. They found that most texts assumed that employees would resist change, which they argue has seeped into common managerial beliefs around the world. By uniformly expecting to encounter resistance to new initiatives, managers create the very resistance they then need to overcome. From the lens of expecting resistance, we're more prone to treat any disagreements (even legitimate ones) as unrelenting opposition to our ideas, making us miss opportunities to respond to helpful suggestions and unfairly sanction the "resisters." Employees who might want to voice valid concerns get silenced or dismissed. Their morale suffers, and they no longer want to help a change initiative—they have already turned into the resisters managers wanted to avoid in the first place.

When managers expect resistance, they also plan for resistance—and that's precisely what they get. They might be tempted to keep change secret or disguise it from others who they reason are inevitably going to sabotage it. When the change finally becomes unmasked, employees resist it because they were kept in the dark.

The reality is that in most change efforts, employees neither support nor resist change—they are neutral. But their neutral stance can shift quickly toward resistance if we *expect* resistance. The same can be said about other areas of our work and personal lives. When we expect the worst—shoddy work, unreliable teams, politically motivated colleagues, or lazy children—we usually get the worst.

# S T R E T C H

It's not a benign description to label someone as incompetent before we meet him or to call a project doomed before it even starts. Instead of putting the dunce cap on other people's heads, we need to follow Madame C. J. Walker's approach and instead beautify their heads.

———

Some people struggle to beautify their own heads. Despite our natural tendency to set positive expectations for ourselves, there are times when *we* put the dunce cap on ourselves. Becoming our own most vicious critics leads us to expect little of ourselves. Negative "tapes" play in our heads, telling us why we can't do something or how we're not good enough, or that we are impostors in situations where we could be leaders.

In one study, Katy DeCelles, Jane Dutton, and I interviewed people who worked tirelessly to improve the environment. These stewards of natural resources took jobs that allowed them to influence how companies changed products to be more sustainable and regularly talked people they knew into being more responsible with natural resources. Besides their remarkable dedication and extensive work to help the environment, many of them shared another common attitude: self-defeat.

Most people we interviewed doubted they were doing enough to make a difference for the environment, which made little sense until we dug deeper. We found that they undermined themselves by insisting their efforts were always short of someone else's. If a person drove a hybrid, he wondered why he didn't take public transportation instead. A woman who took public transportation questioned why she wasn't walking instead. One person we interviewed did an analysis of her meals to determine their full environmental impact and bought carbon offsets for her travel. We found these actions quite notable, but she was far from impressed. She told us, "Knowing the facts I know, I still choose actions that aren't always right. . . . I eat meat. I drink wine and beer. . . . I'll buy Patagonia when I can, but I also buy North Face."*

The antidote to this destructive thinking, our research found, was to plant positive seeds. By reflecting on the resources the environmentalists had—knowledge, experience, and values—we found that they were able to protect themselves from their lingering poor expectations and do more to advance their cause. But without seeding positive expectations, the environmentalists, despite their passion and best intentions, fell short of achieving their goals.

## PLANT POSITIVE SEEDS

Ultimately, our prospects for success and well-being get seeded by expectations. When planting the seeds of positive expectations, we'll harvest fruit, improve performance, strengthen relationships, produce rich opportunities, and pursue the goals we care most dearly about. But when planting the seeds of negative expectations, we'll likely pluck weeds. It's critical to take control of the expectations we set for ourselves and others. After all, if a horse can do math, it's time for us to ask what more we can expect from ourselves and others.

---

* Patagonia and North Face make comparable outerwear, but Patagonia has a reputation for being very environmentally sustainable. In 2011, the company pleaded with its customers to buy fewer new products from them and to buy used stuff instead.

# SEVEN

## MIX IT UP

---

### THE POWER OF UNLIKELY COMBINATIONS

I n 1972, the Choi family immigrated to the United States from Seoul, South Korea, settling in Los Angeles with their toddler son, Roy. The Chois raised him in a traditional Korean, achievement-oriented household, pressuring him to pursue a career in law or medicine. Roy rebelled against his parents' status-driven goal and coped with their strict plans for him by using drugs as a teen and running away from his family several times.

Roy Choi's real dream was to become a chef, and he passionately urged his parents to support his wish. For years, his parents insisted he drop the aspiration, but finally they relented, telling him that if he must, he should go enroll in the Harvard of cooking schools.

Set in picturesque Hyde Park in upstate New York, the Culinary Institute of America houses the nation's top school for promising chefs. When Roy Choi arrived on campus, he channeled his rebellious streak into inventive cooking experiments. Incorporating unusual ingredients into more traditional fare, he annoyed his peers, who were more committed to perfecting classic recipes.

After graduation, Choi worked at upscale hotels on both the East and West Coasts, eventually landing a coveted role as the chef de cuisine at the Beverly Hills Hilton. There he notably had the chance to cook for celebrities and dignitaries such as Barack Obama. But it was working with food and beverage director Mark Manguera that changed the trajectory of his career and life.

One evening, after a night of barhopping, Manguera was sipping champagne and enjoying a late-night taco—an unusual pairing. He wondered aloud to his sister-in-law, Alice Shin, what it'd be like to substitute the traditional meat in a Mexican taco with Korean beef. The next day Manguera challenged Choi to make the hybrid dish.

By replacing the standard ground beef in a taco with Korean BBQ, Choi created an instant hit. Many of his L.A. customers had never sampled Korean food before, but they quickly became hooked on his tasty new dish.

Instead of opening a brick-and-mortar restaurant to sell the new taco, the trio borrowed a truck and traveled around town under the banner KOGI KOREAN BBQ. They were not the first to use a truck to sell food. In 1866, Texas cattle rancher Charles Goodnight converted a former army wagon into a truck packed with kitchenware, food, and supplies to sell meat, beans, coffee, and sundries to men herding cattle to markets in the North and East. By the 1930s, the Oscar Mayer Wienermobile was visiting cities around the country, bringing its twenty-seven-foot-long hot-dog-shaped vehicle stocked with its namesake offering to thousands of welcoming families. Commonplace today, hordes of taco trucks feed construction-site workers with calorically dense, inexpensive food, with detractors nicknaming them "roach coaches" to reflect their reputation for low-quality food and dirtiness.

What separated Kogi from the food trucks that came before it was an unlikely pairing: high-quality foods typically found in up-scale restaurants served from a truck, which historically was considered to offer lower-quality dishes. Choi and his partners transformed the image of the roach coach into a gourmet restaurant on wheels worthy of high-flying ratings from the Zagat food guide. Mobility allowed Choi to extend the reach of his business, bringing delicacies to a wider variety of customers, whether inner-city hipsters looking for the next trend or college students wanting something tastier, and perhaps cooler, than the cafeteria. By virtue of their low-cost structure, Choi and his partners also offered his restaurant-quality items at street-food pricing, charging only two bucks for their signature Korean beef tacos topped with a homemade sauce made from twenty-one ingredients.

In 2008, its first year of operation, Kogi grossed about $2 million in sales, regularly handling hundreds of eager customers, some of whom waited in line for two-plus hours. After an explosive start, the business has grown to three food trucks and two restaurants. The transformation of a food truck into a gourmet restaurant on wheels launched the city's (and eventually the country's) hottest form of dining. Thousands of people from backgrounds as diverse as line cooks to laid-off IT workers gave launching their own gourmet food trucks a try—inspired directly by Choi's success or indirectly through the television shows and movies made about his new form of serving food.

Roy Choi blended ingredients in original ways, a hallmark quality of a good chef. But it was his ability to make improbable combinations outside the kitchen that truly exemplifies the element of stretching I will cover in this chapter. Echoing Aristotle's observation that sometimes the whole is greater than the sum of its parts, we'll learn how expanding the value of our resources comes from combinations we'd least expect.

We'll examine how a wide range of people—everyone from inventors to secretaries—mix all types of resources, from the physical to the intangible. It turns out that bringing together unlikely combinations—competition and friendship, routine work and creativity, and personal and professional identities—leads to remarkable discoveries, better ways of working, and higher levels of well-being. The challenge we face is that it's hard to pair resources that, on first look, appear unrelated or incompatible. To overcome this barrier, we'll learn how to bridge apparent trade-offs and persist until we find just the right combination.

## SLEEPING WITH THE ENEMY

Roy Choi's demonstration that chefs, with far fewer resources than traditional restaurants, could turn out more innovative food, and for far less money, was such a terrific example of resourcefulness that I wanted to learn more about the industry. I quickly realized the magnitude of Choi's impact. When I started a multiyear study in Houston in 2013, there were already more than a hundred gourmet trucks in the city. I visited as many of them as possible, tasted their food (gaining fifteen pounds along the way!), and interviewed their owners and operators. For a foodie like myself, it was an appetizing research project, and what I learned turned out to be even more delightful than what I ate.

Undeniably, the food truckers I met were similar in many ways to other entrepreneurs I've studied, reaching for dreams with limited resources and working incredibly hard, upward of eighteen hours a day. Like other stretchers I've researched, they also relied on less to create more: far fewer pieces of cooking equipment than found in typical commercial kitchens, crammed into a small metal truck where internal temperatures easily soared above 130 degrees.

Beyond the typical struggles of entrepreneurs, I also discovered something quite unusual about the trucks, their prospects for success, and the joy people derived from their work. Food truckers combined competition and friendship.

Ask most people about competition, and you'll likely get an answer similar to former General Electric CEO Jack Welch's, who is often hailed as one of America's greatest executives. His advice to entrepreneurs: "Go out and buy or bury your competition." Through the lens of chasing, Welch's advice makes a lot of sense. Resources are scarce, and competitors might take what we need—customers, promotions, status, or budgets. Psychological research adds some support to Welch's claim. When a resource appears scarce, it strongly motivates people to capture that resource from others.

For stretchers, Welch's advice to crush competitors is not only ill-advised but also downright foolish. Resources are seen as flexible if not abundant to stretchers, so fighting over them crushes the possibilities of creating more. In an experiment, psychologists Peter Carnevale and Tahira Probst told some of their participants to negotiate with a partner but to view them as competitors, trying to capture as much profit as possible. The researchers instructed a second group of participants to cooperate and make as much money as possible, collectively, with their partners.

Before the negotiation was set to begin, Carnevale and Probst gave each participant a book of matches, a cardboard box filled with tacks, and a small candle, and asked a participant to attach the candle to a partition so that it could burn properly and not drip on the table. Participants in the competitor condition were much less likely to find the resourceful solution (removing the tacks from their box, using a tack to attach the box to the wall, and using the box as a platform for the candle) compared to those in the cooperation condition. Carnevale and Probst's study shows that competition can harm people's ability to stretch.

There's an alternative way of viewing competition, one that looks very different from Jack Welch's recommendation. To understand how competition doesn't need to turn into an unavoidable fight over resources requires understanding how competition and friendship can peacefully coexist.

William Ortiz operates a Mexican gourmet taco truck in Houston. As an aspiring chef, he takes tremendous pride in delighting his customers with innovative dishes that push the boundaries of traditional tacos. He spent time experimenting to come up with his own version of a Korean BBQ taco. One day, after perfecting his recipe, he purchased ingredients and marinated beef for hours, hoping this off-the-menu special would sell to rave reviews. All appeared to be going well when he pulled into his parking spot for the day.

Ortiz quickly learned that another truck had staked out a nearby location. He went over to the competitor's truck—as he often did—to say hello. The greeting quickly unfolded into a conversation about what each truck was serving for the day, and Ortiz realized a big problem. He told me: "I did not know the other truck was Korean. . . . I know the guy. He is like my friend. I did not know he is going to be there. I had my Korean meat. I marinate everything and . . . went and said, 'You know what, I am not going to sell my Korean taco, because you are here.' I mean we worked together. We don't work against each other. . . . we are a community. . . . I told [him] I am not going to sell it."

Ortiz's offer to pack up the menu item he had spent so long creating surprised me. Yet, over and over again, I learned of the unbelievable efforts gourmet food truckers made to *help* each other. From running to the store to resupply a pizza maker who ran out of mozzarella cheese (and refusing reimbursement) to fixing a broken truck, they treated each other as close friends rather than competitors to be put out of business. They also taught each other how to fine-tune their operations to become more profitable, volunteered to work on each other's trucks on a rare day off, and advertised on behalf of each other—not to mention grabbed beers together in their little spare time.

All of these friendly gestures didn't eliminate competition. Food truckers fiercely fought for all sorts of accolades—running the most successful business with the most customers, getting the best parking spaces, and having the tastiest food. But adding friendship to an otherwise contentious relationship went a long way in making everyone better off.

The mixture of competition and friendship inspired the food truckers to work harder to strive for excellence, trying to live up to the standards of their friends by serving outstanding products and running smooth operations. I wondered how this unlikely mixture of competition and friendship formed. Why would a group of entrepreneurs struggling to make a living come to befriend the very people and businesses trying to capture the same customers and other scarce resources, such as parking spaces and social media buzz?

# S T R E T C H

In 1954, prominent psychologist Gordon Allport proposed that you can bring together groups inherently distrustful of one another and get them to like one another through social contact. Allport's research examined prejudices that made racial groups hostile to one another and his incredibly straightforward fix seemed almost too easy to believe. Have people with different backgrounds spend a little time with one another, so long as four conditions are met: the two parties need to be of equal status, have common goals, cooperate, and support the law or customs.

More recent research has expanded Allport's contact hypothesis and has shown that the four conditions he initially proposed are usually not even needed. In an analysis of 515 studies on the contact hypothesis, researchers found that mere exposure, and nothing more, to potential rivals increased liking. Why might simple contact with people we dislike transform relationships in such positive ways? The answer may surprise you—it's the same reason why you love that annoying song you keep hearing played over and over again.

Shortly after Allport's work on the contact hypothesis, psychologist Robert Zajonc became intrigued with the idea that when we approach something new, we tend to fear it, but over time our reactions become much more positive. Synthesizing past research pioneered by those who study music, Zajonc found that even for tunes initially considered unpleasant, mere exposure made people warm up to them. This phenomenon is quite simple and doesn't require rewards, such as paying a person to listen to the song. It also doesn't require thinking about the benefits of something. The same goes for people—the more we're around people, the more we tend to like them. It's pretty counterintuitive because we've developed clichés such as "absence makes the heart grow fonder" or "familiarity breeds contempt." When applied to our relationships, it opens up the possibility of liking our rivals, with whom we often share lots of experiences, but who we avoid befriending due to resource competition.

———————

William Ortiz and the other food truckers I studied had a recurring ritual that put them in close contact with each other, helping them warm up to each other over hot meals: the food swap. Whether getting to know a new competitor or catching up with someone not seen for a while, food truckers regularly visit each other and exchange food. There's a pragmatic reason—it allows them to eat a variety of foods through bartering. But there's also an unexpected upside that activates the contact hypothesis. It brings competitors in close physical contact through the intimate act of eating. The interactions soften the edges out of competition and forge more meaningful relationships. These relationships often evolve into genuine friendships.*

When social contact forges friendship with our competitors, it allows us to develop personally satisfying and beneficial relationships in the place we'd least expect it. The people with whom we compete so vigorously often turn out to play a vital role in our own prospects, whether motivating us to do better or even, as William Ortiz and his fellow food truckers illustrate, *directly* helping us do better.

———————

* My research suggests that this type of mixing of competition and friendship is not universal among gourmet food truckers in other cities. For businesses looking to expand to Houston from other markets, they come in assuming it'll be an ultra-competitive environment. But when approached by a competitor to share a meal, they quickly recognize that the norms of the market support both friendship and competition. They had not intended to form friendships with their competitors, and some even stumbled by not being friendly at first. Eventually, they recognized the tremendous help and meaningfulness of forming friendships with competitors and got on board.

# STRETCH

A study by Columbia University professor Paul Ingram and Emory University professor Peter Roberts examined major hotels in Sydney, Australia, comprising fourteen thousand rooms. They interviewed top managers and asked them about any friendships they formed with managers at competing hotels. Afterward, Ingram and Roberts compared the number of friends each manager had to his hotel's performance. Remarkably, each friendship with a competitor was associated with increased revenues of approximately $268,000, boosting sales across the industry by $90 million, or roughly 15 percent. The unexpected friendships among managers at hotels competing for the same customers provided an economic boost because they sparked collaboration, mitigated cutthroat competition, and facilitated sharing knowledge.

In many organizations, teams compete for resources and may even not get along or trust each other. If food trucks and hotels competing for the same customers can form friendships, so, too, can warring teams inside organizations. Putting them in the same room where they can exchange resources—ideas, tools, or even personal objects—can go a long way toward joining together unlikely partners in productive, and even meaningful, relationships.

## FAR FROM "ROUTINE"

If relationships are the heart of organizations—the social fabric that connects us—routines are the organization's brain. They encode the major steps of accomplishing work, directing us to do tasks in very specific ways. For this reason, we both love and hate them. They make our days easier by eliminating much of our active thinking. But they also come with a cost. Few of us want to spend the week without exercising much thought.

When most of us think about routines, we're likely to describe them with adjectives such as "boring," "impersonal," and "inflexible." That might be true, but they also represent much of the work that people in organizations do: hiring, dealing with customers, budgeting—just to name a few. The prevailing view among researchers is that routines provide a steadiness to people's days and allow for consistent and predictable outcomes. Carefully devised and flawlessly executed, it doesn't matter who implements a routine because it will unfold the same way each time, and with the same results. Like a habit or a computer program, routines run on autopilot without much thought, effort, or individuality.

There's a very different way of understanding routines, one that requires adding a concept that just about everyone thinks is the opposite of a routine: creativity. Indeed, a closer look at the seemingly impersonal and uncreative "routine" reveals a very different picture.

Researchers Martha Feldman and Michigan State professor Brian Pentland have been on a mission to change thinking about routines. Their list of adjectives to describe routines: dynamic, creative, and individualized. Far from being mindless, routines provide ample opportunities for people to make a difference with their individuality and creativity. To explain their seismic shift in thinking about routines, Feldman and Pentland distinguish between two aspects of routines.

First, they explain that a routine is an abstract concept—a mental image in our head. We have a broad understanding of any routine we implement, built up from all of the previous times we've performed it. When I get my daughter ready for school—make lunch by placing three slices of turkey in between two pieces of wheat bread, pack her a snack that she'll like, and check over her homework—I label the bundle of actions as the "get my daughter ready" routine. This bundling helps me understand the actions I need to do and allows me to refer to it easily. When I ask my wife, Randi, to get our daughter ready for school, she knows what to do without much thought.

But there's a second part of routines that is less recognized. Routines are not just abstract mental images but specific actions performed by specific people at specific times. Even though we're following the same routine, we insert ourselves into them, making each time we do the routine a little different. Sometimes those differences are deliberate detours. For example, I might decide to leave a note in my daughter's lunch bag wishing her a great day. Other times our deviations are accidental, such as my putting two slices of turkey instead of three on her sandwich. In some situations, current conditions may require different actions—making her sandwich with a roll when I run out of bread. Whether by chance or conscious choice, and however small these deviations are, they have the potential to have an outsized effect. My decision to add a note might brighten my daughter's day, putting her in a good mood and helping her do well on a test. A less-filling sandwich may leave her hungry and with a growling stomach, leading to her bombing a test. The substitution of the roll introduces her to a new kind of sandwich that, if she likes it, might change our routine down the road.

Routines are brought to life by our individuality, personalized by the people performing them. Consider the way Randi's response to not having sandwich bread could have been different. She might have changed the entire meal without the anchor of a sandwich, coming up with her own modification to the established routine.

―――――――――

Now if my daughter didn't like her new lunch at all, it would've ended up in the garbage. We might think that picking up the garbage involves a pretty straightforward routine itself: follow a route, empty residents' trash bins into a truck, and dispose of the waste at the landfill. Collecting data at six North Carolina municipalities, professors Scott Turner and Violina Rindova wanted to figure out what it really takes to pick up the trash.

There's tremendous pressure on sanitation departments to deliver consistent service, especially for the pickup time. Showing up too early means residents miss the chance to get their trash off the front lawn. Coming too late leads to lots of phone calls wondering if a resident's house was skipped.

Even the most seemingly straightforward jobs come with unexpected challenges, and staying on schedule turns out to be anything but routine for trash collectors: trucks break down, detours are necessary during road construction, weather or a fallen tree blocks a street, or people don't show up to work. The researchers found that the garbagemen regularly acted resourcefully to preserve the consistent experience customers demanded. Exercising tremendous discretion and creativity, they followed the routine even as they departed from it. Sometimes they reversed their route, rearranging the sequence of the routine. Other times they reached out to colleagues for assistance, changing who performed it. They even fixed their own trucks to stay on schedule, adding new elements to the routine.

The crews were so good at showing up on time that customers would sometimes "set their watches by the garbage collection." What appears on the outside as straightforward is, on closer examination, full of people acting resourcefully by bringing their own ideas and energies to solve problems.

The intertwinement of routines and creativity helps us realize that individuals make a big difference for even the seemingly dullest types of work. Yet routines are just one avenue where individuals can bring a part of themselves—beliefs, experiences, and unique outlooks—into work situations. Another one is our identities, which not only reflect who we are but also guide just about everything we do. The problem is we often cordon off our different identities, living split lives inside and outside of the office. Combining our different identities allows us to approach problems, opportunities, and changes in more powerful ways.

## OUR MULTIPLE IDENTITIES

A woman by the name of Bette Nesmith Graham was born in Dallas, Texas, in the early 1920s. She became a single mother and high-school dropout, working as a secretary for Texas Bank & Trust to support her young son. It wasn't her first choice of jobs. She wanted to be an artist. After World War II ended, the recently divorced woman learned shorthand and typing to find work that could pay the bills. Through hard work, she moved up to serve as the executive secretary for the bank's chairman of the board.

Around the time of her promotion, electric typewriters started revolutionizing office work. They allowed for a faster and easier way of typing, but they came with a serious drawback. The speedier machines were much less forgiving, leading to more frequent mistakes. Even the smallest mishap rendered an entire page unusable, requiring typists to redo their work.

Graham worried her blunders might lead her to lose her job. One day, she watched painters working on the bank's windows. They had made a few mistakes but had an easy correction. Paint over their errors. Graham made a critical discovery when she combined her two very different identities—secretary and artist—to come up with the idea of using paint to conceal mistakes on paper. It would salvage her work, save a lot of time and money, and put many other secretaries at ease.

She tested out her idea on some documents for her boss. Using a white, water-based, fast-drying permanent paint, she brushed over her errors and typed the correct letters on top. The fix worked, but she kept it to herself, fooling her boss, who never realized his documents had initially contained mistyped letters.

After some experimentation, the secretary and artist perfected one of the bestselling office products of the twentieth century. Her company, Liquid Paper, became a saving grace to typists, turning paper headed for the trash due to a minor mishap into mistake-free work.*

What Bette Nesmith Graham was able to create through using her different backgrounds teaches us about the power that identities have on how we work. Nearly everyone I interview in my research—no matter the project—gets a simple yet revealing exercise to complete. I ask people to fill in five blanks about themselves: I am [blank]. Some people define their blanks with a bundle of social characteristics—gender, age, race, or religion. Other people refer to traits such as intelligence or compassion. Still others point to roles such as secretary or artist. The reality is that our identities include all of these things, and understanding that we're a blend of different characteristics, traits, and roles helps us recognize the versatility we have in how we think about ourselves to solve problems.

Identities allow us to focus on and filter out some things over others. Although most of us have multiple identities (some of mine are: male, husband, parent, researcher, teacher, and squash player), it's hard to access all of them at once. All too often, we're prone

---

* Graham's son went on to fame of his own. Michael Nesmith was a band member and costar of the television series *The Monkees*.

to segmenting our identities, tending to activate only the part that matches our surroundings.

In the MBA classes I teach, which are populated by a lot of engineers, my students sometimes struggle to embrace their managerial identities, approaching technical problems with a singular, engineering focus. Cross-functional teams often lead people to attach to their disciplinary identities—marketing, finance, accounting, operations, R&D—while overlooking their shared organizational identities. Employees remain in silos, unable to think about the bigger picture. For Graham, it took observing painters at the office to trigger her artistic identity. Yet if we could find a way to mix our identities, we could look at problems in new ways—especially when it comes to combining what turns out to be two of many people's most important identities: professional and parent.

―――――――――――

"Parenthood isn't a common topic of discussion among entrepreneurs, because conventional wisdom says that the two simply don't mix," tech entrepreneur and founder of Tapestry.net Andrew Dowling observes. We often feel the need, and organizations often encourage us, to segment our personal lives from our professional lives.

There's good reason for this separation. The common view among researchers for quite some time was that multiple identities psychologically depleted people because they were torn between two very different parts of their lives. Beyond the torment, doing more than one thing well was difficult, so, for example, the better a parent we became, the worse a professional we then became, and vice versa.

Dowling offers a contrasting view, pointing out that while being a parent takes a lot of time, it also creates benefits on the job— teaching skills such as developing patience, dealing with chaos, and providing perspective. His insight is backed up by research. In a study at the Center for Creative Leadership, sixty-one women ranging from middle managers to senior executives sat down for an interview. Responding to questions about how their roles outside of work help on the job, they identified improving interpersonal skills as a critical consequence of non-work experiences. But there was much more to gain from their outside roles. Psychological resources, particularly self-esteem and confidence, received a boost from non-work experiences, carrying over into their jobs.

To get a more rigorous assessment, the researchers followed up with a survey of 276 women, also ranging from middle manager to executive positions. Using a twenty-one-item assessment to measure multiple roles—occupational, marital, parental, community, and friendship—they determined the mix of each person's identity. Afterward, the researchers measured life satisfaction and managerial skills. It turned out that the more diverse the person's roles were, the higher her life satisfaction and the sharper her managerial skills.

The professional skills we learn on the job can equally help our home life—providing organization and conflict-management skills. About a year into our relationship, Randi and I gave each other a formal performance review—taking a tool we learned at work and bringing it into our home. The structure of a business activity provided a way for us to talk about very personal parts of our lives. It turns out we were actually onto something. In a recent study by psychologist James Córdova and his colleagues, the group examined 215 married couples and instructed some of them to complete a Marital Checkup—a type of performance review that assessed each partner's strengths and weaknesses. For couples undergoing the performance review, relational satisfaction, intimacy, and acceptance improved, compared to the control group, for up to two years following the intervention.

A big part of overcoming the division of our identities—and, for that matter, any split between resources—is to understand that we often frame different resources as involving trade-offs: competitive relationships versus friendly relationships, routinized work versus creative work, or work identities versus personal identities. Stretchers find ways of integrating different resources by building pathways that connect the seemingly unconnectable.

## BRIDGING TRADE-OFFS

The stunning Valley of a Thousand Hills lies between the South African cities of Pietermaritzburg and Durban. The area's natural beauty masks the plight of its black residents. Apartheid decimated the impoverished region, and its residents lacked the basic necessities we frequently take for granted, including running water and electricity. In 1998, I spent an evening in the valley's rural village of Maphephethe in a hut with a floor made from hardened dung. Before heading to bed, my host family and I gathered in their smokehouse to share a beer and exchange stories about the remarkable changes unfolding in the community. At nearby Myeka High School, I toured a newly built computer lab, the first solar-powered one in South Africa. Eighteen months after the lab's installation, the passing rates for students soared from 30 percent to 70 percent.

I went to South Africa as part of a multiyear research project to examine how a Washington, D.C.–based organization named the Solar Electric Light Fund brought electricity to the developing world while minimizing any environmental damage. As the twenty-first century approached, many people in the developing world still lacked access to life-changing electricity, missing out on everything from refrigeration for medicine to light for children to do homework by in the evening. For Neville Williams, the organization's leader, electrifying the large swath of the developing world with power brought worries of environmental harm.

Williams traveled to more than fifty developing countries and observed firsthand how electricity could drastically improve people's lives but also could threaten the harmony of the planet. Those who live without power generally don't prioritize the environmental impact decades down the road. In the past, whoever showed up first won the opportunity to provide service, typically delivering electricity using harmful fossil fuels.

Williams faced a second problem—how to pay for electricity. The cost of technology upgrades far exceeded the funds Williams's organization possessed. For individual residents, it amounted to half of their annual income. Besides the financial pragmatics, his personal philosophy held that simply giving away electricity stripped people of the responsibilities of ownership. To electrify the village, residents would need to purchase their equipment at market rates.

Williams thought he could accomplish everything he valued, not seeing any contradictions between economic development and environmental issues, impoverished families and paying customers, and electrification and geographic isolation.

Although the conventional solution at the time was to ask for money, such as from the national government or a power company, to extend the environmentally harmful power grid, Williams took a different approach that allowed him to find harmony. He used solar energy to create environmentally sustainable power and convinced residents of poor communities to pay for it. Demonstration units provided residents with a firsthand look at the transformative powers of the technology, such as at local schools or courthouses. The relatively high cost of the technology encouraged people to care for it much better, while the geographic isolation of the poor communities he empowered lowered the cost of his technology relative to more environmentally harmful technologies. As the technology slowly improved the quality of education, it provided new avenues for economic development, such as sparking local business.

We frequently encounter situations in which we feel compelled to make a choice between two opposing sides of what appears as an unresolvable conflict. Research shows two different ways of approaching these situations. The first approach involves treating both parts as opposing forces. Being more of a parent naturally makes you less of a professional, just like electrifying the developing world necessarily involves harming the environment. Such *bucketing* seeks to place each part of an apparent trade-off into its own, separate category, allowing us to simplify the world by putting things into tidy, clearly defined groups. The reasoning goes that it's futile to mix the different buckets. Like oil and water, they'll naturally separate, no matter how hard we try to prevent it.

Buckets highlight the similarities within a category and the differences across categories, making it harder to see how the two can mix. But there's actually a lot of variety and diversity inside a bucket. There are many ways to be a parent or a professional—or, for that matter, a Republican or a Democrat.

There is a second, and better, way that people can choose to approach potential trade-offs: mixing opposed concepts together. For Neville Williams, economic development and environmental sustainability go hand in hand—when he mixed these together, he was able to create something much more valuable, a business model where increasing incomes allowed people to afford purchasing environmentally friendly technology and then care for it because they had worked hard to pay for it.

University of Delaware professor Wendy Smith has spent much

of her career examining the apparent trade-offs we make. Along with her colleagues, she has found three critical steps to overcome bucketing. First, accept the competing demands of a trade-off. Obviously, there are times when the different sides of a trade-off will conflict. By ignoring these competing demands, we set ourselves up for inevitable disappointment.

Second, recognize the distinct value of each side of the trade-off. To successfully do this, we need to embrace the independent value of each side. What does being a parent contribute to our lives? How might it be a resource for thinking about work out of the house? What does being a dedicated employee contribute to family life—organization, structure, or teamwork?

Third, find synergies between both sides. Ask how one side (such as being a parent) helps with the other side of the trade-off (such as being a dedicated employee), and vice versa. Although our natural tendency is to view the two sides only as opposing forces, Professor Smith invites us to consider how each side can advance the goals of the other side.

Finding ways where different parts of our lives work in harmony is very fulfilling. It allows us to embrace our whole self, but too often we're quick to write off what seem like opposing concepts, ideas, strategies, or other resources. Organizations make the same mistakes, falsely assuming that many goals they have are not reconcilable. Marketing departments focus on sellable products while engineering groups fascinate themselves with the most recent technology. Labor groups seek a fair wage while management pushes for more profits.

Solving some of the world's greatest problems involves unlikely combinations that other people have overlooked, dismissed, and outright said were impossible to make. Of course, as simple as this sounds, it's not easy. Overcoming trade-offs, and for that matter, finding the right mixture for any set of resources, often takes time—as one of America's most influential inventors learned.

## A MOST VALUABLE ACCIDENT YEARS IN THE MAKING

In the 1830s, America fell in love with a new material: rubber. The waterproof substance came from the sap of trees originating in Brazil. First used as a way of rubbing out pencil marks, it quickly became a useful material for waterproofing. Its promise spawned a craze in the United States, with many people staking their family fortunes and livelihoods on it.

Charles Goodyear was the son of a bankrupt hardware merchant in New Haven, Connecticut. Goodyear's finances were not much better than his pop's, and in 1834, he was jailed for failing to pay his debts. It wasn't his first incarceration for delinquincy, and it for sure was not his last. Wanting to join the rubber craze, he asked his wife to bring him some of the promising material along with a rolling pin so that he could learn more about the gummy substance's properties, which started a lifelong fascination with it.

Charles Goodyear's passion was finding the right chemicals to mix into rubber to make the substance more usable. After his release from jail, he created magnesia-dried rubber galoshes, which he hoped might raise his family out of poverty and illustrate the commercial possibilities of rubber. But when the summer came, the Achilles' heel that doomed so many rubber barons during the era also shattered Goodyear's prospects. Rubber, he found out, was highly sensitive to temperature. It melted in the summer, rendering anything made from it a sticky mess with a stinky odor. It didn't fare much better during harsh winters, when the cold made it lose its flexibility.

Down but not out, Goodyear moved to New York, where he sought a new home for his rubber experiments. He believed it would be only a matter of time before he would find the right materials to mix with rubber to stabilize it. One morning, he didn't have enough rubber around so he reused an old sample for his experiment. He had a tendency to decorate his material, so to remove its bronze paint, he applied nitric acid. The piece turned black and ended up in the trash bin. A few days later Goodyear decided to give the black rubber another look. After rummaging through the wastebasket, he found the sample to be smooth and dry, a more usable state than any of the other rubber mixtures he had created. Excited by his latest discovery, a New York financier advanced him several thousand dollars to ramp up production of what seemed like his best rubber yet.

As Goodyear's luck would go, a severe financial panic in 1837 undermined the banking system and took down many businesses, including his rubber operation. Confidence nosedived, and patience by his financial backers for his rubber experiments dropped. Poor again, Goodyear camped in his abandoned rubber factory and caught fish in the nearby harbor for food.

It wouldn't be too long before another backer saw promise in Goodyear's latest work with rubber and helped get him up and running again. Early commercial success came from a contract to produce 150 mailbags using the nitric acid mixture. He also sold several thousand life preservers using the same manufacturing process. He was so confident he had finally mastered the product, he stored the rubber mailbags in a warm room during an extended work trip. Upon returning, the bags had decomposed and their handles had fallen off, making his prospects dimmer than ever.

Despite falling back on hard times, Goodyear continued with his experiments. By now, his family had suffered immensely from his failures, constantly moving from city to city and living in poverty.

# S T R E T C H

Goodyear had come up short . . . until the most fortunate of accidents.

In the winter of 1839, Charles Goodyear was in his kitchen with some family members doing what he often liked to do—describe his latest experiments that he dreamed would one day lead him to solve the rubber puzzle. This time his excitement was hard to contain. With a rapid hand gesture that mirrored his enthusiasm, a piece of rubber accidentally came in contact with the hot stove.

When Goodyear looked down at the rubber, he was surprised by what he found. It didn't melt. Instead, under the stove's extremely high heat, it charred into a leatherlike substance.

Emboldened by his accidental discovery, he nailed the rubber to the outside of his door through a frigid winter night. When morning came, the rubber proved just as flexible as the night before. Goodyear had finally found a way to create a commercially viable product.[*]

Goodyear tried for years to find the right mixture to transform rubber into a more stable, and usable, substance that provided the foundation for the multibillion-dollar industry that revolutionized everything from automobiles to health care. A serendipitous mishap led to his breakthrough, but it was his years of trying that made it likely he'd eventually find the right mixture and have enough awareness to recognize when he found the winning formula.

The more we persist at something, the greater the chances are that we'll come up with a successful combination. In *Originals*,

---

[*] While he proved an able inventor, he was a dismal businessman, squandering away potential fortunes with bad business deals and lapsed patent filings. The company named after him, the world's largest rubber business, Goodyear Tire and Rubber, had no direct connection to him. "Life," he wrote, "should not be estimated exclusively by the standard of dollars and cents. I am not disposed to complain that I have planted and others have gathered the fruits. A man has cause for regret only when he sows and no one reaps."

Adam Grant explains why the best ideas come from those who have the most ideas. Charles Goodyear did not have a stroke of genius and invent rubber. Rather, his invention came from years of attempting new combinations.

## OIL AND WATER

Everyone knows that oil and water don't mix. Water molecules are polar, meaning one end has a slight negative charge and the other a slight positive charge. This property forms hydrogen bonds, allowing it to attach to other molecules that are polar. Oil molecules are nonpolar and can't form hydrogen bonds. When put in the same container, the oil will bunch together and the water will bunch together, forming two separate layers.

The same goes for how we usually treat our resources. We often struggle to take advantage of the value from how resources interact. A hard shake of the bottle will temporary mix oil and water together, but they'll soon separate. Similarly, to find an everlasting and potent mixture of resources, we need more than a short-term shake. We'll need to change the very way we think about and work with our resources.

Adding an emulsifier to water and oil helps bond the two different liquids, achieving a more permanent mixture. When we stretch, this is exactly what we do—seek out experiences, situations, and other catalysts that join resources together, creating overlap and connections while avoiding the trap of treating resources as separate buckets.

Unlikely combinations help us search for friendships when we'd be prone only to compete with others, and find ways of bringing our individuality to the routines we might otherwise consider impersonal and static. They're what also allowed Roy Choi to revolutionize the food industry, Bette Nesmith Graham to transform the office supply market, Neville Williams to electrify the developing world, and Charles Goodyear to perfect one of the most important inventions of modern times. By focusing on unimagined combinations that others overlook or give up on uniting, we mix things up for the better.

# EIGHT

## AVOID INJURIES

### HOW TO GET THE RIGHT STRETCH

We've met stretchers from all walks of life and learned how they've achieved great results at work and beyond by using their available resources. Dick Yuengling's beer empire grew while bigger and better resourced competitors floundered. His competitors chased unbridled growth that never materialized, and Yuengling stepped in to pick up factories, equipment, and market share at a bargain. Bob Kierlin built one of the most successful companies in the world by embracing and promoting frugality. Outsider Gavin Potter lacked the resources of better-equipped opponents in the Netflix prize, but that didn't stop him from being competitive and improving the performance of other teams. Robert Rodriguez's example of moving ahead without a script pushes us into action with what's currently at hand. The wait for the "right" resources can be long or even never ending, but acting immediately teaches us to appreciate and work with what we do have. The horse Clever Hans shows us that positive expectations can make anyone (or anything) better off. Chef Roy Choi's unlikely combinations—inside and outside of the kitchen—demonstrate why the sum is often greater than its parts.

As much success and satisfaction as these people enjoyed, and as much prosperity as they brought to themselves and their organizations—like most scientific phenomena, and for that matter, most things in life, too much of a good thing can turn out to be bad. In this chapter, we'll learn how to avoid five common injuries from overstretching: turning into a cheapskate, wandering on the road to nowhere, leaping without learning, being cursed by high expectations, and making toxic mixtures.

## TURNING INTO A CHEAPSKATE

Nestled within an affluent neighborhood of Los Angeles, peeling roof shingles adorn a one-story stucco home among a group of well-maintained midcentury residences. A blue-and-black tarp patches a leaky roof that neighbors consider a community eyesore. Occasionally, citizens of the Ladera Heights subdivision will spot the unkempt homeowner dressed in a bathrobe tinkering with the tarp, to no avail. Underneath the damaged roof lies a house infested with so much mold that its occupant readily acknowledges the health problems the microbes have caused him. His wife takes up residence across town, refusing to spend time in a toxic house in shambles.

Inside the dilapidated teardown lives Edward Wedbush, the multimillionaire financier who runs the multibillion-dollar security and investment firm that bears his name. The company has more than one hundred offices worldwide, and it runs very differently than the glitz and glamour of its competitors. In his office at the firm's headquarters, there are no lavish furnishings, artwork, or impressive displays of opulence. The spartan space he labels a working office contains a simple desk under bare lighting. The worn carpet used to trip up female workers, whose high heels became lodged in its many holes. After several years of complaints, he patched it with duct tape.

Growing up in the era of the Great Depression taught Edward Wedbush to use his money wisely. This personal philosophy continued when he started his business in 1955 with a partner, when the pair had a combined $10,000 to launch. Even as Wedbush turned into a multimillionaire, he retained this personal philosophy, driving a modest car and turning down fancy meals to enjoy a daily sack lunch. His company avoided excessive debt and spent well within its means.

Despite a successful track record, Wedbush overstretched at times. His obsession with cost controls landed him in hot water with regulators and in the doghouse with many employees. An arbitration panel labeled his firm's behavior as "morally reprehensible" and awarded $3.5 million to a bond trader who, along with other employees, had his pay withheld by the founder. Regulators have also repeatedly fined the company for lax oversight and in 2012 took the unusual step of suspending Wedbush from managing his company for thirty-one days. The Financial Industry Regulatory Authority (FINRA) cited him for failing to adequately disclose terminated employees and unfavorable arbitration rulings. The regulator found no evidence of fraud or intentional deceit. Rather, it considered the firm reckless for not dedicating sufficient resources to its compliance and risk management.

# S T R E T C H

As Aristotle wrote, all virtues can become vices when taken to their extreme. On one end lies what Aristotle called vulgarity—excessive spending beyond what circumstances warrant, often to make a show. It's common among chasers. Equally damning for Aristotle was the other extreme—a focus solely on doing things more cheaply and amassing wealth rather than using that wealth for a higher purpose. It is this vice that leads to a major injury from overstretching: becoming a cheapskate.

Edward Wedbush's stinginess with his firm's resources threatened his company. A lack of investment in compliance and unfair treatment of employees made his firm's resources—such as its reputation and human resources—less valuable. Despite having the means to repair his house, he let it continue to deteriorate while his wife moved across town to avoid its hazards. Was Edward Wedbush frugal or a cheapskate?

There are notable differences between the frugal and the cheap. Frugal people take pleasure in saving and cheap people feel pained by spending. A team of researchers led by University of Michigan professor Scott Rick surveyed more than thirteen thousand people, made up of readers of major U.S. and Canadian newspapers; television viewers in Philadelphia; and students, parents, and staff at two universities in Pittsburgh. They examined differences in how people react to spending money. People they called spendthrifts spent money without recognizing that spending now meant less spending later. They didn't realize any consequences from buying things. These types of folks tend to be chasers, with an unquenchable thirst for consuming goods.

Cheapskates, on the other hand, believed they'd have to give up something in the future to buy something now, a mind-set that often stopped them from opening up their wallets. They recognized that choices in the present would affect their options in the future. On average, roughly a quarter of the people surveyed were cheapskates and 15 percent were spendthrifts.*

It turns out that frugal people have a critical difference in their mind-set compared to cheapskates. Dr. Rick and his team asked 966 people to rate the extent to which they experienced spending money as uncomfortable. Cheapskates felt psychologically pained from spending money. In contrast, frugal people didn't experience this type of emotional pain.

To dig deeper, Rick and his team asked 316 people the extent to which they agreed that saving money was pleasurable. It was the frugal people who took pleasure from saving money, not the cheapskates.

Stretchers aren't pained to spend money; rather, they take pleasure in spending it wisely—and getting the most out of any resource. That's why they tend to be frugal, and not cheap.

In a series of studies with college students, homeowners, food-store customers, Taiwanese workers, and Environmental Protection Agency workers, researchers found that for stretchers, acting frugally was inherently satisfying. It wasn't just a means to an end. This doesn't mean stretchers avoid spending money or deploying resources—they just need to find enough value. Dick Yuengling and Bob Kierlin invested substantial money to grow their businesses, but they avoided the type of unchecked spending that typified the chasers in their marketplaces. Despite their success and eventual access to large amounts of resources, they relished the simple pleasure of getting the most out of what they had.

---

* For the Canadian sample of newspaper readers, the numbers were a bit different: 36 percent were cheapskates, and only 6 percent were spendthrifts.

# S T R E T C H

It's not just turning into cheapskates that causes harm. We'll now examine another injury from overstretching: in accumulating a diversity of experiences, some people wind up wandering on the road to nowhere.

## WANDERING ON THE ROAD TO NOWHERE

Ronald Wayne calls Pahrump, Nevada, a town of thirty-five thousand residents tucked away in the Mojave Desert, home. The self-described "Renaissance Man" lives in a modest $150,000 house where he sells rare coins and stamps to supplement his monthly Social Security check. A talented electromechanical engineer, Wayne holds a dozen patents. Insatiably curious, his forty-plus-year obsession with the intricacies of currencies led him to invest in gold and apply the learnings of his research to politics and governance, penning a book on the topic that he hopes becomes his main legacy.

The illustrator, machinist, and modeler likes to press his luck at the penny slot machines at the town's casinos late into the night. Slot machines hold a particularly fond place in Wayne's heart. One of his proudest accomplishments: designing, fabricating, and assembling a slot machine from the ground up, including the electronic logic, case design, graphics, symbols for the reels, and the electromagnetic backbone. Despite his knowledge of the very different aspects of slot machines, the business he started to build them eventually flopped, leading Wayne to spend a year paying down debts and making investors whole. His refusal to hide behind the corporate veil and instead take responsibility for his failures was morally commendable but personally taxing.

Ronald Wayne's many interests provide him with a very diverse set of experiences. He brings these diverse skills to approach problems in new ways, which has no doubt helped him secure patents. But Wayne's variety of interests and pursuits raises an important question: Is too much diversity of experience a bad thing?

---

MIT researcher Ezra Zuckerman studied how to balance diversity of experience by studying the movies. There are the multitalented actors who star in several genres of film, such as action, drama, and comedy. Diverse experiences can give their characters more complexity, introduce them to new audiences, and push them to try out new parts. They're people like Leonardo DiCaprio, Robert De Niro, or Angelina Jolie. Then there's the single-genre actors—in film parlance, they're typecast to play particular parts. Think Jennifer Aniston for romantic comedies, Jackie Chan for action films, and Will Ferrell for slapstick humor.

Just like actors, we make similar choices in our careers, deciding to become specialists who are very good at a limited number of things or generalists who have knowledge not as deep but much wider in scope. Organizations make the same types of choices, with some focused on a single product line or narrow set of services and others covering a wide variety of offerings.

There's good reason for us to specialize. It sends clear signals about what we can and cannot do. Imagine putting Arnold Schwarzenegger into a romantic comedy. Likewise, we'd be reluctant to hire a doctor to file our taxes or trust a luggage company to make frozen dinners.

Eventually, if we stay in one genre, we get very good at it, but we're likely to get typecast and have a hard time getting different roles or jobs. Although there's a lot of merit in developing an admirable skill set and sound reputation for doing one thing well, breaking out of a typecast brings tremendous benefits—new abilities and challenges and even bigger rewards. But when not done carefully, heading in too many directions leads to a critical injury: wandering to nowhere.

Zuckerman's analysis of the Internet movie database for all films between 1995 and 1997 provides useful guidance on how to avoid being typecast too narrowly or wandering aimlessly. He finds that we first need to establish a coherent core identity—a concentrated career in a specific area or, for organizations, a specific type of product or a signature service. If we diversify too quickly—jumping across industries or functional areas without first establishing credibility where we start—we send confusing signals to others: What type of skill does this person have? Is she committed to anything? What does this company do?

It's only after establishing a core identity that we can diversify. We can follow in the footsteps of actor Matthew McConaughey, who established his credentials in romantic comedies and then played critically acclaimed roles in commercially successful dramas such as *The Lincoln Lawyer* and *Dallas Buyers Club*, for which he won an Oscar for Best Performance by an Actor in a Leading Role. But if we stay too close to home for too long, it's difficult to break the typecast—witness Sylvester Stallone's attempts to branch out of action-adventure films with flops such as *Staying Alive* and *Over the Top*.

Another strategy to avoid wandering aimlessly is to pick up new things that are only somewhat different from our core focus. Eventually, after making a bunch of incremental moves, we end up with some very useful, and pretty varied, experiences. In a study of the online contract labor marketplace Elance, University of California–Berkeley researcher Ming Leung sought to understand techniques to gain a diversity of experience without wandering too far. The Elance platform provided an ideal place to examine this question because it connects people with a variety of skills looking to freelance with other people and businesses in search of part-time talent. Freelancers post profiles that contain their past jobs, skills and training, and client feedback. Clients provide information about the jobs and supply information about pay.

Leung studied all 32,949 jobs posted on Elance in 2004. During the year, 2,779 freelancers bid on at least one of the jobs. Leung found that diverse experiences did help the freelancers get jobs, but there was an important caveat. People who won jobs moved incrementally between similar jobs. They were careful not to bid on a drastically different job from what they had just previously done. Over time, it was possible for these incremental job movers to take on very different types of work, but they had to move step-by-step to build up their portfolio.

The incremental job diversifiers ended up winning far more work than either those who stayed in only one job category or those who moved too erratically between different categories from one job to the next job. Leung's work on the Elance platform matches other research that shows that gradually diversifying our work enables us to be more creative and get promoted faster.

---

Sometimes when pursuing diverse experience, we need to move— either to new jobs or even to new cities. Some important benefits come from these major changes because of the different experiences we'll gain. As valuable as these changes are for diversifying experience, considerable trade-offs come from wandering too frequently.

In 2016, my wife, Randi, faced a major decision. She received two spectacular job offers, which, from a chaser perspective, would be virtually impossible to turn down. They'd dramatically increase her compensation. Her team size would triple to well over a hundred people. She'd work for a bigger company, with higher status—not to mention a bigger office. After a lot of temptation, she turned down both jobs.

As enticing as the positions were, they failed her critical test: What do I find more exciting—getting the job or learning from the job? Once framed in the language of a stretcher—with a focus on learning, not acquiring—the difficult decision turned out to be quite easy.

The first opportunity would have meant leading several types of teams she had already led before—there was little opportunity for new experiences. She'd be doing a job she'd done before. The second opportunity would have involved a switch to such a different industry that it might have led her to wander too far. Her lack of enthusiasm for the industry only added to her reservations.

Another part of her decision also weighed on me. Both jobs would have required a cross-country move—something that excited us at times but also could have meant a disruption to our family.

Psychologist Shigehiro Oishi at the University of Virginia finds that when people move frequently, they uproot their lives and social relations. They focus on the novelty of experience, which is important, but underestimate the value of what's already around them, especially their relationships. Gaining new colleagues and friends can be very exciting, but losing good ones is equally trying.

In one study, Oishi examined 7,108 American adults over a ten-year period. They ranged in age from twenty to seventy-five and included a roughly even split between men and women. Oishi measured their life satisfaction using questions such as "How satisfied are you with your life?" at the start of the study and ten years later. He also measured psychological well-being by having participants rate their level of agreement or disagreement with statements such as "For me, life has been a continuous process of learning, changing, and growth."

Next, Oishi evaluated the degree that each person was introverted or extraverted, as well as their social relationships (friendship quality, family relationships, and neighborhood relationships). Finally, he asked participants about the number of residential moves they had made as children.

For introverts, the news was not very good. The frequency of residential moves was negatively related to life satisfaction and psychological well-being, but for extroverts, there was no relationship between moving and well-being. After diving deeper, Oishi found that introverts struggled to form positive social relationships upon moving, which decreased their well-being. It turned out that moving cost introverts in an even more substantial way. Introverts who moved a lot as children also had a greater risk of death.* As the lone introvert in our family, I was most worried.

In line with Oishi's findings, some medical research shows positive correlations between frequent job switching and adverse health effects such as greater incidences of smoking, alcohol consumption, and less-frequent exercise.

It's important to calibrate how much or how frequently we diversify experiences—too much (especially for introverts) is just as dangerous as too little. And believing the only way to diversify experiences is through major life changes that undermine existing resources, especially relationships, is sometimes (literally) perilous. It's possible to find much less disruptive ways of gaining different experiences while staying put. We need to look for novel situations that also allow us to maintain some sense of constancy.

———————————

* Moving did not affect the chances of death for extroverts.

# S T R E T C H

For all of his moving back and forth, in the early 1970s, Ronald Wayne laid the seeds for what could have forged a very different life for him—one that would have taken him far away from living off government assistance. He had a promising computer career and spent time as chief draftsman at Atari, where he met an ambitious and brilliant computer whiz named Steve Jobs. Jobs, along with his partner, Steve Wozniak, dreamed of building the personal computing industry. The two Steve geniuses clashed interpersonally, so they turned to Wayne, twenty years their senior, and someone they immensely respected, to help arbitrate their disputes and provide adult supervision for their venture. On April 1, 1976, the three signed a contract to create Apple Computer. Wayne designed Apple's original logo and authored the manual for the company's first product, the Apple I.

Ronald Wayne helped found one of the largest, most successful, and most innovative companies in the world—but he left twelve days after joining. He worried that strong initial interest in its computers would, ironically, lead the underresourced company to follow the fate of his slot machine business—it'd run out of resources and wouldn't be able to fulfill orders. Wayne also wanted to satisfy his need for involvement in all aspects of product development, reflecting his diverse skills and even more diverse interests. He would later explain, "I went off and did my own thing, having fun in doing it and taking off in any direction that seemed appropriate at the time." Upon departure, Wayne sold his 10 percent ownership of the company for $2,300, a stake that would have reached billions of dollars today. He reflected more recently, "My whole life has been a day late and a dollar short." At the end of 2014, he auctioned off his remaining connection to Apple to help pay his bills—an archive of documents from the early days of the company that fetched $25,000.

Ronald Wayne learned the hard way about the dangers of wandering aimlessly. His early work at Apple helped found a remarkably successful company, but he benefited very little from his contributions as he floated on to his next venture. Apple grew to become a tech giant, with Wayne on the sidelines.

## LEAPING WITHOUT LEARNING

In 2011, a struggling iconic retailer thought it had found its savior. The company was slowly dying, and it had just hired a hotshot CEO with a ridiculously successful track record. His name was Ron Johnson, the executive who had turned Ronald Wayne's Apple into a retail giant, pulling in about $6,000 in sales per square foot, more than double the next highest retailer, jewelry maker Tiffany & Co. Before joining Apple, Johnson helped transform Target from a dull discounter into a hip merchandiser that combined style and value. On paper, Johnson appeared to be a perfect fit to rescue his new company: JC Penney.

So promising was the news that, upon the hiring announcement, JC Penney saw its stock soar 17.5 percent in a single day. Only seventeen months would go by before JC Penney was on the verge of financial collapse. During Johnson's brief tenure, JC Penney lost about half of its market value and saw sales decline roughly 30 percent. It posted close to a billion dollars in losses.

Shortly after arriving at JC Penney, Ron Johnson knew he needed to shake things up, and he went right to work. To turn around the sluggish company, he rapidly introduced an entirely new approach to selling, called "fair-and-square" pricing. The everyday low-pricing strategy eliminated artificially high list prices and the endless sales and coupons that brought those prices back down to earth.

Johnson's approach had him jump right in, relying on his gut instincts about how to run the business. He reasoned that JC Penney had become too bogged down in planning and quickly eliminated meetings to review data, store performance, and other metrics. He saw no need to pilot his idea. This wasn't the first time Johnson took a leap of faith. When he created the Genius Bar at Apple—the store hub that provides help and support for customers—he stuck to his instincts about the merit of the idea despite disappointing data: "What you can't do is chicken out. . . . If you had looked at the data on the Genius Bar after a year and a half, we should have taken it out of the store. But it was something I believed in with every bone in my body."

Johnson's instincts about fair-and-square pricing carried the same degree of confidence as he had with his Genius Bar at Apple. His bravado was met with some skepticism by a few members of the company's leadership, who questioned his blind faith in the strategy. They wanted to back out, and Johnson fought back. He liked to say, "We didn't test at Apple." Instead, he wanted to follow his gut, observing, "My ideas just sort of come. I don't know [how] to explain it. It's all intuitive. . . . It's not like you go out and go study something and go, 'What am I going to do?' You just kind of have an instinct for this stuff."

When the numbers started rolling in showing that Johnson's instincts were wrong, he blamed customers, sticking resolutely to his fair-and-square pricing much the same way he stuck with his gut for the Genius Bar. Customers just needed to be better educated, and then they'd take a liking to the new JC Penney. Unfortunately, sales continued to plummet, and customer satisfaction dropped. JC Penney management continued living in a different reality, explaining, "Customers love the new JCP they discover in our stores." The sales numbers told a very different story.

As good as Ron Johnson's ideas were in theory, and as right as his instincts had been in the past, he had a grave misunderstanding of JC Penney's customers, who enjoyed the thrill and satisfaction of scoring a great deal from their savvy bargain hunting. Fair-and-square pricing was superior to Johnson because it was straightforward, but customers enjoyed showing off what skilled shoppers they were by maximizing their coupon and sale discounts. They wanted to win the game of shopping.

The investor Bill Ackman, who had wooed Johnson away from Apple to JC Penney, acknowledged, "One of the big mistakes was perhaps too much change too quickly without adequate testing on what the impact would be." Ron Johnson and JC Penney leaped to a potentially new and exciting direction—but it turned out they had jumped into an empty pool and were unable, or unwilling, to learn from previous mistakes.

Nobel Prize winner Daniel Kahneman and intuition expert Gary Klein investigated all of the benefits and downsides of using the type of gut instincts that shaped how Ron Johnson ran JC Penney. They concluded that the most important requirement for effectively jumping right in was a learning focus. By learning from our actions, we can make critical adjustments down the road. Unfortunately, Ron Johnson kept doubling down on his bad bet, struggling to comprehend how his choices were decimating JC Penney. When asked if he'd start over again if given a chance, he replied, "No, of course not."

The filmmaker Robert Rodriguez embraced a very different mind-set when jumping in—he constantly learned. He approached making *El Mariachi* as an inexpensive film school, allowing him to build on his mistakes and calibrate his instincts. Like Johnson, Rodriguez leaped, but unlike Johnson, he also looked and learned.

Strategy scholars Chet Miller and Duane Ireland recommend a

fast-feedback, slow-learning approach to minimize the injuries that can come from acting too quickly. JC Penney needed fast action, but the company also needed to learn from its actions. Miller and Ireland point out that by evaluating feedback immediately, it's possible to fine-tune actions rapidly. Although it often takes a long time to learn fully about the complex situations JC Penney faced, gradual adjustments in our actions bring us a step closer each time.

Miller and Ireland raise another important safeguard Johnson didn't follow at JC Penney. They advocate avoiding leaps that, if they turn out badly, would be catastrophic. The reason is quite simple: we still have an ability to recover if our leaps don't work, as long as we learn from them. At Apple, had Johnson's bet on the Genius Bar soured, it would have only represented a very small share of the company's business. But when Johnson aggressively rolled out his fair-and-square strategy across JC Penney, and then resolutely stuck with it, he was betting the entire company on an untested and unproven idea.

We don't just wager on ideas. We also bet on people. And when we bet on people, we send signals to them that either spark positive prophecies or, when done ineffectively, curse people with high expectations.

## BEING CURSED BY HIGH EXPECTATIONS

In 1998, two of the best quarterbacks ever to play college football entered the NFL draft, with lots of teams wanting to take a chance on them. Racking up impeccable records, the first quarterback broke forty-two NCAA, conference, and school records. He finished second in voting for the Heisman Trophy, the award that goes to college football's best player. The other quarterback led his college team to its first Rose Bowl appearance in sixty-seven years, came in third in the Heisman Trophy, and won the prestigious Sammy Baugh Trophy, given to the nation's top college passer.

The Indianapolis Colts had already secured the first overall pick in the draft, and the San Diego Chargers wanted a shot at signing one of the star quarterbacks. Trading two first-round draft picks, a second-round pick, and an existing player, the Chargers moved up to the second overall selection, just behind the Colts.

To no one's surprise, both rising quarterbacks were first-round draft picks, with one going first overall to the Colts and the other going second overall to the Chargers.

To say that the Colts and Chargers were struggling at the time was an understatement. The Colts finished the previous season with three wins and thirteen losses. The Chargers fared a bit better, winning four games and losing twelve.

The Colts' choice, Peyton Manning, went on to become one of the league's all-time greatest quarterbacks, living up to the enormous expectations people had of him and helping the Colts win their first Super Bowl since 1971. Manning would go on to take his teams to three Super Bowls, win two of them, and be named the league's most valuable player five times.

The Chargers signed the other top prospect—a Washington State University superstar named Ryan Leaf. So much promise did the Chargers see in their young prodigy that they awarded him an $11.25 million signing bonus, at the time the most lucrative deal for a rookie player.

Like Manning, the expectations for Leaf were through the roof—illustrated by all of the efforts the Chargers made to get a shot at him, the media buzz about his promise, and the terms of his contract. Brushing off any potential roadblocks to his success, he declared, "I don't know what all the fuss is about NFL defenses. I have seen about everything they can throw at me and it's no big deal."

# STRETCH

Leaf's debut pitted his San Diego Chargers against the Buffalo Bills. The Chargers ended up winning the game 16–14, but Leaf's performance was far from stellar. He fumbled his first snap in front of a home crowd that expected a great game from their newly hired superstar. He went on to throw two interceptions during the game, and another two that were overturned by Buffalo penalties.

Despite his promise, Ryan Leaf turned out to be no Peyton Manning. Leaf won only four games as a starting quarterback and threw fourteen touchdowns compared to thirty-six interceptions. He played in only twenty-five games across four seasons. His winning record before joining the NFL had not prepared him to lose in the pros, and his early struggles sent him into a downward spiral. "I had never lost, and I didn't know how to handle it," he recalls.

The collapse of Ryan Leaf was just as remarkable as the triumph of Peyton Manning. Their different trajectories help us understand when positive prophecies work and when they don't. Both players had high expectations about their professional careers but ended up on very different sides of the field.

Peyton Manning never felt personal pressure from others' high expectations. "You don't feel pressure if you study the game plan and know what to do," he liked to tell people. He recognized the connection between hard work and self-improvement, approaching the game with what the psychologist Carol Dweck calls a growth mind-set.

Ryan Leaf struggled with living up to the high expectations others had of him, and he was painfully aware of his disappointing start. As he put it, "The way things turned out, the expectations that the city had on me, the way I let them down, I always felt some apprehension about doing that." The physical play beat up his body as much as the emotional toll of losing beat up his mind—and he couldn't get back in the game.

Making matters worse, Leaf turned to pain medication to soothe his worries. "I became anti-social, isolated, and it just takes away all the bad feelings. You know, all the criticisms of why you weren't a great quarterback, or how you let down your university, or how you let down so and so, or your family. It was a way to cope," he reflects. Eventually, his addiction would lead to an arrest along the Canadian border for trying to carry illegal painkillers into the United States. Leaf pleaded guilty to eight charges—not his first time getting into trouble with the law for drugs and, unfortunately, not his last.

His drug addiction cost him a second chance as a promising college football coach. Leaf would observe, "I was good at two things, athletics and lying. I was always worried about what others were thinking about me or how I was being perceived . . . soon lying, to make the story more about who I wanted people to think I was, ultimately won out." Ryan Leaf was cursed by high expectations, always wanting to please others.

---

High expectations, when calibrated correctly, can create positive prophecies but when imposed without safeguards can trip up even the most promising people. Ryan Leaf expected to have a successful NFL career because that's what others expected from him. But his early struggles eroded his own high expectations. Eventually, others' high expectations simply provoked his insecurities. An audience that expects success will be disappointed by failure. Ryan Leaf was well aware of all of the spectators who came to watch with high hopes, and he started focusing on not letting others down.

When people set positive expectations for us, they give us two different types of information. First, there's information that shapes our own expectations. To the degree that we believe in the expectations others set for us, we're more likely to live up to them. We reason that if others expect great things of us, we must be capable of delivering.

Second, there's a social aspect of a positive expectation—and with it comes the dark side that sacked Ryan Leaf: performance pressure. Performance pressure distracts us with worrying about satisfying what others want from us.

An experiment by a research team led by psychologist Roy Baumeister studied when expectations create positive prophecies and when they lead to performance pressures. They reasoned that a high expectation of someone else would trigger performance pressure if that expectation wasn't believed by that person. It wouldn't create any of the benefits from shaping a person's own expectations but would come with all of the downsides of social pressures.

Thirty undergraduate students were told there was a positive correlation between a personality test they took and their ability to solve difficult problems. The test was really a ruse. The researchers told all participants they received a score of 75 on it, regardless of their results. Those in a control group received no information about how to interpret the 75, whereas all of the other participants were told based on their 75 score, the researchers expected them to solve difficult problems very well. Of the group told that researchers expected them to solve problems very well, half were given reinforcing additional information—a graph that verified the claim (the credible information group). The other half received a graph that showed that past research didn't support the claim (the noncredible information group).

Both the credible and noncredible information groups believed that the researchers expected them to do well. The big difference was that participants in the credible information group internalized the positive expectation of the researchers much more than the noncredible group and, as a result, had more favorable private expectations—they had received both the internalized and social aspects of the expectation. The noncredible information group just experienced performance pressure from social expectations.

When the researchers tallied performance of members of each group, the pattern was striking. The average number of problems solved by the control condition—the group that didn't get any information about their "75" score—was okay. Members of this group averaged solving 5.2 problems. But the group that received credible information solved many more, an average of 7.1 problems. Just as striking, the noncredible group solved even fewer than the control group, only 3.4 problems. For the noncredible information group, the researchers had created performance pressure that didn't translate into a positive belief among participants, making them crumple under pressure.

It turns out that debuting his professional career on his home turf of San Diego might have also inadvertently contributed to Leaf's problems. Although we tend to think of a home field advantage for sports, during critical games, the results are more intriguing. In a separate study, Professor Baumeister examined baseball's World Series and validated our intuitions: home field advantage helps World Series teams. Analyzing results from 1924 to 1982, he finds that in games one and two, the home team wins 60.2 percent of the time. Yet, the home team chokes in decisive games, winning only 40.8 percent of the last game of the series. Zooming into perhaps the most telling data—a game seven, winner-take-all situation—the home team tops the visitors only 38.5 percent of the time.

Another explanation for the patterns of wins Baumeister found could simply be that the visiting team excelled—not that the home team choked under performance pressure. Maybe there is something about being on the road that brings the best out of the guest team—because of the boos and jeers!

A look at fielding errors helps sort out whether home teams choke under performance pressure or visiting teams prevail on the road. In principle, the home team should have a constant error rate on the field—they know the idiosyncrasies of the field they've been playing on all year. The visitors should do slightly better as the series progresses because they get used to the field—its winds, surface, and dimensions. But no matter how much they learn over the course of a best of seven series, visitors, on average, technically shouldn't outperform the home team that knows the field inside out.

Baumeister finds that for the first two games of the World Series, that's exactly what happens. The home team averaged .65 errors compared to 1.04 for the visiting team. The home team also had thirty-three errorless games, compared to only eighteen for the visiting team. Yet, by the decisive game seven, the home field advantage not only disappeared but also turned into a disadvantage. The home team's error rate doubled to 1.31, while the visitor's rate declined to .81. The visiting team also had twice as many error-free games (twelve) as the home team.[*]

To harness the power of positive prophecies and avoid the curse of high expectations, it's important that those expectations be credible and delivered in ways that avoid unnecessary performance pressure. It might be comfortable to play on our home turf, but as the stakes get higher, we're better off working in an environment where we have supportive fans, but not overly zealous ones watching our every move and expecting perfection.

---

[*] Baumeister finds a similar effect when examining free throws in the NBA semifinals and championship games. The free throw percentage for home and visiting teams is virtually identical, except in the final game when the visiting team outperforms the home team (despite the likely loud crowds trying to distract visiting players with noise and signs).

Another way of avoiding the curse of high expectations is to get some early "small wins." Our instincts often favor getting a big win—making it to the Super Bowl, completing a project better than anyone's seen before, or signing up the company's largest customer. But big wins early further enlarge expectations before we've even had a chance to live up to initial expectations reliably. Finding small wins—having an interception-free game, finishing a first project, or landing a new account—goes a long way toward internalizing others' positive expectations about us, while minimizing performance pressure. Ryan Leaf's problems started when the high hopes he had for himself quickly faded following a string of small losses—and eventually, the small losses led to a big defeat.

Having examined some serious injuries from overstretching—turning into a cheapskate, wandering aimlessly, leaping without learning, and now being cursed by high expectations—we'll turn to our final injury: what happens when we mix unlikely combinations that result in a blowup?

## MAKING TOXIC MIXTURES

In 1974, the baby-food maker Gerber thought it had a winning idea that could jump-start its growth. Take the best of what the company already did, using its existing facilities—sourcing, processing, and jarring produce for babies—and combine it with a new marketing spin to serve an entirely different type of customer. Gerber Singles launched with much fanfare, and the company's products, a staple in the baby aisle, now had a presence elsewhere in the grocery store. The product largely looked and tasted like Gerber's existing ones but was meant for time-pressured college students and working adults.

Instead of filling an important niche by providing a quick and healthy meal for grown-ups living on their own, the company pulled the product from grocery stores only three months after launching it. Eating mushy food out of a small jar with a tiny spoon—in flavors such as creamed beef and blueberry delight—wasn't what most people considered a good meal at home. Calling the product Gerber Singles only added to its stigma. One commentator remarked, "They might as well have called it, 'I Live Alone and Eat My Meals from a Jar.'"

Robert McMath started the New Products Showcase and Learning Center in Ithaca, New York. He calls it the world's largest Library of Losers. It not only catalogued flops like Gerber Singles but also thousands of failed product combinations: Maalox Whip (an antacid dispensed as an aerosol whip), edible deodorant, and flavored bottle water for pets—to name just a few. Not all mixtures turn out good—sometimes the sum is less valuable than the individual parts. Baby food and adult single-serving meals are both good products. Combining them was a disaster.

———

When we botch up a mixture, it's often because we struggle to manage successfully an underlying tension needed for the most successful combinations: novelty and usefulness. The idea of adult meals packaged in a baby jar was novel. It just wasn't very useful to potential customers, who were turned off by both the name and packaging. Without novelty, there is little value in mixtures, as someone has already thought about how to combine that set of resources. But without usefulness, there's no purpose for a mixture.

Researchers have found that coming up with both novel and useful mixtures requires two very different orientations to our work. When we're intrinsically motivated, we tend to come up with novel ideas. We enjoy learning and experimenting to find new combinations. In contrast, when we focus on performance, we tend to come up with useful ideas. We take the perspective of others and rely on more familiar ideas likely to be accepted by others.

In one study, 189 people came into a university lab, and each received a diverse set of resources: two origami papers, six popsicle sticks, one lollipop stick, two paper clips, four pipe cleaners, one baking cup, two small plastic cups, one small clothespin, one glue stick, and a roll of Scotch tape. The researchers asked each participant to design a novel and useful decor product in twenty minutes with the resources at hand.

Before having the participants start their product design, the researchers provided different sets of instructions depending on which group they randomly assigned a participant to join. Some groups received instructions to focus on learning from the exercise (for example, telling participants it's okay to make mistakes that are a natural part of learning); other groups received instructions to focus on performing during the exercise (for example, telling participants to make a product better than other participants); and another group received both learning and performing instructions. There was also a control group that didn't receive any information about learning or performing.

After each participant finished the product design, the researchers measured a couple of other important concepts. First, they counted the number of unique items each participant used in his or her mixture, a way of evaluating how flexibly participants viewed their resources. Second, the researchers surveyed each participant's desire for closure—the degree to which he or she tended to stick to a solution early in the process or remained open to new ideas in the middle of the task. Third, independent judges evaluated the novelty and usefulness of each person's decor product.

The researchers found that a learning focus made people flexible with their mixing, leading them to develop more novel products. On the other hand, the performance goal led people to seek closure, sticking to earlier ideas and not exploring new ideas as they emerged. This tended to lead to more useful product designs. However, members of both groups failed to design novel *and* useful products.

The third set of participants who received both learning and performing instructions ended up designing both novel and useful products. But how they received their instructions mattered a lot. One set of participants received instructions to trigger both goals at the same time, while another set received instructions to focus either on learning first and then, midway through the product design, on performance, or on performance first, followed by learning midway through.

People created more novel and useful products when simultaneously receiving both learning and performing goals, compared to those receiving the different goals over time. Instead of separating what are often unique goals (learning and performance), the researchers found that it's critical to mix both goals together throughout the task.

Unthinkable combinations can foster not only innovative products but also new relationships and ways of working. But we need to be careful not to overstretch by too cleverly mixing resources at the expense of producing something that's not useful. Sometimes, despite our cleverness, it's best to stay single with our resources and not join them together.

## THE RIGHT STRETCH

In this chapter, I've shown you how to avoid some critical injuries from overstretching. Edward Wedbush, Ronald Wayne, Ron Johnson, Ryan Leaf, and the designers of Gerber Singles had the foundations of a good stretch, but they all went a little too far. Learning from their mistakes helps separate a good stretch from a bad one.

Having introduced you to studies to explain the basis for stretching, the stories to illustrate its positive consequences, and the boundaries of its application, we're now ready for our final step—to learn some exercises that help us strengthen a stretch.

# NINE

## WORKOUT

===

### EXERCISES TO STRENGTHEN A STRETCH

n the 1960s, tetanus posed a health threat to college-age students. It's a serious disease spread by bacteria that enter the body, usually through a wound, and can lead to muscle contractions and an interruption of breathing. Step on a rusty nail and the odds are pretty good you'll get infected. In the best cases, it's fairly uncomfortable. In the worst cases, it kills. Although there's no cure for tetanus, there's a very simple way of preventing it: get a vaccine.

For most college students, visiting the student health clinic is not how they want to spend an afternoon. A group of Yale psychologists came up with an idea: scare the hell out of the students to get them to the clinic.

The researchers had participants come to a building where they were told they'd be evaluating a health pamphlet. Depending on their random placement in a group, some students received a booklet that described the disease in horrifying terms. If that wasn't enough, the materials also included graphic pictures of people who had contracted the disease. The pamphlets were so disturbing that some participants were visibly shaken and turned pale while reading them. Another group was spared the scary language and visuals but received the same basic facts about the dangers of contracting the disease.

All participants received information that explained that an immunization would be the only way to protect against the disease, and indicated that the university was even providing the vaccine free of charge at the nearby campus health clinic.

The tactics appeared to work well. Participants exposed to the fearful language and gory pictures were more scared than other participants. They also had higher levels of anger, nervousness, discomfort, and tension—just the type of emotions we might think would prompt action.

Researchers asked two important questions to evaluate the effectiveness of scaring them: "How important do you think it is to get a tetanus shot?" and "Do you intend to get a tetanus shot?"

Participants in the fear group thought getting the shot was much more important than the other participants. They also had stronger intentions to get vaccinated. Mission accomplished!

Or was it?

The researchers checked student health records during the weeks between the experiment and the end of classes. What they found seemed to make no sense at all. Participants exposed to the fearmongering didn't get vaccinated at a higher rate than other participants, despite their fright and intentions to get immunized. The materials had scared them and increased their desire to get the shot—but didn't actually change their behavior.

It turns out there was a group of participants who got immunized at a much higher rate than any of the other participants—and it had nothing to do with their level of fear. These were the students who were provided with a map to the health clinic. Even though almost all of the students knew where the health clinic was before the study, giving them a map provided the extra push to transform their intentions into actions. Participants handed the map were more than eight times as likely to get vaccinated compared to those who didn't receive the map.

As a professor and social scientist who's spent much of the past decade teaching and researching change, I'm well aware that it's one thing to shift attitudes and beliefs and quite another thing to change behaviors. Even if you've read this book, recognize the harm from chasing, and embrace the value of stretching, the scientific record would predict you won't do anything about it—unless I provide you with a proverbial "map to the clinic." I'm going to hand you exactly that—a dozen exercises to get you to stop chasing and start stretching right now—whether you want to advance in your career, boost the performance of your organization, raise resourceful children, or live a more satisfying life. Like a muscle, your stretch will strengthen with practice, but you can start enjoying some of the benefits of this powerful way of working and living now.

## JUST SAY NO

When I was growing up, the television airwaves were filled with pleas to "just say no." Nancy Reagan accidentally discovered the catchy slogan when answering a question from a child during a school visit. Asked what to do when somebody offers you drugs, the First Lady famously replied, "Well, you just say no."

For chasers, getting more resources is an addiction to feed—they develop an unhealthy dependence on acquiring more, endorsing the false belief that having more resources = getting better results.

Once we shift our mind-set to using resources better, we will realize that what we do with what we've got matters more than what we have at hand—making it much easier to just say no and expand the value of what's already there.

In 1957, author Theodor Geisel started a book with a "just say no" bet. His editor, Bennett Cerf, wagered $50 that Geisel couldn't write a book using only fifty unique words. For most people, these constraints would've been devastating. They'd demand to use more words. For Geisel, the constraints turned out to be liberating. Saying no to limitless words gave him a focused dictionary that enabled him to be creative with the words he could use. The result: Geisel, also known as Dr. Seuss, penned his most successful book, the blockbuster *Green Eggs and Ham.*

Instead of falling into the typical, "If I only had this, I could" thinking, try taking the opposite approach. Just say no to more resources. Take it one step further: Ask for *fewer* resources: "If I only *didn't* have this resource, I could . . ."

Whether it's intentionally short-changing a project team with one fewer member, moving forward a deadline, limiting a project's budget, preparing a special meal with only those ingredients already in the fridge, or planning a kid's birthday party for $25, reject believing that something can't be done without extra resources.

---

* For the curious, the fifty words are: a, am, and, anywhere, are, be, boat, box, car, could, dark, do, eat, eggs, fox, goat, good, green, ham, here, house, I, if, in, let, like, may, me, mouse, not, on, or, rain, Sam, say, see, so, thank, that, the, them, there, they, train, tree, try, will, with, would, you.

Must-have resources we think we depend on often aren't as important as we think. That's exactly what many of the stretchers we've met in the book learned. They lacked resources that others in similar positions depended on, first turning to stretching out of necessity. Dick Yuengling didn't have the marketing budgets of the big brewers, and the artist Phil Hansen didn't have two steady hands. Their constrained environments left them with little choice, but they eventually realized how much more they could do with what they had. We don't need physical or economic limitations to recognize the power of stretching. By saying no to more resources, we're saying yes to an entirely new outlook on working and living.

## FIND A SLEEPING BEAUTY

Disney's iconic 1959 film *Sleeping Beauty* tells the tale of Aurora, a princess who falls under the curse of a villain named Maleficent. On the princess's sixteenth birthday, she will prick her finger on the spindle of an enchanted spinning wheel and die. The quick thinking of a fairy named Merryweather layers on her own spell so that, instead of dying from the spindle prick, Aurora will fall into a deep sleep until she's awakened by a true love's first kiss.

Merryweather and two other fairies shelter Aurora as a peasant girl in the woods to keep her out of harm's way, far from the dangerous spindle. But Maleficent lures Aurora from safety and tricks her into touching the spinning wheel on her sixteenth birthday, putting her into a deep, and potentially eternal, sleep.

It takes the kiss of a true love, a prince named Phillip, to revive the princess. The seemingly lifeless Aurora awakens as a vivacious princess and the couple live happily ever after.

As I've already shown, in the world beyond fairy tales, a lot of resources lie dormant. If we look hard enough, we'll find resources all around us waiting to be activated. We just need to awaken them to benefit from more than we thought we had, allowing us to solve different problems and pursue promising opportunities that otherwise might be impossible. Indeed, research by the consulting firm Bain finds that the overwhelming number of organizational renewals—times when companies redefine their core business—come from hidden assets they no longer used.

My firsthand experience with dormant resources comes from the vast wealth of knowledge produced by the scientific community that regularly gets put into storage. A recent study by researchers at Indiana University found that some of the most important scientific papers in a variety of fields were "sleeping beauties"—they were published but quickly forgotten by other researchers for decades. One of Albert Einstein's influential papers, published in 1935, didn't become widely cited in the scientific literature until almost sixty years after its publication. The greatest hibernation periods in science occur in fields such as physics, chemistry, mathematics, and general and internal medicine—with deep sleeps lasting upwards of seventy years!

The researchers find that it often takes an outsider to awaken a sleeping beauty. The different background of an outsider is more likely to lead her to notice a dormant resource and bring it back to life.

The same type of awakening happens with products that fall out of fashion. Madame C. J. Walker, the first African American woman millionaire we met in chapter 6, started a very successful cosmetics business at a time when black people had few legal rights. Her business languished after she passed away, unable to sustain itself without its energetic and savvy founder. Spending decades off the shelf, the brand fell into a deep sleep until awakened, renewed, and placed on the shelves of cosmetics retailer Sephora in 2016. The new line, called Madame C. J. Walker Beauty Culture, based on the original products and intended to reach the same underserved customers, opened up an additional market for Sephora—bringing new shoppers through its doors.

To find your own sleeping beauties, ask: What personal resources (skills, knowledge, connections, and so on) and organizational resources (products, routines, equipment, and so on) have been shelved for years? Better yet, have outsiders ask the same questions about your situation. Then make a list of potential ways the dormant resource can help advance an objective, followed by at least one action you can take immediately to revive it.

## GO EXPLORE

As a twenty-seven-year-old accepting an award at the Academy of Achievement, Steve Jobs proclaimed that the difference between you and your dumb friend is the bag of experiences you carry around with you. Making a bag of experiences more compelling often comes from changing where we spend the most time—the place we work, the city we live in, and the areas we visit.

It's possible to embrace the multi-c rule (introduced in chapter 4) without making such drastic changes. Dedicate a few hours each week, or even each month, to reading something different (such as a new magazine, book, or website), attending a workshop or conference outside of your industry, or spending time working alongside new colleagues (such as by trading office space with someone for a day). Go have lunch with someone in a similar job but different industry. Find a study buddy where you learn together about a field different from your own. I've personally found tremendous benefit from learning about different fields. I was mentored by a philosopher as an undergraduate, an economist as a master's student, and one of the most intellectually diverse professors as a PhD student.

To take this exercise to the next level, consider what Fred Cook, CEO of Golin, one of the country's largest public relations firms, has done. His explorations include time as a chauffeur, teacher, rock band agent, and doorman. Recognizing the value from following the multi-c rule, Cook launched Golin's "unternship" program in late 2014. Using a contest open to all, he had a simple request: with $40 and a video crew, experience something different.

The winner, Akinbola Richardson, spent time panhandling and driving a taxi in Chicago, believing that these two perspectives would bring him closer to the pulse of a city. His reward: a paid summer unternship during which he planned an itinerary of diverse experiences—skydiving in Georgia, running a Tough Mudder race in Virginia, building a house for homeless people in New Orleans, and living with the Amish and a Native American community. Of his unternship, Richardson says, "I chose to do a combination of things that would scare me, expose me to new cultures, and provide a way I could be of service." Cook has high hopes for the unternship program, reasoning that the diverse experiences will allow participants to bring back new ideas that can help the firm's clients.

If you can't take the time off or sponsor someone to do the same, find better ways to tap into people's diverse experiences around you. Rite-Solutions, a software company that performs highly classified work for the military, came up with its own solution to take advantage of people's diverse experiences. It created an internal ideas market. Any employee can pitch an idea such as adopting a new technology, launching a new product, or developing an alternative process. The proposals become "stocks" that other employees can buy and sell with $10,000 of opinion money the company provides. Each idea lists at $10, and employees can bid up (or down) the value of an idea. This novel approach utilizes the diverse experiences of employees who collectively, but also independently, influence the direction of the company.

Whether you go explore directly or indirectly by assembling a group of outsiders, it's important to sometimes leave comfortable territory.

## TAKE A BREAK (AND PAY LESS ATTENTION)

Drilled into our heads from a very early age is the importance of paying attention—and for good reason. It's hard to learn and perform when we're daydreaming. We spend about half of our time thinking about something other than what we're currently doing, which research finds makes us unhappy. In its most dangerous form, our mindlessness even causes car crashes.

Yet, too much focus can undermine creativity, and distractions can actually enhance creativity. At the extreme, people diagnosed with attention deficit hyperactivity disorder (ADHD) tend to score higher on creativity assessments than other people. Why? They let their minds wander, often making connections others overlook.

A study by a team of psychologists asked 145 participants to list as many unusual uses for an object as possible. Each participant initially worked with two out of a possible four objects: a paper clip, a sheet of paper, a toothpick, and a screwdriver. The exercise allowed the researchers to evaluate participants' baseline resourcefulness from the number of novel uses each person found. Next, the researchers randomly put participants into one of four groups. For three of these groups, participants had twelve minutes to complete a task. One group received a mentally challenging activity, a second group received a mentally unchallenging task, and a third group simply rested. Afterward, participants completed questions about how much their mind wandered. A fourth group, the no-break group, skipped the activity period and immediately started on the next step.

Participants in all four groups completed a second resourcefulness task. The researchers allocated two minutes to come up with as many novel uses for each of four objects—the two resources participants earlier worked on during the baseline exercise and the two other resources they didn't get during the baseline exercise.

When researchers examined the data, they found that participants in the mentally unchallenging task mind wandered more than the other groups. The low levels of working memory required for the easy task gave them the capacity to think about other things. But this turned out to help them a lot, without sacrificing their performance on the mentally unchallenging activity. These mind wanderers showed a 40 percent improvement in coming up with new uses for the same objects they'd worked on earlier, substantially better than the groups doing demanding work, resting, or getting no break. The mindless work had helped them subconsciously expand how they viewed the objects when they later returned to them.*

Management professors Kim Elsbach and Andrew Hargadon offer some counterintuitive advice: give overworked people more mindless work. This appears ridiculous at first glance. Besides having enough on our plates already, why bother ourselves with mindless stuff when we could be working on more interesting projects? Dating back to the 1970s, organizational psychologists have been lobbying to do the exact opposite of Elsbach and Hargadon's recommendation: design challenging jobs to create more meaningful work, make people more satisfied with their jobs, and make them more effective.

---

* For the new resources, there were no differences in performance change across the four groups. One possible explanation is that participants were not subconsciously thinking about these new resources because they hadn't encountered them before. It was only the two repeated resources that they were thinking about.

Although designing challenging jobs reaps these advantages, it can also cause undue pressure and mental exhaustion. To give people a break, Elsbach and Hargadon advocate rotating between difficult work and mindless work—mindless work recharges our batteries, readies us to do more down the road, and lets our mind wander to find new connections among our resources.

First, occasionally do work you're overqualified for—these are easily mastered and less demanding tasks but ones that are still important to complete. I'll often break up my day of researching and writing, a pretty mentally draining task for me, by doing thirty minutes of e-mail, and I often find that in the middle of responding to an unrelated project or e-mail, a new idea will pop into my head. If you're an executive, leave the corporate office and spend time with customers. If you're an engineer, spend some time doing routine maintenance. Find time to do some clerical work. Pick up an adult coloring book. Clean your office. Cook a simple meal. Play solitaire.

Or try one of my favorite daily rituals—go for a walk. A group of Stanford University psychologists find that people are at least 81 percent more effective when it comes to devising novel and appropriate uses for resources while walking compared to sitting. Walking, the researchers reason, frees the mind to wander.

Second, go on the clock. For most professionals, clocking in and out is for blue-collar workers. That's because professionals usually define their workday not based on hours but rather on projects or activities. Despite the apparent flexibility from not clocking in or out, there's often less flexibility with structuring our days around activities—we simply move from one urgent task to the next with little rest. Going on the clock provides mandatory beginnings and endings to our work, something that not only can make us feel better but also allows us some time for our mind to wander. Try setting a specific number of hours to work for at least one day, once a month—and stick with it, even when you leave the office and get tempted to eat and sleep with your smartphone. Afterward, take it to the next level and read Tim Ferriss's *The 4-Hour Workweek* to try to get the same amount of work done in substantially less time.

## PICK NEW NEIGHBORS

Our fifth exercise recognizes that to strengthen a stretch, we first need to break free from the chase. It's incredibly hard to do—especially when we have the wrong neighbors.

We surround ourselves with other people all the time—not just our neighbors next door but also our colleagues at work, the children our kids go to school with, and the people we mingle with during our free time.

Whom we choose to spend time with shapes a lot of our behavior. In a recent study, psychologists examined state-level income-inequality data with Google search terms for residents of each state. They asked a team of independent raters to identify searches that focused on purchases that signaled wealth or success, something economists call positional goods. Searches for positional goods such as Ralph Lauren menswear, David Yurman earrings, and fur vests more frequently occurred in cities with higher income inequality, while search terms in low-inequality states focused on non-positional goods such as romantic comedies, flower names, and lemon bar recipes. Even the non-wealthy in states with high inequality searched more for positional goods compared with peers in states with less income inequality. Regardless of our absolute income level, having big relative differences in income increases our pursuit of positional goods because the less well heeled try to keep up with wealthier people.

When my wife, Randi, and I moved from Silicon Valley to the

small college town of Ann Arbor, Michigan, our income dropped by more than half, but we felt a lot richer being surrounded by lots of grad students and a vibrant campus culture.

Perhaps no part of the country exemplifies the chase more than Hollywood, where actors try to outdo one another with everything from how they look to who's got the most Twitter followers. That's one reason why Oscar winner Brie Larson keeps her distance from Hollywood. Her philosophy about avoiding Hollywood neighbors: "I don't really feel like I've been part of the industry, I don't feel like I've been part of some weird machine. I've actually made a conscious effort to not be a part of it. I don't live in Los Angeles, I work in Los Angeles, and even that—I audition in Los Angeles, I very rarely film in Los Angeles."

You don't need to move across the country, or even change cities or jobs, to get new neighbors. Instead, identify one stretcher you admire and already know. Commit to spending at least one hour with him or her once a month. Do this for different parts of your life: a friend, a colleague, a parent of one of your child's friends, or someone who works out where you do.

## APPRECIATE

Alex Turnbull, the founder of customer service software maker Groove, whom we met in chapter 6, thinks that people too frequently say thank you to others without truly showing appreciation. As Groove grew, Turnbull remained as appreciative as ever, and he liked to let his most important stakeholders—employees, customers, and family—know how deeply grateful he was for their support. Gratitude, Turnbull told me, helped him also value free time more—leading him to recognize the great expense of chasing that many entrepreneurs do and disciplining him to stick to a relatively modest average nine-hour workday.

As Alex Turnbull grew the business, he went public with his expression of gratitude, penning a blog about his struggles and successes in building Groove. He wanted to help other start-ups wrestling with similar issues so they wouldn't make his same mistakes.

Psychology research finds that when people are grateful, they expand how they think about their resources, often in ways that try to help others. Turnbull's blog reflected an effort to give back to others in an unusual but incredibly effective way. Sharing valuable experiences with his stakeholders gave a rare inside look at the company; in turn, Turnbull's transparency created trust with his readers, transforming some of them into customers. Roughly 10 percent of people who subscribe to his blog sign up for a free trial of Groove, compared to only 5 percent of visitors on his more traditional marketing website. Blog subscribers also become paid users at a rate roughly 50 percent greater than non-subscribers. Generosity guided Turnbull to think expansively about helping others and, in turn, ended up helping him grow his business on his own terms.

By appreciating what he has, it makes it much easier to say no to tempting things he lacked but doesn't really want or need. Yet for many of us, a narrow focus on the pleasures of today thwarts us from achieving a more satisfying tomorrow. What helped Alex Turnbull avoid these temptations?

In a study of thirty-two males and forty-three females, psychologists randomly grouped participants into one of three conditions—those asked to recall an event that made them grateful, those asked to recall an event that made them happy, or those asked to recall simply a typical day (which served as a control group). After writing about their topic for five minutes, participants completed questionnaires to ensure that the researchers had successfully put them into their assigned emotional state of gratitude or happiness, or had no emotional impact in the case of the control group. Afterward, participants made twenty-seven choices between receiving small amounts of cash now compared to larger cash amounts down the road. Participants in both the happy and control groups, on average, chose a $55 payout now to forgo an $85 payout three months away.

Participants who wrote about gratitude had significantly lower levels of economic impatience. They required a higher payout, $63, to forgo the same $85 three months later. Their gratitude in the present helped them prioritize the future—making them more patient to wait for things down the road and less likely to be tempted in the present. Alex Turnbull knew this lesson well. He turned down a short-term windfall for selling his company to build the one of his dreams.

Researchers Robert Emmons and Michael McCullough designed a very easy but effective exercise to express gratitude. Find time once a week to write down five things about your life that you are grateful for—these can be really mundane things such as simply waking up to more consequential milestones such as a promotion, the achievement of a sales goal, or the enjoyment of a meaningful family vacation. Emmons and McCullough found that when compared to a group of participants who alternatively listed five hassles or five events that unfolded during the week, the gratitude group reported higher levels of well-being and fewer symptoms of physical illness. People in the gratitude condition also exercised more during the week. Regularly following this simple activity will condition us to appreciate what we have, big and small.

## SHOP YOUR CLOSET

Courtney Carver lived a life of chasing, becoming caught up in thinking she always needed more to be successful and happy. When diagnosed with multiple sclerosis, she gave up chasing and started Project 333, which challenges people to whittle down their wardrobe to only thirty-three items for three months. Besides recognizing that she didn't need more than thirty-three items to dress stylishly and comfortably, Carver freed up time to focus on the more important experiential aspects of her life, such as spending time with her family. She also stretched herself by coming up with new possibilities for what was already in her closet, finding unique combinations and uses for her thirty-three items.

Like Courtney Carver, Lauri Ward grew frustrated with needlessly wasting resources. When Ward graduated from design school, she quickly became dissatisfied that all her job prospects revolved around getting people to buy more stuff. To her, interior design was really about the experiences of living and not the consumption of furniture and blinds. Instead of getting a job, she founded an interior design company based on a philosophy of "use what you have."

In 2014, Marie Kondo introduced the world to the Japanese art of decluttering and organizing. Her blockbuster book captivated millions of readers who learned that satisfaction doesn't come from accumulating lots of things, but rather from organizing the most essential stuff in our lives. Once we organize our stuff, it makes it easier to use what's already in hand.

We can draw inspiration from Courtney Carver, Lauri Ward, and Marie Kondo by shopping our closets already full of valuable resources. Look around the office and take stock of the unnoticed or underutilized talents and skills your colleagues have, instead of asking for another head count. At home, take note of stuff that could be put to better use—a newspaper to wrap a birthday present, a mouse pad that could be used as a trivet, or old bent silverware that could be repurposed to create kitchen hooks.

Many of the best-known inventions also came from existing

products. Play-Doh started as a wallpaper cleaning compound that became obsolete with the rise of vinyl wallpaper in the 1950s; the corkscrew came from a military tool to remove bullets; and Pyrex came from material from train lantern glass the wife of a scientist at Corning Glass Works experimented with to bake a cake. The baby carrot was the result from transforming damaged carrots customers would not buy by running them through potato peelers and green bean cutters to create a sweeter, juicier, and more profitable product.

When writing this book, I used a "scraps" file of stories, studies, and examples that I came across in my research but that didn't seem to fit in the chapters I had intended. I put them into a Microsoft Word file that I read at least monthly to see if they might be helpful for later chapters in the book. That's where I found all of the examples in the previous paragraph.

## PLAN BACKWARD

Our eighth exercise takes us back to chapter 5, where I introduced two music metaphors to describe very different ways of thinking about work, organizations, and life. Most of us are more comfortable making symphonic music: we plan first and act afterward. We can do great things when operating this way. The familiarity of routines and having a solid plan in hand is reassuring—but it also comes with a cost. Making symphonic music depends on having everything worked out before doing anything. Without a plan, it becomes difficult to get anything done.

Jazz music replaces a plan with improvisation, teaching us to act and respond more spontaneously. Once we get moving, we free ourselves from worrying about plotting and following a plan and focus on observing and learning from our actions. Although we'll make mistakes, they become important opportunities to improve, rather than stressful departures from what we planned out. The great jazz musician Miles Davis used mistakes as a launching pad to explore new melodies, rather than treating them as a problem to fix.

To play jazz music metaphorically, reverse the typical relationship between planning and acting. Act first and plan afterward. The organizational scholar Karl Weick poses an intriguing question: "How can I know what I think until I see what I say?" He's pointing out that we usually don't know what we think until after we reflect on what we've already said—or, for that matter, done. Planning robs us from the benefits of careful reflection as we have a tendency to move to the next step, if all goes according to plan.

Start a project, work toward a goal, take a trip, or leave the house for the day without a plan. Keep a journal of what you did, but only *after* doing it. Repeat as you make progress toward your project, goal, trip, or day. At its completion, your journal will contain a list of actions you took—it's what I like to call a backward-looking plan.

Take time to evaluate your backward-looking plan. Compare it to your typical forward-looking plan. What new things did you learn? Did you act quicker? How much did you end up missing by not planning in advance? What did you gain by not planning?

## SCRAMBLE THE BACK ROW

In the summer of 1996, one of the world's greatest chess players made a big announcement. Hundreds of journalists and chess fans flocked to Buenos Aires, Argentina, to hear from Bobby Fischer. His message: the game he loved and mastered was under serious threat. The best players spent countless hours analyzing past games and memorizing opening moves. Extensive planning became the key to success, not skill, originality, and adaptability. The focus on preparation was so strong that many players struggled in the middle and end part of the games, after they exhausted their memorized moves.

Fischer wanted chess to return to being a game that involved skill, and he proposed a critical rule change: randomly scramble the back row. Fischer was not the first to propose randomly placing pieces on the board, but he found the complete randomization of the board in what's known as Shuffle Chess to lead to too much anarchy. Too much change, too fast, can unravel people just as too much familiarity can make them stale and unable to adapt.

He found a happy medium. His game, called Chess960 (or Fischer Random Chess), randomly mixes up the back pieces, making it impossible to preplan the game. With 960 potential opening boards, players need to rely on skills and on-the-spot thinking to win. They learn to adapt as they experience a new board they've never seen before, focusing on learning how to manipulate pieces and not just memorize moves.

If we find ourselves too regularly on autopilot, it might be time to scramble our back rows. There's comfort in habits, but it's critical to avoid being complacent with how things are, closing off the possibility of imagining how things might be better. Scramble the back row by shuffling the people you put on teams—put a few outsiders in the group. Run your weekly meeting from a different room, on a different day, or with a different room layout or seating arrangement. How do the dynamics of the group change? Go visit another person's office and hash things out in person, rather than over e-mail. Drive to work or school following a different route and park in a new spot. Change your hours for a few days to come in earlier or leave later, running into new people in the hallway.

# S T R E T C H

## MAKE MIDYEAR RESOLUTIONS

Four thousand years ago, the Babylonians celebrated the planting of their crops and the beginning of a new year. Crowning a twelve-day religious festival called Akitu, they used the holiday to reaffirm their support for the reigning king or pick a new leader. They also did something that has shaped how many people spend January 1: they made promises. For the Babylonians, this meant paying off debts and returning borrowed objects. Many religions now couple resolutions for self-improvement with the beginning of a new year. It's also a part of many secular cultures.

Psychologist John Norcross has studied resolutions for years. He finds that about 40 percent of adults make New Year's resolutions. Despite our perceptions, he estimates that making a New Year's resolution increases the success rate for making positive changes tenfold.

Why wait until the beginning of the year to make a pledge? Health journalist Linda Andrews prefers making July Fourth resolutions. She reasons that the stress of preparing for the holidays, spending time with extended family, or simply being hung over from a nice bottle of champagne might sour our mood to make resolutions. The midyear resolutions also allow us to take stock of how we did with our New Year's resolutions and set additional goals from a presumably clearer head space.

Every year starting on June 1, for six weeks, Randi and I eat healthier meals and try to exercise more. It's part of an annual ritual we started almost fifteen years ago to get into top shape before our wedding. The June 1 resolution stuck with us, and we now follow it every year with a fun twist. We celebrate our anniversary by transforming ourselves from a many years' married couple to newlyweds. We spend a night on the town—in our original wedding clothes. To add to the experience, I remake Randi's bouquet, and she orders me a boutonniere.

All sorts of people come up to us—wishing us a happy marriage. We smile, usually play along as newlyweds, and savor the moment, appreciating that not only did our relationship make it another year but also that we still fit into the same clothes more than a decade later. Getting all those extra uses out of a wedding dress and tux that might otherwise lie dormant forever is only icing on the wedding cake!

## BREAK IT DOWN

In a very poor part of the Philippines, people living in dilapidated houses were using what little money they had to purchase electricity to light their homes—in the middle of the day. The desire to conserve precious resources led to a neat invention: put an empty two-liter soda bottle, filled with water, through a hole in the roof. The water-filled bottle would refract the sunlight throughout the house, making electric lights unnecessary on sunny days.

During his studies for a PhD in psychology at the University of Massachusetts, Anthony McCaffrey realized that, like the makeshift soda-bottle light, almost all of the world's most important inventions followed along a similar path. Inventors discover obscure functions or features by breaking down a resource into tiny building blocks.

To help us learn how to break down a resource, he developed a very effective and practical technique, and it works like this. Pose two questions about any resource: (1) Can it be broken down further? and (2) Does the description of the broken-down part imply a use? The trick is to break down the resource into its smallest components, something that allows us to understand lots of hidden uses.

McCaffrey's technique works on all sorts of resources, but start simple in order to get more comfortable with it. Take an ordinary household object, such as a candle, and practice the technique. A candle is composed of wax and a wick. Wax implies a use (it provides fuel). He points out then that when we view resources based only on their uses, it prevents us from imagining atypical uses. Instead, we can reduce the wax to cylindrically shaped lipids. A wick implies something we light—it's a use. Reduce it to interwoven fibrous strands, and you'll start to see lots of different uses for it.

In his research, McCaffrey trained people on his two-part technique and provided them with several resource-constrained challenges. One asked how to fasten together two heavy steel rings using only a candle, match, and two-inch cube of steel. Because melted wax is not strong enough to bond the steel rings, one correct solution involves recognizing that the wick reduces down into a string, and that a string can tie the two rings together. Participants trained in his two-step technique solved problems like the ring challenge 67.4 percent more frequently than people without the training.

## TURN TRASH INTO TREASURE

In chapter 3, we met Jenny Dawson, who transformed blighted produce headed for the trash bin into artisanal food that launched a successful business. She's not the only one Dumpster diving to create treasures. Tom Szaky started a sustainable fertilizer company from worm poop packaged in used Coca-Cola bottles. This was the beginning of a multimillion-dollar business called TerraCycle that repurposes all kinds of waste materials, such as turning empty juice pouches into tote bags. John Bradburn leads General Motors' landfill-free initiative, where he's tasked with turning trash into treasure. "At GM, we view waste as a resource out of place," he says. "When we look at waste streams from our facilities, we don't ask how we dispose of this waste, we ask how can we find a better use for it." His personal residence is dotted with newfound treasure—two sheds built from the scraps of shipping containers and nineteen car batteries turned into nests for wildlife. At GM, he has led initiatives to turn paint sludge into shipping crates, oil-soaked booms into parts for the Chevy Volt, and used tires into air and water deflectors.

We can also create treasure by mobilizing people to do new things. In 2014, Hurricane Odile decimated Los Cabos, Mexico, destroying many of the hotels the local economy depended on. Mauricio Martinez, general manager of a luxury resort in the city, needed to shut down his hotel for months to repair critical infrastructure. He no longer needed his hospitality and leisure staff because there were no customers. Instead of firing them, he turned his staff—everyone from his tennis pro to bartenders—into construction workers and kept them employed. The devastated hotel was rebuilt at a substantially faster pace than any of its competitors because it had a bigger "construction crew." He also retained valuable staff who might have found another job while the hotel remained closed.

To find treasure in the trash bin, start by keeping a benefits diary. List key events, activities, or experiences. Next to each item, write at least one unexpected benefit. For blatantly positive experiences—a promotion at work and birthday celebration with my daughter—this is fairly easy. For more neutral experiences—cooking dinner or writing a research proposal—this becomes a bit harder. For situations we likely experience with negative emotions—visiting the doctor or, for me, grading papers—this becomes almost impossible. However, if we look hard enough, we will find hidden benefits, whether becoming motivated to live healthier based on a checkup or learning something new from students' writings. Once we find a hidden benefit in something, we can turn it into treasure.

## ANY MAP WILL DO

In this chapter, we covered exercises that will help strengthen a stretch. Some exercises will immediately sound more enticing than others. That's okay. We always need a place to start. Treat each exercise as a resource that you can build on and adapt to your own circumstances.

Back in chapter 5, we learned about a group of missing soldiers who inadvertently used the wrong map to navigate their way back home. Despite being lost in the Alps with a map of the Pyrenees, they safely returned because the map first calmed them down and then got them moving, communicating, and learning. In this chapter, I've handed you a map to strengthen your stretch, but what's important is not so much which exercises you do, or even if you follow them to a T. Instead, I'd just like to see you get moving. Like a muscle, our stretch gets stronger each time we use it.

# CONCLUSION

## YOUR STRETCH

Almost all of us have experienced chasing in parts of our lives—or at the very least have been tempted by its pull. I personally know how difficult it can be to break free from the grip of chasing, especially when we're surrounded by people who evangelize it. But I also know firsthand that it is possible and worthwhile to give up chasing and start stretching.

I've learned that one of the biggest reasons why we chase is that we don't think there's an alternative. In this book, I've shared studies and stories to help you reject chasing and embrace stretching as a better way to work, live, and build organizations.

People we've met in this book choose to stretch because it delivers outstanding results, professionally and personally. Dick Yuengling built a beer empire he took joy in passing on to his children; Van Man became a better baseball player on and off the field; Jenny Dawson created a more meaningful and impactful career by turning waste into chutney; Madame C. J. Walker used beauty products to make over an oppressed group of African Americans into businesswomen; Robert Rodriguez used a smaller crew to produce critically acclaimed and commercially lucrative movies while enjoying his work more than most of his contemporaries; and Alex Turnbull walked away from an offer of millions for his tech business to make plenty more in all parts of his life. All of these stretchers had successful careers or businesses, but more important, they've found deeper satisfaction in their lives.

As helpful as stretching is for these people, for many there's an even greater urgency to start stretching because a world of chasing has brought a devastating reality. We're under more pressure than ever. Seventy percent of Americans bear at least one of three major financial challenges: (a) They spend more than they make, (b) Their debt payments consume almost half of their monthly gross income, and (c) They lack enough cash to last at least one month.

For other people, time serves as a major obstacle. Leisure time used to be a privilege of the educated and rich. In 1965, college-educated men had slightly more leisure time than their counterparts who had only high school diplomas. By 2005, college-educated men had eight fewer hours of leisure time per week than high school graduates had.

Most American children now live in households with either two working parents or a single working parent.

In a world of constant change, we're frequently asked to do things we've never been trained to do. Yet a recent Harris poll of two thousand adults found that 41 percent of Americans had not received any skills training at work in the past two years. As we increasingly find ourselves in tough situations, it becomes even more essential to adjust, build upon, and transform our resources quickly—to learn how to stretch.

The road to stretching starts with a simple but significant shift in mind-set—giving up the belief that having more resources = getting better results and replacing it with the conviction that a better use of resources = getting better results. This change in mind-set takes us away from a dehumanizing rat race for resources that is impossible to win and provides us with a way to make do with and magnify what we already have.

Develop the skills to stretch after abandoning the chase. Become an outsider and seek out new experiences in order to put resources to use in atypical ways. Get comfortable with working without a plan some of the time. Spark positive prophecies to enhance the value of resources. And combine resources in novel ways to make the whole much greater than the sum of the parts.

In the last chapters of the book, I've shown you how to find the right stretch by avoiding five injuries from overstretching—becoming a cheapskate, turning into a wanderer, relying on false intuitions, being cursed by others' expectations, and making toxic mixtures. I've also provided you with a dozen exercises to give up chasing and start stretching.

Imagine how liberating it would be to stop worrying about what you don't have and instead appreciate what you do have. Dream of inspiring everyone—from your colleagues to your children—to learn how to use what they have, rather than always asking for what they don't have. Picture how satisfying it would be to expand the value of resources already available to you at work, in your teams, and at home. Envision how much better you can adapt to a changing world because you've learned to stretch in any situation.

There are so many rewards of a good stretch. If you practice its principles daily, you'll give up an endless craving for more resources. In its place, you'll enjoy work more, build stronger organizations, and achieve greater well-being using what you already have. It won't always be easy, but the changes stretching brings will make it worth it. This book is a map. Take it and start moving to reach your own stretch.

# ACKNOWLEDGMENTS

Completing this book was truly a collective effort, and there're plenty of people to thank. Let me start with the most significant person—my wife, Randi. Living with such an extraordinary stretcher was a great inspiration. My ideas became much clearer when I reflected on how she practiced them. Randi also brought wisdom to every page of the book, editing, several times, everything I wrote—all while being an adoring partner, attentive parent, and accomplished professional. This book is a lot better because of her—and so am I.

My agent, Richard Pine, stretched my thoughts from our very first conversation. He patiently started working with me when I had written just a paragraph, and his curiosity and constructive feedback nurtured it into a book. I'm incredibly grateful to Richard and all of his terrific colleagues at InkWell Management, especially Eliza Rothstein.

I would've never started writing this book if it weren't for three people. Jane Dutton, my doctoral adviser, taught me so much about research and resourcefulness. She approached me after I gave a keynote address at the 2013 Positive Organizations Conference. Upon my leaving the stage, she simply told me, "Go write a book about this now." That's exactly what I did. Adam Grant spent many hours educating me about book publishing and convincing me I should, and could, bring my research and ideas to a broader audience—and I'd have a great time doing it. I owe tremendous thanks for his encouragement, generosity, and advice—not to mention his introduction to Richard. Marc Epstein, a colleague of mine formerly at Rice, offered sage counsel and nonstop support as I figured out whether I wanted to write a book—and how to write one.

Hollis Heimbouch's enthusiasm for the book was apparent the first time we met. I'm indebted to her for championing *Stretch* throughout the entire publishing process, while making it clearer and more compelling. I'm also thankful to the rest of the Harper-Collins team, including Stephanie Hitchcock.

A group of talented research assistants found examples to bring my points to life. Matt Stein joined as I formulated the initial framework of the book. It was my good fortune that he was eager to learn something new and so quickly transformed himself into a skilled researcher. Matt found some of the most important stories, provided valuable feedback, and contributed in countless other ways. He's a great stretcher and even better friend for bringing all of his energy and knowledge to the book.

Jessica Yi took over where Matt left off, skillfully and passionately assisting me with finishing the project. Deyanira Verdejo found some excellent examples before I even knew I was writing a book. I'm also grateful to Kristen Nault and Asiya Kazi for their support with some of my scientific studies I used in the book, and to Pat Victor and Janelle Farabaugh for clerical assistance.

Katy DeCelles and Utpal Dholakia are two of the best research collaborators anyone could ever have. I've learned so much from them and am grateful they enthusiastically read every page of the book. When they were satisfied, I knew the book was ready for a larger audience. My colleague Erik Dane offered extremely useful advice on a couple of chapters.

I also relied on some outsiders for their comments on the book. Derren Barken read every page of the book, sometimes more than once. He also sent some excellent examples my way. Thanks also to Claudia Kolker, Nelli Nikova, and Seth Topek for their superb feedback on the entire manuscript.

For years, I've benefited from many discussions about resourcefulness. I want to thank Ryan Quinn, Martha Feldman, Christian Mealey, and Monica Worline, whose research and insights stimulated my own thinking. I also learned so much from Karl Weick. His influence on the book can be found throughout its pages, especially in chapter 5, where I elaborate on several examples he introduced to me.

My colleagues at Rice University couldn't have been any more supportive of the book. The school was an ideal setting for my research, teaching, and writing. I'm also deeply indebted to the entire marketing team at the Jones Graduate School of Business, especially Kathleen Clark, Claudia Kolker, Kevin Palmer, and Liana Lopez, for their help spreading the ideas in the book.

My two delightful daughters, Myaan and Noa, showed an endearing interest about my book (and eagerly offered their help with the Sleeping Beauty exercise in chapter 9). The joy from spending time with them constantly reminded me why success comes in so many different forms.

Lastly, my parents, Jane and Ron, raised me to be resourceful, teaching me not to worry about what others had and to make the most out of what I had. It took me a while to realize it, but they were right.

**Note to the reader:** I welcome your ideas and am especially interested in learning how you've kicked the chase and embraced stretching. I'd love to hear from you: e-mail me at Scott@ScottSonenshein.com or visit www.ScottSonenshein.com.

# NOTES

## INTRODUCTION: MY STRETCH

ix    *The New New Thing*: Michael Lewis, *The New New Thing: A Silicon Valley Story* (New York: W. W. Norton, 1999).

xi    **brave fight with what little they had:** Ryan W. Quinn and Monica C. Worline, "Enabling Courageous Collective Action: Conversations from United Airlines Flight 93," *Organization Science* 19, no. 4 (2008): 497–516.

xi    **Positive Organizations:** University of Michigan, the Center for Positive Organizations, accessed April 11, 2016, http://positiveorgs.bus.umich.edu; Kim S. Cameron, Jane E. Dutton, and Robert E. Quinn, eds., *Positive Organizational Scholarship* (San Francisco: Berrett-Koehler, 2003).

xii   **$19.2 trillion of household wealth destroyed:** United States Department of Treasury, "The Financial Crisis Response in Charts," April 2012, accessed September 5, 2015, http://www.treasury.gov/resource-center/data-chart-center/Documents/20120413_FinancialCrisisResponse.pdf.

## CHAPTER 1: A TALE OF TWO BEERS

2    **return home:** Lone Geier, "Yuengling Marches to Different Drummer," *Republican Herald*, July 2, 2012, http://republicanherald.com/news/yuengling-marches-to-different-drummer-1.1336503.

3    **started campaigns to appeal:** Rod Kurtz. "Knowing When to Say When," *Inc.* 26, no. 7 (July 2004): 64–71.

3    **3 percent of family businesses:** Adrian Wooldridge, "To Have and to

Hold," *Economist*, April 18, 2015, http://www.economist.com/news/special-report/21648171-far-declining-family-firms-will-remain-impor tant-feature-global-capitalism.

3    **D. G. Yuengling & Son:** Richard Yuengling Jr. (owner and president of D. G. Yuengling & Son), in discussion with author, September 1, 2015; Mark A. Noon, *Yuengling: A History of America's Oldest Brewery* (Jefferson, NC: McFarland, 2005); Robert A. Musson, *D.G. Yuengling & Son, Inc.* (Charleston, SC: Arcadia, 2013).

3    **grew into America's largest:** International conglomerates Anheus er-Busch Inbev and MillerCoors brew the most beer in the United States but are not American companies. Pabst Brewing rounds out the top three sellers of beer, but Pabst contracts out its brewing to other companies.

3    **"Our game is longevity":** Spencer Soper. "Yuengling Becomes Big gest U.S.-Owned Brewery," *Morning Call*, January 12, 2012, accessed March 7, 2016, http://articles.mcall.com/2012–01–12/business/mc allentown-yuengling-sales-20120112_1_yuengling-boston-beer-beer-marketer-s-insights.

3    **net worth of close to $2 billion:** "The World's Billionaires, Richard Yuengling, Jr." *Forbes*, accessed May 7, 2016, http://www.forbes.com/profile/richard-yuengling-jr/.

3    **"They say I'm cheap . . . but I'm economical":** Richard Yuengling Jr. (owner and president of D. G. Yuengling & Son), in discussion with author, September 1, 2015.

4    **adapting to major changes:** Scott Sonenshein and Utpal Dholakia, "Explaining Employee Engagement with Strategic Change Implemen tation: A Meaning-Making Approach," *Organization Science* 23, no. 1 (January 2012): 1–23; Scott Sonenshein, "Treat Employees as Resources, Not Resisters," in J. Dutton and G. Spreitzer (eds.), *How to Be a Posi tive Leader: Insights from Leading Thinkers on Positive Organizations* (San Francisco: Berrett-Koehler, 2014), pp. 136–46.

4    **everyday routines:** Scott Sonenshein, "Routines and Creativity: From Dualism to Duality," *Organization Science* 27, no. 3 (2016): 739–758.

4    **meaningful careers and lives:** Scott Sonenshein, Jane E. Dutton, Adam M. Grant, Gretchen M. Spreitzer, and Kathleen M. Sutcliffe, "Growing at Work: Employees' Interpretations of Progressive Self-

Change in Organizations," *Organization Science* 24, no. 2 (2013): 552–70; Gretchen Spreitzer, Kathleen Sutcliffe, Jane Dutton, Scott Sonenshein, and Adam M. Grant. "A Socially Embedded Model of Thriving at Work," *Organization Science* 16, no. 5 (2005): 537–49.

6    **"lived like kings":** Frances Stroh, *Beer Money: A Memoir of Privilege and Loss* (New York: Harper, 2016), p. 14.

6    **"grow or go":** Ibid., p. 45.

6    **"as big as we can get":** Ibid., p. 44.

6    **"It was like going to a gunfight with a knife":** Kerry A. Dolan, "How to Blow $9 Billion: The Fallen Stroh Family," *Forbes*, July 21, 2014, http://www.forbes.com/sites/kerryadolan/2014/07/08/how-the-stroh-family-lost-the-largest-private-beer-fortune-in-the-u-s/.

6    **"antiquated Detroit plant":** Dustin Walsh, "For Stroh's, the Bell's Tolled: The Crumbling of a Detroit Institution Rang in the Era of Craft Breweries," *Crain's Detroit Business*, February 11, 1985.

6    **family fortune that could have approached $9 billion:** Kerry A. Dolan, "How to Blow $9 Billion."

6    **"it overwhelmed them":** Brian Yaeger, *Red, White, and Brew: An American Beer Odyssey* (New York: St. Martin's Press, 2008), p. 21.

8    **family that disappeared forty-two years earlier:** Mike Dash, "For 40 Years, This Russian Family Was Cut Off from All Human Contact, Unaware of World War II," *Smithsonian Magazine*, January 28, 2013; Vasily Peskov, *Lost in the Taiga: One Russian Family's Fifty-Year Struggle for Survival and Religious Freedom in the Siberian Wilderness* (New York: Doubleday, 1994).

10    **Constraints can motivate:** Scott Sonenshein, "How Organizations Foster the Creative Use of Resources," *Academy of Management Journal* 57, no. 3 (June 2014): 814–48; Irene Scopelliti, Paola Cillo, Bruno Busacca, and David Mazursky, "How Do Financial Constraints Affect Creativity?" *Journal of Product Innovation Management* 31, no. 5 (2014): 880–93.

10    **"engineering" . . . "bricolage":** Claude Lévi-Strauss, *The Savage Mind* (Chicago: University of Chicago Press, 1966).

11    **makes good use of the tools around:** Ted Baker and Reed E. Nelson, "Creating Something from Nothing: Resource Construction Through Entrepreneurial Bricolage," *Administrative Science Quar-*

*terly* 50, no. 3 (2005): 329–66; Raghu Garud and Peter Karnøe, "Bricolage Versus Breakthrough: Distributed and Embedded Agency in Technology Entrepreneurship," *Research Policy* 32, no. 2 (2003): 277–300.

11  **psychological discomfort . . . from using things in different ways:** Karl Duncker, "On Problem-Solving," *Psychological Monographs* 58, no. 5 (1945): i–113.

12  **repair it with duct tape:** Eli Saslow, "The Man in the Van," ESPN .com, accessed March 5, 2015, http://espn.go.com/espn/feature/story/_/id/12420393/top-blue-jays-prospect-daniel-norris-lives-own-code; Vice Sports, "The Millionaire Pitcher That Lives in a Van," YouTube video, 5:46, accessed March 25, 2015, https://www.youtube .com/watch?t=17&v=wKPa3uVddbU; John Lott, "Toronto Blue Jays Prospect Daniel Norris Drives an Old Van in Search of Good Waves: 'I've Been Different My Whole Life,'" *National Post*, March 11, 2014, http://news.nationalpost.com/sports/mlb/toronto-blue-jays-prospect-daniel-norris-drives-an-old-van-in-search-of-good-waves-ive-been-different-my-whole-life.

13  **"you have to appreciate what you have":** Daniel Norris, "More Than Just the 'Man in the Van,'" *Players' Tribune*, April 7, 2016, http://www .theplayerstribune.com/daniel-norris-tigers-pitcher-baseball-van/, accessed July 28, 2016.

13  **"Life is like the ocean to me":** Sharleen Rydie, "Interview with an Outdoorsman: Daniel Norris + Johnson City, TN," *London Red*, 2014, http://www.newlondonred.com/INTERVIEWS/Interview-Daniel-Norris.

13  **"Just cuz money's there":** Saslow, "The Man in the Van."

13  **monthly stipend:** Ibid.

13  **"Never once did I not have":** Lott, "Toronto Blue Jays Prospect Daniel Norris Drives an Old Van in Search of Good Waves."

14  **He got a second job:** Aniseh Hamour, "Those Who Know Daniel Norris Call Him Humble, Competitive, Extremely Talented." WVTM-TV Birmingham, AL, April 8, 2015, http://wvtm.membercenter.worldnow .com/story/28756554/those-who-know-daniel-norris-call-him-humble-competitive-extremely-talented.

14  **sports stars bankrupt and depressed:** Pablo S. Torre, "How (and

Why) Athletes Go Broke," *Sports Illustrated*, March 23, 2009, accessed April 18, 2016, http://www.huffingtonpost.com/bill-johnson-ii/beyond winning-and-losing-athletes-and-depression_b_8174292.html.

14 **knocked the ball out of the park:** "MLB Notebook: Daniel Norris Is 19th Pitcher to Hit Home Run in First Major League at-Bat," Associated Press, August 20, 2015, accessed September 5, 2015, http://www .ohio.com/sports/mlb/mlb-notebook-daniel-norris-is-19th-pitcher-to-hit-home-run-in-first-major-league-at-bat-1.617833; "Tigers Pitcher Homers in First MLB at-Bat," SI.com, accessed September 5, 2015, http://www .si.com/mlb/2015/08/19/daniel-norris-home-run-video-tigers-cubs.

15 **Facit:** William H. Starbuck, "Organizations as Action Generators," *American Sociological Review* 48 (February 1983): 91–102.

17 **Success blinds us and reinforces:** Barbara Levitt and James G. March, "Organizational Learning," *Annual Review of Sociology* 14, no. 1 (1988): 319–40; Andrea E. Abele and Daniel Spurk, "The Longitudinal Impact of Self-Efficacy and Career Goals on Objective and Subjective Career Success," *Journal of Vocational Behavior* 74, no. 1 (February 2009): 53–62, doi:10.1016/j.jvb.2008.10.005.

17 **naturally prefer the status quo:** William Samuelson and Richard Zeckhauser, "Status Quo Bias in Decision Making," *Journal of Risk and Uncertainty* 1 (1988): 7–59.

## CHAPTER 2: THE GRASS IS ALWAYS GREENER

22 **California's worst drought of the modern era:** Lisa Krieger, "California Drought: Woodside, Fremont on Opposite Ends of Water-Saving Spectrum," *San Jose Mercury News*, April 4, 2015.

22 **wrestle with his municipality over water usage:** Barney Brantingham, "Harold Simmons Dies: Dallas Money Man and Montecito Resident Was 82," *Santa Barbara Independent*, December 30, 2013.

23 **homeowners to direct so many resources to get greener grass:** Amanda R. Carrico, James Fraser, and Joshua T. Bazuin, "Green with Envy: Psychological and Social Predictors of Lawn Fertilizer Application," *Environment and Behavior* 45 (2013): 427–54.

24 **2012 summer games in London:** "There Is No Silver Lining: The Hilarious Pouts of the Olympians Who Went for the Gold—But Wound Up in Second Place," DailyMail.com, accessed August 26, 2015,

http://www.dailymail.co.uk/news/article-2185554/London-Olympics
Hilarious-pouts-athletes-took-silver-medals.html.

24    **bronze medalists had a much higher tendency to be close to ecstasy
compared to silver medalists:** Victoria H. Medvec, Scott F. Madey,
and Thomas Gilovich, "When Less Is More: Counterfactual Thinking
Among Olympic Medalists," *Journal of Personality and Social Psychology*
69, no. 4 (October 1995): 603–10.

25    **look to others to get a better sense of ourselves:** Leon Festinger, "A
Theory of Social Comparison Processes," *Human Relations* 7 (1954):
117–40; Susan Fiske offers a more recent overview of social comparison
perspectives in her book *Envy Up, Scorn Down: How Status Divides Us*
(New York: Russell Sage Foundation, 2011).

26    **"you're nobody here at $10 million":** Gary Rivlin, "The Millionaires
Who Don't Feel Rich," *New York Times*, August 5, 2007, p. A1.

28    **the more time people spent using Facebook, the worse they felt:**
Ethan Kross, Philippe Verduyn, Emre Demiralp, Jiyoung Park, David
Seungjae Lee, Natalie Lin, Holly Shablack, John Jonides, and Oscar
Ybarra, "Facebook Use Predicts Declines in Subjective Well-Being
in Young Adults," *PLOS One*, August 14, 2013, doi: 10.1371/journal
.pone.0069841; Sang Yup Lee, "How Do People Compare Themselves
with Others on Social Network Sites?: The Case of Facebook," *Computers in Human Behavior* 32 (March 2014): 253–60, doi: 10.1016/j.
chb.2013.12.009.

29    **parable told by scientist and teacher Alexander Calandra:** Alexander Calandra, "Angels on a Pin," *Saturday Review*, December 21, 1968,
p. 60.

30    *functional fixedness:* Karl Duncker, "On Problem-Solving," *Psychological Monographs* 58, no. 5 (1945).

30    **help Bobo by using only the tools provided:** Tim P. German and
Margaret Anne Defeyter, "Immunity to Functional Fixedness in Young
Children," *Psychonomic Bulletin and Review* 7, no. 4 (December 2000):
707–12.

32    **CEO of Borders, Greg Josefowicz:** Matt Townsend, "Borders' Bezos
Champagne Toast Marked Start of Chain's Demise," Bloomberg, July
19, 2011.

33    **mindless accumulation:** Christopher K. Hsee, Jiao Zhang, Cindy F.

Cai, and Shirley Zhang, "Overearning," *Psychological Science* 24, no. 6 (2013): 852–59.

35 **"you have to be asleep to believe it":** *Time*, "Top 10 George Carlin Quotes," accessed August 26, 2015, http://content.time.com/time/specials/packages/article/0,28804,1858074_1858085_1858083,00.html.

35 **American dream is harder to achieve:** Center for a New American Dream, "New American Dream Survey 2014," http://newdream.s3.amazonaws.com/19/d9/7/3866/NewDreamPollFinalAnalysis.pdf.

36 **Chasing kept pushing Joshua Millburn:** Millburn turned things around dramatically and adopted a minimalist lifestyle where he abandoned many of his possessions for a simpler but more meaningful life, something he now regularly writes about at theminimalists.com and has detailed in a book: Joshua Fields Millburn and Ryan Nicodemus, *Minimalism: Live a Meaningful Life* (Missoula, MT: Asymmetrical Press, 2011).

36 **"hadn't focused on the things that were most important":** Michael Posner, "Does a Less Is More Life Bring Happiness?" *Globe and Mail*, December 13, 2012.

37 **career chasing negatively predicted career satisfaction seven years later:** Andrea E. Abele and Daniel Spurk, "The Longitudinal Impact of Self-Efficacy and Career Goals on Objective and Subjective Career Success," *Journal of Vocational Behavior* 74 (February 2009): 53–62, doi: 10.1016/j.jvb.2008.10.005.

37 **largest destructions of wealth in history:** Burton G. Malkiel, "Bubbles in Asset Prices," in Dennis C. Mueller, ed., *The Oxford Handbook of Capitalism* (New York: Oxford University Press, 2012), pp. 405–25.

37 **$12 million on advertising to generate a whopping $619,000 in sales:** Arun Rao and Piero Scaruffi, *A History of Silicon Valley: The Greatest Creation of Wealth in the History of the Planet* (Palo Alto, CA: Omniware, 2011).

37 **sold goods below cost:** Accessed April 11, 2016, http://www.cnet.com/news/pets-com-latest-high-profile-dot-com-disaster/.

38 **Digital Archive of the Birth of the Dot Com Era:** Leslie Berlin, "Lessons of Survival, from the Dot-Com Attic," *New York Times*, November 23, 2008. Professor Kirsch also makes his archive available at http://www.businessplanarchive.org/.

39    **twenty bucks a square foot:** Evelyn M. Rusli, "Free Spending by Startups Stirs Memories of Dot-Com Era Excesses," *Wall Street Journal*, October 5, 2014.

39    **"solve your problems by spending":** Ibid.

40    **"Revenues solve all problems" and "fire hose of cash":** Accessed May 10, 2016, http://www.bloomberg.com/features/2016-yahoo/.

40    **Bill Demas:** Personal conversation, August 24, 2015.

40    **Fab.com:** FastCompany.com, "How Fab.com's Jason Goldberg Hustled His Way to $325 Million," accessed August 25, 2015, http://www.fastcodesign.com/3016913/how-fabcoms-jason-goldberg-hustled-his-way-to-325-million.

41    **offer to switch seats for $100:** Jim Edwards, "Fab.com Founder Baffled by Passenger Who Declined $100 to Switch Seats with Him on Plane," *Business Insider*, July 15, 2013, accessed August 25, 2015, http://www.businessinsider.com/fabcom-founder-baffled-by-passenger-who-declined-100-to-switch-seats-with-him-on-plane-2013–7.

42    **Departments with too many spare resources become less likely to improve:** Nitin Nohria and Ranjay Gulati, "Is Slack Good or Bad for Innovation?" *Academy of Management Journal* 39, no. 5 (1996): 1245–64.

42    **escalation of commitment:** Barry Staw, "Knee-Deep in the Big Muddy: A Study of Escalating Commitment to a Chosen Course of Action," *Organizational Behavior and Human Performance* 16, no. 1 (1976): 27–44.

44    **quest for the greenest grass:** Ted Steinberg, *American Green: The Obsessive Quest for the Perfect Lawn* (New York: W. W. Norton, 2006).

## CHAPTER 3: ALL THINGS RICH AND BEAUTIFUL

45    **BoutiqueCo:** For this example, I am using pseudonyms for the names of the organization and its employees.

48    **Things are very regimented:** Ethan Peters (pseudonym), in discussion with the author, April 20, 2010.

49    **"cut off the straps":** Scott Sonenshein, "How Organizations Foster the Creative Use of Resources," *Academy of Management Journal* 57, no. 3 (2014): 814–48.

49    **psychological ownership:** Amitai Etzioni, "The Socio-Economics of Property," in F. W. Rudmin, ed., "To Have Possessions: A Handbook

on Ownership and Property," Special Issue, *Journal of Social Behavior and Personality* 6, no. 6 (1991): 465–68.

49　**a feeling of possessiveness:** Jon L. Pierce, Tatiana Kostova, and Kurt T. Dirks, "Toward a Theory of Psychological Ownership in Organizations," *Academy of Management Review* 26, no. 2 (2001): 288–310.

50　**self-perception processes:** Daryl Bem, "Self-Perception: An Alternative Interpretation of Cognitive Dissonance Phenomena," *Psychological Review* 74 (1967): 183–200.

50　**Its CEO told me:** In conversation with the author, June 3, 2010.

50　**accounted for 16 percent of a person's job satisfaction:** Linn Van Dyne and Jon L. Pierce, "Psychological Ownership and Feelings of Possession: Three Field Studies Predicting Employee Attitudes and Organizational Citizenship Behavior," *Journal of Organizational Behavior* 25, no. 4 (2004): 439–59.

51　**strong psychological beliefs and owner-like behaviors predicted improved financial performance:** Stephen H. Wagner, Christopher P. Parker, and Neil D. Christiansen, "Employees That Think and Act Like Owners: Effects of Ownership Beliefs and Behaviors on Organizational Effectiveness," *Personnel Psychology* 56, no. 4 (December 2003): 847–71.

52　**"become more creative . . . by looking for limitations":** Phil Hansen, "Embrace the Shake," TED video, at 9:40, posted May 2013, accessed December 17, 2015, https://www.ted.com/talks/phil_hansen_embrace_the_shake/transcript?language=en#t-198180.

53　**Monet's art as having one constant:** Patricia D. Stokes, *Creativity from Constraints* (New York: Springer, 2006); Patricia D. Stokes, "Variability, Constraints, and Creativity: Shedding Light on Claude Monet," *American Psychologist* 56, no. 4 (2001): 355–59.

54　**forced rodents to press a bar:** Patricia D. Stokes, "Learned Variability," *Animal Learning and Behavior* 23, no. 2 (1995): 164–76.

54　**"little c" creativity:** James C. Kaufman and Ronald A. Beghetto, "Beyond Big and Little: The Four C Model of Creativity," *Review of General Psychology* 13, no. 1 (2009): 1–12.

54　**constraints served as a barrier to using resources creatively:** Teresa M. Amabile, *Creativity in Context* (Boulder, CO: Westview Press, 1996).

54    **feeling that our work is not a priority:** Teresa M. Amabile, Regina Conti, Heather Coon, Jeffrey Lazenby, and Michael Herron, "Assessing the Work Environment for Creativity," *Academy of Management Journal* 39, no. 5 (October 1996): 1154–84.

55    **freedom to use resources in less conventional ways:** Ravi Mehta and Meng Zhu, "Creating When You Have Less: The Impact of Resource Scarcity on Product Use Creativity," *Journal of Consumer Research* (October 2015).

56    **constraints that direct us to make the best:** Christopher M. McDermott and Gina Colarelli O'Connor, "Managing Radical Innovation," *Journal of Product Innovation Management* 19, no. 6 (2002): 424–38; Ronald Finke, *Creative Imagery: Discoveries and Inventions in Visualization* (Hillsdale, NJ: Lawrence Erlbaum Associates, 1990).

56    **"path of least resistance" model:** Thomas B. Ward, "Structured Imagination: The Role of Category Structure in Exemplar Generation," *Cognitive Psychology* 27, no. 1 (1994): 1–40.

56    **dedicate our mental energy:** Ronald A. Finke, Thomas B. Ward, and Steven M. Smith, *Creative Cognition: Theory, Research and Applications* (Cambridge, MA: MIT Press, 1992).

56    **budgets significantly increased how resourceful people:** Irene Scopelliti, Paola Cillo, Bruno Busacca, and David Mazursky, "How Do Financial Constraints Affect Creativity?" *Journal of Product Management Innovation* 31, no. 5 (2014): 880–93.

57    **"sticks with you":** Marc Ballon, "The Cheapest CEO in America," *Inc.*, October 1, 1997, p. 52.

57    **cheapest CEO in America:** Ibid.

57    **performance was second best:** Analysis using FactSet database retrieved on June 4, 2015.

57    **earned a nickel a day:** Fastenal Company, "Our History," accessed October 7, 2015, https://www.fastenal.com/en/99/our-history; Harvey Meyer, "Cheap and Cheerful: Fastenal's Strategy Is to Pinch Every Penny Twice Before Letting It Go. So Far, It's Working." *Journal of Business Strategy* 22, no. 5 (2001): 14–17.

60    **keep turnover at an impressive 7 percent:** United States Securities and Exchange Commission, Fastenal Company Prospectus, filed August 20, 1987.

60    **"We're not afraid to spend":** Meyer, "Cheap and Cheerful," 16.

60    **vending machines at customers' locations:** Dyan Machan, "Sweating the Small Stuff," *Barrons*, March 10, 2014, 38–39.

61    **understand their mind-set:** John L. Lastovicka, Lance A. Bettencourt, Renee Shaw Hughner, and Ronald J. Kuntze, "Lifestyle of the Tight and Frugal: Theory and Measurement," *Journal of Consumer Research* 26, no. 1 (1999): 85–98.

62    **Stanford Financial Group:** Jennifer Dawson, "Behind the Scenes at Stanford's Old Office," *Houston Business Journal*, December 29, 2010.

63    **800 million people lack enough food:** World Food Programme, accessed March 10, 2016, http://www.wfp.org/hunger/stats.

63    **billions of dollars to manage food waste:** Susan Swift, "Jenny Dawson, Founder of Rubies in the Rubble," *Business Feminism*, July 17, 2014; Tim Fox, "Global Food: Waste Not, Want Not," *Institution of Mechanical Engineers*, 2013.

63    **bazaar hardly emblematic of a global food crisis:** Jo Fairley, "Why Jenny Relishes Rubbish: How a Former Hedgefund Manager Got into a Pickle Over Discarded Fresh Produce," *Daily Mail*, September 21, 2013.

63    **"how can we afford to be this wasteful?":** Adam Pescod, "Rubies in the Rubble: The Chutney Company Taking the Fight to Food Waste," *Economist*, August 4, 2014.

64    **more than a quarter of all produce:** http://www.huffingtonpost .com/entry/walmart-food-waste-petition_us_57768c61e4b0a629c1a-9bacd? (accessed July 28, 2016).

64    **company's mantra:** Johanna Derry, "First Person: Jenny Dawson," *Financial Times*, October 4, 2013.

64    **"we judge a person by their looks":** Lydia Slater, "The High-Flying Banker Who Gave It All Up to Turn Throwaway Veg into Posh Pickles," *Daily Mail*, May 19, 2014, accessed October 18, 2014, http://www.dai lymail.co.uk/femail/article-2633364/The-high-flying-banker-gave-turn-throwaway-veg-posh-pickles.html.

66    **to become anything valuable requires action:** Martha S. Feldman, "Resources in Emerging Structures and Processes of Change," *Organization Science* 15, no. 3 (2004): 295–309; Martha S. Feldman and Monica C. Worline, "Resources, Resourcing, and Ampliative Cycles

in Organizations," in *The Oxford Handbook of Positive Organizational Scholarship*, ed. Gretchen M. Spreitzer and Kim S. Cameron (Oxford: Oxford University Press, 2011), pp. 629–41, doi: 10.1093/oxfordhb/9780199734610.013.0047.

66    **can also create valuable resources:** Jane E. Dutton, Monica C. Worline, Peter J. Frost, and Jacoba Lilius, "Explaining Compassion Organizing," *Administrative Science Quarterly* 51, no. 1 (2006): 59–96; M. A. Glynn and K. Wrobel, "My Family, My Firm: How Familial Relationships Function as Endogenous Organizational Resources," in J. E. Dutton and B. R. Ragins eds., *Positive Relationships at Work* (Mahwah, NJ: Erlbaum, 2006).

66    **employees as resisters:** Scott Sonenshein, "Treat Employees as Resources, Not Resisters," in *How to Be a Positive Leader: Insights from Leading Thinkers on Positive Organizations*, ed. Jane Dutton and Gretchen Spreitzer (San Francisco: Berrett-Koehler, 2014), pp. 136–46; Jeffrey D. Ford, Laurie W. Ford, and Angelo D'Amelio, "Resistance to Change: The Rest of the Story," *Academy of Management Review* 33, no. 2 (2008): 362–77.

67    **large retail company we'll call EntertainCo:** For this example, I am using pseudonyms for the names of the organization and its employees. This example is based on the following article: Scott Sonenshein, and Utpal Dholakia, "Explaining Employee Engagement with Strategic Change Implementation: A Meaning-Making Approach," *Organization Science* 23, no. 1 (2012): 1–23.

## CHAPTER 4: GET OUTSIDE

72    **Netflix collects a trove of data:** Gavin Potter, in discussion with the author, October 23, 2015; Eliot Van Buskirk, "How the Netflix Prize Was Won," *Wired*, September 2009; Andreas Töscher, Michael Jahrer, and Robert M. Bell, "The Big Chaos Solution to the Netflix Grand Prize," Commendo Research & Consulting GmbH, http://www.commendo .at/UserFiles/commendo/File/GrandPrize2009_BigChaos.pdf; Clive Thompson, "If You Liked This, You're Sure to Love That," *New York Times*, November 23, 2008; Jordan Ellenberg, "This Psychologist Might Outsmart the Math Brains Competing for the Netflix Prize," *Wired*, February 25, 2008.

72    **emperor offered a prize:** Angelika Cosima Bullinger and Kathrin Moeslein, "Innovation Contests—Where Are We?" *AMCIS 2010 Proceedings*, 2010, Paper 28, http://aisel.aisnet.org/amcis2010/28.

74    **anchoring:** Amos Tversky and Daniel Kahneman, "Judgment Under Uncertainty: Heuristics and Biases," *Science* 185, no. 4157 (September 27, 1974): 1124–31.

75    **"teamed up with one of the mathematics teams":** Gavin Potter, in discussion with the author, October 23, 2015.

75    **stream of psychology research:** Malcom Gladwell, *Outliers: The Story of Success* (New York: Little, Brown and Co., 2008).

76    **expertise depends on extensive practice:** Anders Ericsson and Robert Pool Peak, *Secrets from the New Science of Expertise* (New York: Eamon Dolan Books, 2016).

76    **hard to become an expert at something always changing:** Frans Johnson, *The Click Moment: Seizing Opportunity in an Unpredictable World* (New York: Portfolio, 2012).

76    **relationship between the number of hours of practice and performance:** Brooke N. Macnamara, David Z. Hambrick, and Frederick L. Oswald, "Deliberate Practice and Performance in Music, Games, Sports, Education, and Professions: A Meta-Analysis," *Psychological Science* 25, no. 8 (2014): 1608–18.

78    **expertise sometimes sways people too far:** Robert B. Cialdini, *Influence: The Psychology of Persuasion*, rev. ed. (New York: Harper Business, 2006); Cialdini takes the example from Neil M. Davis and Michael Richard Cohen, *Medication Errors: Causes and Prevention* (Philadelphia: George F. Stickley, 1981).

78    **experts were no better than the average person in forecasting future:** Philip E. Tetlock, *Expert Political Judgment: How Good Is It? How Can We Know?* (Princeton, NJ: Princeton University Press, 2006).

79    **whether people with the most expertise for the specific challenge would come out on top:** Lars Bo Jeppesen and Karim R. Lakhani, "Marginality and Problem-Solving Effectiveness in Broadcast Search," *Organization Science* 21, no. 5 (2010): 1016–33.

79    **Experts come with a significant liability:** Erik Dane, "Reconsidering the Trade-Off Between Expertise and Flexibility: A Cognitive Entrenchment Perspective," *Academy of Management Review* 35, no. 4 (2010): 579–603.

80     **Cheves Perky conducted a series of experiments:** Cheves West Perky, "An Experimental Study of Imagination," *American Journal of Psychology* 21, no. 3 (July 1910): 422–45.

81     **British biochemist Sir Tim Hunt shocked:** Sarah Knapton, "Sexism Row: Scientist Sir Tim Hunt Quits over 'Trouble with Girls' Speech," *Telegraph*, June 11, 2015.

81     **unconscionable truth about women in science:** Henry Etzkowitz, Carol Kemelgor, and Brian Uzzi, *Athena Unbound: The Advancement of Women in Science and Technology* (Cambridge: Cambridge University Press, 2000).

82     *The Difference*: Scott E. Page, *The Difference: How the Power of Diversity Creates Better Groups, Firms, Schools, and Societies* (Princeton, NJ: Princeton University Press, 2008).

83     **Story Musgrave:** I developed this example from multiple sources: Story Musgrave, "Lessons for Life," *STEAM Journal* 2, no. 1 (2015); Claudia Dreifus, "A Conversation with F. Story Musgrave: Watching from Sidelines as NASA Regains Spotlight," *New York Times*, October 20, 1998; Gary Pinnell, "A Life Story, According to Story Musgrave from High School Dropout to NASA, One Step at a Time," *Highlands Today*, January 18, 2015; Ann E. Lenehan, *Story: The Way of Water* (Westfield, Australia: Communications Agency, 2004).

85     **"So I could operate on the Hubble of course":** David Shayler and Colin Burgess, *NASA's Scientist-Astronauts* (Berlin, New York: Springer, published in association with Praxis, 2007), p. 464.

85     **Musgrave's ability to solve complex challenges:** Susan M. Barnett and Barbara Koslowski, "Adaptive Expertise: Effects of Type of Experience and the Level of Theoretical Understanding It Generates," *Thinking and Reasoning* 8 (2002): 237–67; Erik Dane and Scott Sonenshein, "On the Role of Experience in Ethical Decision Making at Work: An Ethical Expertise Perspective," *Organizational Psychology Review* 5, no. 1 (2015): 74–96.

86     **division of labor:** Adam Smith, *An Inquiry into the Nature and Causes of the Wealth of Nations,* vol. 1 (Oxford: Oxford University Press, 1976).

87     **Industrial Revolution ushered in an era:** Robin Leidner, *Fast Food, Fast Talk: Service Work and the Routinization of Everyday Life* (Berkeley: University of California Press, 1993).

87   **Increasing specialization:** Gillian Tett, *The Silo Effect: The Peril of Expertise and the Promise of Breaking Down Barriers* (New York: Simon & Schuster, 2015).

87   **people who manage to gain this diverse experience:** Cláudia Custódio, Miguel A. Ferreira, and Pedro Matos, "Generalists Versus Specialists: Lifetime Work Experience and Chief Executive Officer Pay," *Journal of Financial Economics* 108 (May 2013): 471–92.

88   **Multi-c executives earned a 19 percent pay premium:** Other research has replicated these results with chief financial officers, finding that even among executives in a single functional area those who follow the multi-c rule get paid more. Sudip Datta and Mai Iskandar-Datta, "Upper-Echelon Executive Human Capital and Compensation: Generalist vs Specialist Skills," *Strategic Management Journal* 35 (2014): 1853–66.

88   ***A Whole New Mind*:** Daniel H. Pink, *A Whole New Mind: Why Right-Brainers Will Rule the Future* (New York: Riverhead Books, 2005).

88   **increasingly specialized experiences:** From 2000 to 2010, the number of academic programs reported to the Department of Education grew by more than 30 percent. The University of Michigan, where I obtained my PhD, offers more than 250 majors. Cecilia Capuzzi Simon, "Major Decisions," *New York Times*, November 2, 2012.

89   ***Valdez* oil spill:** Scott Pegau, e-mail message to the author, October 29, 2015; Cornella Dean, "If You Have a Problem, Ask Everyone," *New York Times*, July 28, 2008, accessed October 21, 2015, https://www.innocentive.com/johndavis; InnoCentive, "InnoCentive—Oil Spill Cleanup Part 1—Challenge Overview," YouTube, at 2:26, December 21, 2007, accessed November 13, 2015, https://www.youtube.com/watch?v=5_ucQKWmxdk.

90   **small worlds:** Duncan J. Watts, *Small Worlds: The Dynamics of Networks Between Order and Randomness* (Princeton, NJ: Princeton University Press, 1999).

90   **IDEO:** Andrew Hargadon and Robert I. Sutton, "Building an Innovation Factory," *Harvard Business Review*, May–June 2000, 157–166; Andrew Hargadon, "Brokering Knowledge: Linking Learning and Innovation," *Research in Organizational Behavior* 24, no. 41 (2002): 85.

91   **use analogical reasoning:** Mary L. Gick and Keith J. Holyoak, "Analogical Problem Solving," *Cognitive Psychology* 12 (1980): 306–55.

92   **Nobel Prize–winning scientists:** Robert Root-Bernstein et al., "Arts Foster Scientific Success: Avocations of Nobel, National Academy, Royal Society and Sigma Xi Members," *Journal of Psychology of Science and Technology* 1, no. 2 (2008): 51–63.

92   **Google's chairman Eric Schmidt:** James Robinson, "Eric Schmidt, Chairman of Google, Condemns British Education System," *Guardian*, August 26, 2011.

93   **hiring managers want both:** Hart Research Associates, "It Takes More Than a Major: Employer Priorities for College Learning and Student Success," Commissioned by the Association of American Colleges and Universities, April 10, 2013, accessed November 17, 2015, http://www.aacu.org/sites/default/files/files/LEAP/2013_EmployerSurvey.pdf.

94   **more diverse . . . the more resourceful:** Kimberly S. Jaussi, Amy E. Randel, and Shelley D. Dionne, "I Am, I Think I Can, and I Do: The Role of Personal Identity, Self-Efficacy, and Cross-Application of Experiences in Creativity at Work," *Creativity Research Journal* 19 (2007): 247–58.

94   **we favor people like us:** Miller McPherson, Lynn Smith-Lovin, and James M. Cook, "Birds of a Feather: Homophily in Social Networks," *Annual Review of Sociology* 27, no. 1 (2001): 415–44.

95   **"no gain if both teams were simply duplicating":** Robert Bell, Yehuda Koren, and Chris Volinsky, "Statistics Can Find You a Movie, Part 2," *AT&T Research*, May 19, 2010.

### CHAPTER 5: TIME TO ACT

97   **Robert Rodriguez:** Robert Rodriguez, *Rebel Without a Crew: Or How a 23-Year-Old Filmmaker with $7,000 Became a Hollywood Player* (New York: Penguin Books, 1995); "Wizard of Hollywood, Robert Rodriguez," Narrated by Tim Ferriss, *The Tim Ferriss Experiment*, August 23, 2015, http://fourhourworkweek.com/2015/08/23/the-wizard-of-hollywood-robert-rodriguez/; Will Hodgkinson, "Robert Rodriguez, Director of *From Dusk Till Dawn* and the Smash Hit *Spy Kids*," *Guardian*, April 11, 2001.

98   **"bleed for your money":** Robert Rodriguez, *Rebel Without a Crew*, p. 11.

99    **"act first before inspiration":** "Wizard of Hollywood, Robert Rodri-
      guez," *The Tim Ferriss Experiment*, quoted at 43:15.

99    **"all the time and money in the world":** Ibid., quoted at 19:24.

99    **"working with what you got":** Ibid., quoted at 35:35.

101   **"creative person with limitless imagination":** Robert Rodriguez,
      *Rebel Without a Crew*, 203–4.

101   **"edited it in my garage":** Will Hodgkinson, "I'm Probably the Only
      Guy Who Really Enjoys Being in the Movies," *Guardian*, April 11, 2001,
      accessed April 19, 2016, http://www.theguardian.com/culture/2001/
      apr/11/artsfeatures1.

102   **"enjoys being in the business":** Ibid.

103   **The Battle of Antietam:** Rick Beard, "A Terminal Case of the 'Slows,'"
      *New York Times*, November 5, 2012; *Freedom: A History of US*, Webisode
      6: "A War to End Slavery," "Biography George B. McClellan," PBS.org,
      accessed January 6, 2016, http://www.pbs.org/wnet/historyofus/web06/
      features/bio/B06.html; "George McClellan," History.com, 2009, http://
      www.history.com/topics/american-civil-war/george-b-mcclellan.

103   **"does not want to use the Army":** PBS.org, accessed April 15, 2016,
      http://www.pbs.org/wnet/historyofus/web06/features/bio/B06.html.

104   **Lincoln jokingly wrote:** J. Matthew Gallman, "Three Roads to Antie-
      tam: George McClellan, Abraham Lincoln, and Alexander Gardner,"
      *Lens of War: Exploring Iconic Photographs of the Civil War*, ed. J. Mat-
      thew Gallman and Gary W. Gallagher (Athens: University of Georgia
      Press, 2015), pp. 41–50.

104   **Lincoln wryly questioned:** Christopher Heam, *Lincoln and McClellan
      at War* (Baton Rouge: Louisiana State University Press, 2012), p. 199.

105   **thoroughness just causes a greater delay:** James W. Fredrickson and
      Terence R. Mitchell, "Strategic Decision Processes: Comprehensiveness
      and Performance in an Industry with an Unstable Environment," *Acad-
      emy of Management Journal* 27 (1984): 399–423; Henry Mintzberg,
      Duru Raisinghani, and André Théorêt, "The Structure of 'Unstruc-
      tured' Decision Processes," *Administrative Science Quarterly* 21, no. 2
      (June 1976): 246–75.

106   **modest correlation between planning and organizational performance:**
      Brian K. Boyd, "Strategic Planning and Financial Performance: A Meta-An-
      alytic Review," *Journal of Management Studies* 28, no. 4 (1991): 353–74.

106 **how businesses navigated these trade-offs:** Kathleen M. Eisenhardt, "Making Fast Strategic Decisions in High-Velocity Environments," *Academy of Management Journal* 32, no. 3 (September 1989): 543–76.

108 **lost in the Alps:** Miroslav Holub, "Brief Thoughts on Maps." *Times Literary Supplement*, February 4, 1977.

108 **"any old map will do":** Karl E. Weick, *Sensemaking in Organizations* (Thousand Oaks, CA: Sage, 1995), p. 54.

109 **Fighting a tendency for inertia:** Warren Berger, "Dan Wieden, Wieden + Kennedy," Inc.com, accessed January 6, 2016, http://www.inc.com/magazine/20040401/25wieden.html.

109 **Dan Wieden:** Ibid.

109 **governor a "moral coward":** Accessed April 15, 2016, http://content.time.com/time/subscriber/article/0,33009,918554–1,00.html.

109 **"Let's do it":** Lily Rothman, "The Strange Story of the Man Who Chose Execution by Firing Squad," *Time*, March 12, 2015; "Gary Gilmore Biography," Biography.com, accessed December 24, 2015, http://www.biography.com/people/gary-gilmore-11730320; "The Law: Much Ado About Gary," *Time*, December 13, 1976, p. 87.

109 **Wieden pitched a potential slogan:** "Nike's 'Just Do It' Slogan Is Based on a Murderer's Last Words, Says Dan Wieden," dezeen.com, accessed January 6, 2016, http://www.dezeen.com/2015/03/14/nike-just-do-it-slogan-last-words-murderer-gary-gilmore-dan-wieden-kennedy/.

110 **regulatory modes:** A. W. Kruglanski, E. P. Thompson, E. T. Higgins, M. N. Atash, A. Pierro, J. Y. Shah, and S. Spiegel, "To 'Do the Right Thing' or to 'Just Do It': Locomotion and Assessment as Distinct Self-Regulatory Imperatives," *Journal of Personality and Social Psychology* 79, no. 5 (2000), 793–815; A. W. Kruglanski, E. Orehek, E. T. Higgins, A. Pierro, and I. Shalev, "Modes of Self-Regulation: Assessment and Locomotion as Independent Determinants in Goal-Pursuit," in R. Hoyle, ed., *Handbook of Personality and Self-Regulation* (Boston: Blackwell, 2010), pp. 374–402.

110 **In a study of seventy employees:** Antonio Pierro, Arie Kruglanski, and Tory Higgins, "Regulatory Mode and the Joys of Doing: Effects of 'Locomotion' and 'Assessment' on Intrinsic and Extrinsic Task Motivation," *European Journal of Personality* 20, no. 5 (2006): 355–75.

112 **The Trukese:** *Explorations in Cultural Anthropology: Essays in Honor*

*of George Peter Murdock*, ed. Ward H. Goodenough (New York: Mc-Graw-Hill, 1964).

113 **shift people's regulatory modes:** Tamar Avnet and E. Tory Higgins, "Locomotion, Assessment, and Regulatory Fit: Value Transfer from 'How' to 'What,'" *Journal of Experimental Social Psychology* 39, no. 5 (2003): 525–30.

115 **set a speaking order:** Malcolm Brenner, "The Next-in-Line Effect," *Journal of Verbal Learning and Verbal Behavior* 12, no. 3 (1973): 320–23.

116 **Viola Spolin:** Viola Spolin, *Improvisation for the Theater: A Handbook of Teaching and Directing Techniques* (Evanston, IL: Northwestern University Press, 1972).

117 **Del Close:** Lyle Deixler, "Theater; Honoring a Mentor with Laughter," *New York Times*, August 19, 2001.

117 **"Yes, and":** Kelly Leonard and Tom Yorton, *Yes, And: How Improvisation Reverses "No, But" Thinking and Improves Creativity and Collaboration—Lessons from the Second City* (New York: Harper Business, 2015).

119 **Paula Dickson:** W. Angus Wallace, T. Wong, A. O'Bichere, and B. W. Ellis, "Managing in Flight Emergencies: A Personal Account," *British Medical Journal* 311, no. 7001 (August 5, 1995): 374–75.

120 **symphony and jazz:** Frank J. Barrett, "Creativity and Improvisation in Jazz and Organizations: Implications for Organizational Learning," *Organization Science* 9, no. 5 (1998): 605–22.

## CHAPTER 6: WE ARE WHAT WE EXPECT

123 **a horse named Hans:** Edward T. Heyn, "Berlin's Wonderful Horse: He Can Do Almost Everything But Talk—How He Was Taught," *New York Times*, September 4, 1904; Robert Rosenthal and Christine M. Rubie-Davies, "How I Spent My Last 50-Year Vacation: Bob Rosenthal's Lifetime of Research into Interpersonal Expectancy Effects," in *The Routledge International Handbook of Social Psychology of the Classroom*, ed. Christine M. Rubie-Davies, Jason M. Stephens and Penelope Watson (New York: Routledge, 2015), pp. 285–95; Benjamin Radford, "The Curious Case of Clever Hans," Discovery.com, January 7, 2012, accessed January 26, 2016, http://news.discovery.com/history/smartest-horse-hans-120107.htm.

124 **a commission:** Heyn, "Berlin's Wonderful Horse.

126 **free-falling stock market:** "False Rumor Leads to Trouble at Bank," *New*

*York Times*, December 11, 1930, p. 5; Christopher Gray, "Streetscapes: The Bank of the United States in the Bronx: The First Domino in the Depression," *New York Times*, August 18, 1991, http://www.nytimes.com/1991/08/18/realestate/streetscapes-bank-united-states-bronx-first-domino-depression.html.

127 **Bank of the United States:** Robert K. Merton, "The Self-Fulfilling Prophecy," *Antioch Review* 8, no. 2 (Summer 1948): 193–210.

128 **wrote up his results for a generalist readership:** Robert Rosenthal, "On the Social Psychology of the Psychological Experiment: 1, 2 the Experimenter's Hypothesis as Unintended Determinant of Experimental Results," *American Scientist* 51, no. 2 (June 1963): 268–83.

129 **"gifted" students were chosen at random:** Robert Rosenthal and Lenore Jacobson, *Pygmalion in the Classroom: Teacher Expectation and Pupils' Intellectual Development* (New York: Holt, Rinehart, and Winston, 1968).

130 **a manager's expectations:** Jean-François Manzoni and Jean-Louis Barsoux, "Inside the Golem Effect: How Bosses Can Kill Their Subordinates' Motivation," INSEAD Working Paper, 1998.

130 **Pygmalion effect:** Dov Eden, "Self-Fulfilling Prophecy and the Pygmalion Effect in Management," *Oxford Bibliographies*, 2014; Dov Eden, "Self-Fulfilling Prophecies in Organizations," in *Organizational Behavior: The State of the Science*, 2nd ed., ed. Jerald Greenberg (Mahwah, NJ: Lawrence Erlbaum Associates, 2003), pp. 91–122.

130 **soldiers designated as "high performers" objectively performed better:** Dov Eden and Abraham B. Shani, "Pygmalion Goes to Boot Camp: Expectancy, Leadership, and Trainee Performance," *Journal of Applied Psychology* 67, no. 2 (April 1982): 194.

130 **manager sets high expectations, they raise their own expectations:** Nicole M. Kierein and Michael A. Gold, "Pygmalion in Work Organizations: A Meta-Analysis," *Journal of Organizational Behavior* 21, no. 8 (December 2000): 913–28.

131 **stronger marriages:** James K. McNulty and Benjamin R. Karney, "Positive Expectations in the Early Years of Marriage: Should Couples Expect the Best or Brace for the Worst?" *Journal of Personality and Social Psychology* 86, no. 5 (May 2004): 729–43.

131 **higher test scores:** U.S. Department of Education, "Tested Achievement

of the National Education Longitudinal Study of 1998 Eighth Grade Class" (NCES 91–460). Washington, DC: Office of Educational Research and Improvement, 1991.

131 **how expectations shape newly forming relationships:** M. Snyder, E. D. Tanke, and E. Berscheid, "Social Perception and Interpersonal Behavior: On the Self-Fulfilling Nature of Social Stereotypes," *Journal of Personality and Social Psychology* 35, no. 9 (September 1977): 656.

133 **impressions formed . . . had a substantial effect on the candidate's prospects:** Thomas W. Dougherty, Daniel B. Turban, and John C. Callender, "Confirming First Impressions in 'The Employment Interview: A Field Study of Interviewer Behavior," *Journal of Applied Psychology* 79, no. 5 (1994): 659–65.

134 **setting expectations for ourselves:** D. Brian McNatt and Timothy A. Judge, "Boundary Conditions of the Galatea Effect: A Field Experiment and Constructive Replication," *Academy of Management Journal* 47, no. 4 (August 2004): 550–65.

134 **Sarah Breedlove Walker:** Bundles, *On Her Own Ground: The Life and Times of Madame C. J. Walker* (New York: Scribner, 2001); A'Lelia Bundles, *Madam C. J. Walker: Entrepreneur, Philanthropist, Social Activist,* http://www.madamcjwalker.com; Obituary, "Wealthiest Negress Dead," *New York Times,* May 26, 1919, p. 15; National Park Service, "Two American Entrepreneurs: Madam C. J. Walker and J. C. Penney," accessed March 14, 2016, http://www.nps.gov/subjects/teachingwithhistoricplaces/index.htm.

135 **"I couldn't see how":** A'Lelia Bundles, *On Her Own Ground,* p. 48.

136 **"unveiled the vast economic potential":** Henry Louis Gates Jr., "Madam C. J. Walker: Her Crusade," *Time,* December 7, 1998, p. 165.

136 **Many people expect to discover opportunities:** Sharon A. Alvarez and Jay B. Barney, "Discovery and Creation: Alternative Theories of Entrepreneurial Action," *Strategic Entrepreneurship Journal* 1, no. 1–2 (November 2007): 11–26.

136 **"get up and make them!":** National Park Service, "Two American Entrepreneurs: Madam C. J. Walker and J. C. Penney"; A'Lelia Bundles, *Madam C. J. Walker: Entrepreneur* (New York: Chelsea House Publishers, 1991), p. 105.

137 **"product of the constraints that she faced":** Martha Lagace, "HBS

Cases: Beauty Entrepreneur Madam Walker," *HBS Working Knowledge*, June 25, 2007.

137 **threat rigidity:** Barry M. Staw, Lance E. Sandelands, and Jane E. Dutton, "Threat Rigidity Effects in Organizational Behavior: A Multilevel Analysis," *Administrative Science Quarterly* 26, no. 4 (December 1981): 501–24.

138 **Alex Turnbull picked up his phone:** Alex Turnbull (founder and CEO of Groove), in e-mail to the author, October 9, 2015; Alex Turnbull, *Groove*, https://www.groovehq.com/blog.

139 **Simon Sinek calls a "why":** Simon Sinek, *Start with Why: How Great Leaders Inspire Everyone to Take Action* (New York: Portfolio, 2009).

140 **"nobody breathing down my neck":** Alex Turnbull, in e-mail to the author, May 10, 2016.

141 **Wizards wore similarly shaped hats:** Cecil Adams, "What's the Origin of the Dunce Cap?" *Straight Dope*, accessed January 17, 2016, http://www.straightdope.com/columns/read/1793/whats-the-origin-of-the-dunce-cap; Eric Grundhauser, "The Dunce Cap Wasn't Always So Stupid," *Atlas Obscura*, accessed January 17, 2016, http://www.atlasobscura.com/articles/the-dunce-cap-wasnt-always-so-stupid.

141 **Forest Fields:** Telegraph reporters, "School Shames My Son by Making Him Wear Fluorescent Jacket Like the Old Dunce's Cap," *Telegraph*, November 20, 2012.

142 **attribute their failures to things they control:** Lee Ross, "The Intuitive Psychologist and His Shortcomings: Distortions in the Attribution Process," *Advances in Experimental Social Psychology* 10 (1977): 173–220.

143 **failure rate of organization change initiatives at almost 70 percent:** Carolyn Aiken and Scott Keller, "The Irrational Side of Change Management," *McKinsey Quarterly*, April 2009, accessed February 6, 2016, http://www.mckinsey.com/insights/organization/the_irrational_side_of_change_management.

143 **most texts assumed that employees would resist change:** Eric B. Dent and Susan Galloway Goldberg, "Challenging 'Resistance to Change,'" *Journal of Applied Behavioral Science* 35, no. 1 (March 1999): 25–41.

143 **managers expect resistance . . . plan for resistance:** Jeffrey D. Ford and Laurie W. Ford, "Decoding Resistance to Change," *Harvard Business Review* 87, no. 4 (April 2009): 99–103, https://goo.gl/lqqviG.

144 **doubted they were doing enough:** Scott Sonenshein, Katy De-Celles, and Jane Dutton, "It's Not Easy Being Green: The Role of Self-Evaluations in Explaining Support of Environmental Issues," *Academy of Management Journal* 57, no. 1 (February 2014): 7–37.

**CHAPTER 7: MIX IT UP**

147 **Roy Choi's real dream:** Katy McLaughlin, "The King of the Streets Moves Indoors," *Wall Street Journal*, January 15, 2010; Biography, "Community Award Winner Chef Roy Choi," StarChefs.com, accessed March 21, 2016, http://www.starchefs.com/chefs/rising_stars/2010/los-angeles-san-diego/chef-roy-choi.shtml; Jonathan Gold, "How America Became a Food Truck Nation," SmithsonianMag.com, March 2012, accessed January 8, 2016, http://www.smithsonianmag.com/travel/how-america-became-a-food-truck-nation-99979799/; Nicole LaPorte, "How Roy Choi Built an Empire from One Beat-Up Taco Truck," *Fast Company*, accessed January 20, 2016, http://mobilecuisine.com/business/historyofamericanfoodtrucks/.

148 **Texas cattle rancher:** "Invention of the Chuck Wagon," American Chuck Wagon Association, accessed February 29, 2016, http://www.americanchuckwagon.org/chuck-wagon-invention.html.

148 **Oscar Mayer Wienermobile:** "Smile, It's the Wienermobile," Oscar Mayer, accessed February 29, 2016, http://www.oscarmayer.com/wienermobile.

151 **combined competition and friendship:** Scott Sonenshein, Kristen Nault, and Otilia Obdaru, "Competition of a Different Flavor: How a Strategic Group Identity Shapes Competition and Cooperation" (working paper, Jones Graduate School of Business, Rice University, 2016).

151 **"buy or bury your competition":** Mike Hogan, "Jack Welch Gives 'Em Hell at VF/Bloomberg Panel," *Vanity Fair*, May 29, 2009, accessed March 21, 2016, www.vanityfair.com/news/2009/05/jack-welch-gives-em-hell-at-vfbloomberg-panel.

151 **When a resource appears scarce:** Robert B. Cialdini, *Influence: The Psychology of Persuasion*, rev. ed. (New York: Harper Business, 2006).

152 **competition can harm people's ability to stretch:** P. J. Carnevale and T. M. Probst, "Social Values and Social Conflict in Creative Problem Solving and Categorization," *Journal of Personality and Social Psychology* 74, no. 5 (May 1998): 1300–9.

# NOTES

152 **William Ortiz:** A pseudonym to disguise the identity of someone in my research study who was promised anonymity in exchange for participating in my research.

154 **social contact:** G. W. Allport, *The Nature of Prejudice* (Cambridge, MA: Perseus Books, 1954).

154 **515 studies on the contact hypothesis:** Thomas F. Pettigrew and Linda R. Tropp, "A Meta-Analytic Test of Intergroup Contact Theory," *Journal of Personality and Social Psychology* 90, no. 5 (May 2006): 751–83.

154 **mere exposure:** Robert B. Zajonc, "Attitudinal Effects of Mere Exposure," *Journal of Personality and Social Psychology* 9, no. 2, part 2 (June 1968): 1–27.

156 **unexpected friendships among managers at hotels:** Paul Ingram and Peter W. Roberts, "Friendships Among Competitors in the Sydney Hotel Industry," *American Journal of Sociology* 106, no. 2 (September 2000): 387–423.

157 **habit:** Richard R. Nelson and Sidney G. Winter, *An Evolutionary Theory of Economic Change* (Cambridge, MA: Harvard University Press, 1982); E. Stene, "An Approach to the Science of Administration," *American Political Science Review* 34, no. 6 (December 1940): 1124–37.

157 **computer program:** James G. March and Herbert A. Simon, *Organizations* (New York: Wiley, 1958).

157 **mission to change thinking about routines:** Martha S. Feldman and Brian T. Pentland, "Reconceptualizing Organizational Routines as a Source of Flexibility and Change," *Administrative Science Quarterly* 48, no. 1 (March 2003): 94–118.

158 **Routines are brought to life:** S. Sonenshein, "Routines and Creativity: From Dualism to Duality," *Organization Science* 27, no. 3 (May–June 2016): 739–58.

159 **what it really takes to pick up the trash:** Scott F. Turner and Violina Rindova, "A Balancing Act: How Organizations Pursue Consistency in Routine Functioning in the Face of Ongoing Change," *Organization Science* 23, no. 1 (January 2012): 24–46.

159 **The crews were so good:** Ibid., 38.

160 **Bette Nesmith Graham:** "About Us," accessed February 28, 2016, http://www.liquidpaper.com/about_us.html; Jessica Gross, "Liquid Paper," *New York Times Magazine*, Innovations Issue, June 7, 2013,

accessed March 21, 2016, http://www.nytimes.com/packages/html/magazine/2013/innovations-issue/#/?part=liquidpaper.

162 **remain in silos:** Gillian Tett, *The Silo Effect: The Peril of Expertise and the Promise of Breaking Down Barriers* (New York: Simon & Schuster, 2015).

162 **mix our identities:** Stephanie Creary, "Making the Most of Multiple Worlds: Multiple Identity Resourcing in the Creation of a Coordinated System of Care" (working paper, 2016); Stephanie J. Creary, "Resourcefulness in Action: The Case for Global Diversity Management," in *Positive Organizing in a Global Society: Understanding and Engaging Differences for Capacity-Building and Inclusion*, ed. L. M. Roberts, L. Wooten, and M. Davidson (Routledge: New York, 2015), pp. 24–30; Jeffrey Sanchez-Burks, Matthew J. Karlesky, and Fiona Lee, "Psychological Bricolage: Integrating Social Identities to Produce Creative Solutions," in *The Oxford Handbook of Creativity, Innovation, and Entrepreneurship*, ed. Christina Shalley, Michael Hitt, and Jing Zhou (Oxford: Oxford University Press, 2015), pp. 93–102.

162 **"Parenthood isn't a common topic":** Andrew Dowling, "Why Parents Make Better Entrepreneurs," VentureBeat.com, June 29, 2013, accessed February 27, 2016, http://venturebeat.com/2013/06/19/why-being-a-parent-can-make-you-a-better-entrepreneur/.

162 **segment our personal lives:** Tracy Dumas and Jeffrey Sanchez-Burks, "The Professional, the Personal and the Ideal Worker: Pressures and Objectives Shaping the Boundary Between Life Domains," *Academy of Management Annals* 9, no. 1 (March 2015): 803–43; Lakshmi Ramatajan, "Past, Present, and Future Research on Multiple Identities: Toward an Interpersonal Approach," *Academy of Management Annals* 8, no. 1 (2014): 589–659.

162 **different parts of their lives:** Jeffrey H. Greenhaus and Nicholas J. Beutell, "Sources of Conflict Between Work and Family Roles," *Academy of Management Review* 10, no. 1 (1985): 76–88.

162 **the better a parent:** It also doesn't help that organizations have a tendency to dichotomize women as either friendly but incompetent stay-at-home parents or competent but cold professionals. See Amy J. C. Cuddy, Susan T. Fiske, and Peter Glick, "When Professionals Become Mothers, Warmth Doesn't Cut the Ice," *Journal of Social Issues* 60, no. 4 (2004): 701–18.

163  **Psychological resources . . . received a boost:** Marian N. Ruderman, Patricia J. Ohlott, Kate Panzer, and Sara N. King, "Benefits of Multiple Roles for Managerial Women," *Academy of Management Journal* 45, no. 2 (2002): 369–86.

163  **professional skills we learn on the job:** James V. Cordova, C. J. Fleming, Melinda Ippolito Morrill, Matt Hawrilenko, Julia W. Sollenberger, Amanda G. Harp, Tatiana D. Gray, et al., "The Marriage Checkup: A Randomized Controlled Trial of Annual Relationship Health Checkups," *Journal of Consulting and Clinical Psychology* 82, no. 4 (June 2014): 592.

167  **examining the apparent trade-offs:** Wendy K. Smith and Marianne W. Lewis, "Toward a Theory of Paradox: A Dynamic Equilibrium Model of Organizing," *Academy of Management Review* 36, no. 2 (March 2011): 381–403.

167  **different parts of our lives work in harmony:** Michael L. Tushman and Charles A. O'Reilly, "The Ambidextrous Organizations: Managing Evolutionary and Revolutionary Change," *California Management Review* 38, no. 4 (Summer 1996): 8–30.

168  **new material: rubber:** "Our Company, History: The Charles Goodyear Story," Goodyear.com, accessed February 14, 2016, https://corporate.good year.com/en-US/about/history/charles-goodyear-story.html; Charles Slack, *Noble Obsession: Charles Goodyear, Thomas Hancock, and the Race to Unlock the Greatest Industrial Secret of the Nineteenth Century* (New York: Hyperion, 2002); Cai Guise-Richardson, "Redefining Vulcanization: Charles Goodyear, Patents, and Industrial Control, 1834–1865," *Technology and Culture* 51, no. 2 (March 2010): 357–87; Bradford K. Peirce, *Trials of an Inventor: Life and Discoveries of Charles Goodyear* (New York: Phillips & Hunt, 1866).

171  **the best ideas come from those:** Adam Grant, *Originals: How Non-Conformists Move the World* (New York: Viking Press, 2016).

171  **oil and water:** Sarah Zielinski, "Oil and Water Do Mix," Smith sonianMag.com, November 17, 2010, accessed March 21, 2016, http://www.smithsonianmag.com/science-nature/oil-and-water-do-mix-38726068/.

**CHAPTER 8: AVOID INJURIES**

174  **too much of a good thing:** Adam M. Grant and Barry Schwartz, "Too Much of a Good Thing: The Challenge and Opportunity of the In-

verted U," *Perspectives on Psychological Science* 6, no. 1 (January 2011): 61–76.

174 **Nestled within an affluent neighborhood:** Walter Hamilton, "Edward Wedbush's Roof Leaks, But His Wallet Doesn't," *Los Angeles Times*, November 16, 2010.

175 **His obsession with cost controls:** Walter Hamilton, "Wedbush Inc. Ordered to Pay Former Trader $3.5 Million," *Los Angeles Times*, June 29, 2011.

175 **Regulators have also repeatedly fined:** Suzanne Barlyn, "Wall Street Watchdog Suspends Wedbush Securities President," Reuters, August 7, 2012.

176 **There are notable differences between the frugal and the cheap:** Scott I. Rick, Cynthia E. Cryder, and George Loewenstein, "Tightwads and Spendthrifts," *Journal of Consumer Research* 34, no. 6 (2008): 767–82.

177 **Stretchers aren't pained to spend money:** John L. Lastovicka, Lance A. Bettencourt, Renée S. Hughner, and Ronald J. Kuntze, "Lifestyle of the Tight and Frugal: Theory and Measurement," *Journal of Consumer Research* 26 (June 1999): 85–98.

177 **acting frugally was inherently satisfying:** Raymond De Young, "Some Psychological Aspects of Reduced Consumption Behavior: The Role of Intrinsic Satisfaction and Competence Motivation," *Environment and Behavior* 28, no. 3 (May 1996): 358–409.

178 **Ronald Wayne:** Ronald G. Wayne, *Adventures of an Apple Founder: Atari, Apple, Aerospace & Beyond*, (Valencia, CA: 512K Entertainment, LLC, 2010); Benny Luo, "Ronald Wayne: On Co-Founding Apple and Working with Steve Jobs," NextShark.com, September 12, 2013, accessed June 16, 2015, http://nextshark.com/ronald-wayne-interview; Dan Simon, "The Gambling Man Who Cofounded Apple and Left for $800," CNN.com, June 23, 2010, accessed June 16, 2015, http://www.cnn.com/2010/TECH/web/06/24/apple.forgotten.founder; Brian Heater, "Two Days in the Desert with Apple's Lost Founder, Ron Wayne," Engadget.com, December 19, 2011, accessed June 16, 2015, http://www.engadget.com/2011/12/19/two-days-in-the-desert-with-apples-lost-founder-ron-wayne.

178 **main legacy:** Ronald G. Wayne, *Insolence of Office: SocioPolitics, Socio-*

*Economics and the American Republic* (Valencia, CA: 512k Entertainment, LLC, 2010).

180  **attempts to branch out of action-adventure films:** Mike Thompson, "Sylvester Stallone: All Films Considered," metacritic.com, August 9, 2010, accessed March 30, 2016, http://www.metacritic.com/feature/sylvester-stallone-best-and-worst-movies.

180  **diversity of experience without wandering too far:** Ming D. Leung, "Dilettante or Renaissance Person? How the Order of Job Experiences Affects Hiring in an External Labor Market," *American Sociological Review* 79, no. 1 (2014): 136–58.

181  **be more creative and get promoted faster:** Lee Flemming, Santiago Mingo, and David Chen, "Collaborative Brokerage, Generative Creativity, and Creative Success," *Administrative Science Quarterly* 52, no. 3 (September 2007): 443–75, Daniel J. Brass, "Being in the Right Place: A Structural Analysis of Individual Influence in an Organization," *Administrative Science Quarterly* 29, no. 4 (December 1984): 518–39.

182  **when people move frequently, they uproot their lives:** Shigehiro Oishi and Ulrich Schimmack, "Residential Mobility, Well-Being, and Mortality," *Journal of Personality and Social Psychology* 98, no. 6 (2010): 980–94.

183  **positive correlations between frequent job switching and adverse health effects:** C. Metcalfe, G. D. Smith, J. A. Sterne, P. Heslop, J. Macleod, and C. Hart, "Frequent Job Change and Associated Health," *Social Science and Medicine* 56, no. 1 (January 2003): 1–15.

184  **"did my own thing":** Matt Brian, "Apple's Co-Founder Ron Wayne on Its Genesis, His Exit and the Company's Future," TheNextWeb.com, September 11, 2011, accessed March 31, 2016, http://thenextweb.com/apple/2011/09/11/apples-co-founder-ron-wayne-on-its-genesis-his-exit-and-the-companys-future/#gref.

184  **"a day late and a dollar short":** Bruce Newman, "Apple's Third Founder Refuses to Submit to Regrets," *Los Angeles Times*, June 9, 2010.

184  **fetched $25,000:** Christie's Auction, "Apple Computer Company (founded April 1, 1976), the Personal Archive of Apple Co-Founder Ronald Wayne," Christies.com, December 11, 2014, Sale 3459, Lot 35, accessed March 31, 2016, http://www.christies.com/lotfinder/lot/apple-computer-company-the-personal-archive-5855176-details.aspx.

185  **$6,000 in sales per square foot:** Seth Fiegerman, "Apple Has Twice the Sales per Square Foot of Any Other U.S. Retailer," Mashable.com, November 13, 2012, accessed March 30, 2016, http://mashable.com/2012/11/13/apple-stores-top-sales-per-square-foot//#4JXmmQMTmuq1.

185  **"fair-and-square" pricing:** Brad Tuttle, "The 5 Big Mistakes That Led to Ron Johnson's Ouster at JC Penney," Time.com, April 9, 2013, accessed March 20, 2016, http://business.time.com/2013/04/09/the-5-big-mistakes-that-led-to-ron-johnsons-ouster-at-jc-penney.

186  **eliminated meetings to review data:** Dana Mattioli, "For Penney's Heralded Boss, the Shine Is Off the Apple," *Wall Street Journal*, February 24, 2013.

186  **"What you can't do is chicken out":** Jennifer Reingold, "Ron Johnson: Retail's New Radical," Fortune.com, March 7, 2012, accessed March 30, 2016, http://fortune.com/2012/03/07/ron-johnson-retails-new-radical.

186  **"We didn't test at Apple":** Mattioli, "For Penney's Heralded Boss, the Shine Is Off the Apple."

186  **"an instinct for this stuff":** Danielle Sacks, "Ron Johnson's 5 Key Mistakes at JC Penney, in His Own Words," FastCompany.com, April 10, 2013, accessed March 30, 2016, http://www.fastcompany.com/3008059/ron-johnsons-5-key-mistakes-jc-penney-his-own-words.

186  **"Customers love the new JCP":** Brad Tuttle, "Why JCPenney's 'No More Coupons' Experiment Is Failing," *Time*, May 17, 2012.

187  **"One of the big mistakes":** Steve Denning, "JCPenney: Was Ron Johnson's Strategy Wrong?" *Forbes*, April 9, 2013.

187  **most important requirement for effectively jumping right in:** Daniel Kahneman and Gary Klein, "Conditions for Intuitive Expertise: A Failure to Disagree," *American Psychologist* 64, no. 6 (September 2009): 515–26.

187  **if he'd start over again:** Joann S. Lublin and Dana Mattioli, "Penney CEO Out, Old Boss Back In," *Wall Street Journal*, April 8, 2013.

188  **fast-feedback, slow-learning approach:** C. Chet Miller and R. Duane Ireland, "Intuition in Strategic Decision Making: Friend or Foe in the Fast-Paced 21st Century?" *Academy of Management Executive* 19, no. 1 (February 2005): 19–30.

188  **two of the best quarterbacks:** Clyde Haberman, "Manning or Leaf? A Lesson in Intangibles," *New York Times*, May 4, 2014.

# NOTES

189 **"I don't know what all of the fuss is":** Wonko, "NFL Draft History: Why Ryan Leaf Didn't Work Out," *SB Nation*, April 23, 2012, accessed March 15, 2016, http://www.boltsfromtheblue .com/2012/4/23/2965217/nfl-draft-history-chargers-why-ryan-leaf-didnt-work-out.

190 **fumbled his first snap:** Bernie Wilson, "Leaf Survives Big Mistakes in NFL Debut," Associated Press, September 8, 1998.

190 **"I had never lost":** Michael Bean, "Ryan Leaf's Quest for Personal Redemption Is Well Underway," SportsRadioInterviews.com, April 15, 2010, accessed March 31, 2016, http://sportsradiointerviews .com/2010/04/15/the-first-chapter-of-the-ryan-leaf-redemption-story-is-complete-and-impressive.

190 **You don't feel pressure if you study the game plan:** accessed May 14, 2016, http://www.achievement.org/autodoc/steps/prp?target=mar0–004.

190 **growth mind-set:** Carol Dweck, *Mindset: The New Psychology of Success* (New York: Random House, 2006).

190 **"I let them down":** Michael David Smith, "Ryan Leaf Looks Back on the Draft: I Should Have Stayed in School," NBCSports.com, September 9, 2014, accessed March 15, 2016, http://profootballtalk.nbcsports .com/2011/04/28/ryan-leaf-looks-back-on-the-draft-i-should-have-stayed-in-school/.

191 **"I became anti-social":** Bean, "Ryan Leaf's Quest for Personal Redemption Is Well Underway."

191 **pleaded guilty to eight charges:** Betsy Blaney, "Ex-NFL QB Ryan Leaf Sentenced to 5 Years," GreatFallsTribune.com, September 9, 2009, accessed March 31, 2016, http://www.greatfallstribune.com/story/news/ local/2014/09/09/ex-nfl-qb-ryan-leaf-sentenced-years/15350625/.

191 **"I was good at two things":** Ryan Leaf, *596 Switch: The Improbable Journey from the Palouse to Pasadena* (Pullman, WA: Crimson Oak Publishing, 2011), p. 25.

192 **performance pressures:** Roy F. Baumeister, James C. Hamilton, and Dianne M. Tice, "Public Versus Private Expectancy of Success: Confidence Booster or Performance Pressure?" *Journal of Personality and Social Psychology* 48, no. 6 (June 1985): 1447–57.

193 **home team chokes:** Roy F. Baumeister and Andrew Steinhilber, "Paradoxical Effects of Supportive Audiences on Performance Under Pres-

sure: The Home Field Disadvantage in Sports Championships," *Journal of Personality and Social Psychology* 47, no. 1 (1984): 85–93.

195 **"small wins":** Karl E. Weick, "Small Wins: Redefining the Scale of Social Problems," *American Psychologist* 39, no. 1 (January 1984): 40–49.

195 **Gerber Singles:** Maxwell Wessel, "Why Big Companies Can't Innovate," September 27, 2012, *Harvard Business Review*, accessed March 31, 2016, https://hbr.org/2012/09/why-big-companies-cant-innovate.

196 **"I Live Alone":** Susan Casey, "Everything I Ever Needed to Know About Business I Learned in the Frozen-Food Aisle," *eCompany Now*, October 2000, p. 96.

196 **Library of Losers:** Robert M. McMath, *What Were They Thinking: Marketing Lessons You Can Learn from Products That Flopped* (New York: Times Books, 2011).

196 **intrinsically motivated:** Teresa M. Amabile, "Motivating Creativity in Organizations: On Doing What You Love and Loving What You Do," *California Management Review* 40, no. 1 (Fall 1997): 39–58.

197 **learning and experimenting:** G. Hirst, D. V. Van Knippenberg, and J. Zhou, "A Cross-Level Perspective on Employee Creativity: Goal Orientation, Team Learning Behavior, and Individual Creativity," *Academy of Management Journal* 52, no. 2 (April 2009): 280–93.

197 **more familiar ideas:** O. Janssen and N. W. Van Yperen, "Employees' Goal Orientation, the Quality of Leader-Member Exchange and the Outcomes of Job Performance and Job Satisfaction," *Academy of Management Journal* 47, no. 3 (June 2004): 368–84.

197 **design a novel and useful:** Ella Miron-Spektor and Gerard Beenen, "Motivating Creativity: The Effects of Sequential and Simultaneous Learning and Performance Achievement Goals on Product Novelty and Usefulness," *Organizational Behavior and Human Decision Processes* 127 (2015): 53–65.

198 **it's critical to mix both goals:** Ibid.

## CHAPTER 9: WORKOUT

201 **serious disease:** "Diseases and Conditions: Tetanus," MayoClinic .org, accessed April 5, 2016, http://www.mayoclinic.org/diseases-conditions/tetanus/basics/definition/con-20021956.

203 **Participants handed the map:** Howard Leventhal, Robert Singer, and

# NOTES

Susan Jones, "Effects of Fear and Specificity of Recommendation upon Attitudes and Behavior," *Journal of Personality and Social Psychology* 2, no. 1 (July 1965): 20–29.

203 **"just say no":** "Just Say No," Ronald Reagan Presidential Foundation & Library, accessed April 6, 2016, http://www.reaganfoundation.org/details_f.aspx?p=RR1008NRHC&tx=6.

204 **write a book using fifty specific words:** Stacy Conradt, "10 Stories Behind Dr. Seuss Stories," CNN.com, January 23, 2009, accessed March 31, 2016, http://edition.cnn.com/2009/LIVING/wayoflife/01/23/mf.seuss.stories.behind; Daven Hiskey, "Dr. Seuss Wrote 'Green Eggs and Ham' on a Bet That He Couldn't Write a Book with 50 or Fewer Words," TodayIFoundOut.com, accessed March 31, 2016, http://www.todayifoundout.com/index.php/2011/05/dr-seuss-wrote-green-eggs-and-ham-on-a-bet-that-he-couldnt-write-a-book-with-50-or-fewer-words.

206 **organizational renewals . . . come from hidden assets:** Chris Zook, *Unstoppable: Finding Hidden Assets to Renew the Core and Fuel Profitable Growth* (Cambridge, MA: Harvard Business Review Press, 2007).

206 **"sleeping beauties":** Qing Ke, Emilio Ferrara, Filippo Radicchi, and Alessandro Flammini, "Defining and Identifying Sleeping Beauties in Science," *Proceedings of the National Academy of Sciences* 112, no. 24 (2015): 7426–31, accessed March 31, 2016, http://news.indiana.edu/releases/iu/2015/05/sleeping-beauties.shtml.

206 **shelves of cosmetics retailer Sephora:** Allison Keyes, "Sephora Teams Up with Iconic Black Hair Brand," Marketplace.org, accessed April 11, 2016, http://www.marketplace.org/2016/03/15/world/sephora-teams-iconic-black-hair-brand.

207 **bag of experiences:** Steve Jobs, Academy of Achievement, Genius.com speech, 1982, accessed April 10, 2016, http://genius.com/Steve-jobs-academy-of-achievement-speech-1982-annotated.

209 **half of our time thinking about something other than what we're currently doing:** Matthew A. Killingsworth and Daniel T. Gilbert, "A Wandering Mind Is an Unhappy Mind," *Science* 330, no. 6006 (November 12, 2010): 932.

209 **makes us unhappy:** Ibid.

209 **causes car crashes:** Cédric Galéra, Ludivine Orriols, Katia M'Bailara,

264

Magali Laborey, Benjamin Contrand, Régis Ribéreau-Gayon, Françoise Masson et al., "Mind Wandering and Driving: Responsibility Case-Control Study," *British Medical Journal* 345 (December 13, 2012): e8105.

209 **distractions can actually enhance creativity:** Ap Dijksterhuis and Teun Meurs, "Where Creativity Resides: The Generative Power of Unconscious Thought," *Consciousness and Cognition* 15, no. 1 (March 2006): 135–46.

209 **(ADHD) tend to score higher on creativity assessments:** G. A. Shaw and L. M. Giambra, "Task Unrelated Thoughts of College Students Diagnosed as Hyperactive in Childhood," *Developmental Neuropsychology* 9, no. 1 (1993): 17–30; H. A. White and P. Shah, "Creative Style and Achievement in Adults with Attention-Deficit/Hyperactivity Disorder," *Personality and Individual Differences* 50, no. 5 (April 2011): 673–77.

210 **40 percent improvement in coming up with new uses:** Benjamin Baird, Jonathan Smallwood, Michael D. Mrazek, Julia W. Y. Kam, Michael S. Franklin, and Jonathan W. Schooler, "Inspired by Distraction, Mind Wandering Facilitates Creative Incubation," *Psychological Science* (August 31, 2012): 1117–22.

210 **give overworked people more mindless work:** Kimberly D. Elsbach and Andrew B. Hargadon, "Enhancing Creativity Through 'Mindless' Work: A Framework of Workday Design," *Organization Science* 17, no. 4 (August 1, 2006): 470–83.

210 **design challenging jobs:** J. Richard Hackman and Greg R. Oldham, "Motivation Through the Design of Work: Test of a Theory," *Organizational Behavior and Human Performance* 16, no. 2, (1976): 250–79.

211 **Walking . . . frees the mind to wander:** Marily Oppezzo and Daniel L. Schwartz, "Give Your Ideas Some Legs: The Positive Effect of Walking on Creative Thinking," *Journal of Experimental Psychology: Learning, Memory, and Cognition* 40, no. 4 (2014): 1142.

211 **one urgent task to the next:** Joanne B. Ciulla, *The Working Life: The Promise and Betrayal of Modern Work* (New York: Crown, 2001).

212 **sleep with your smartphone:** Leslie A. Perlow, *Sleeping with Your Smartphone: How to Break the 24/7 Habit and Change the Way You Work* (Boston: Harvard Business Press, 2012).

212 *The 4-Hour Workweek:* Timothy Ferriss, *The 4-Hour Workweek: Es-*

*cape 9–5, Live Anywhere, and Join the New Rich* (New York: Crown, 2007).

212 **having big relative differences in income increases our pursuit of positional goods:** Lukasz Walasek and Gordon D. A. Brown, "Income Inequality and Status Seeking: Searching for Positional Goods in Unequal US States," *Psychological Science* 26, no. 4 (April 2015): 527–33.

213 **Her philosophy about avoiding Hollywood neighbors:** Jordan Zakarin, "Brie Larson Might Be the Geekiest It Girl Ever," BuzzFeed.com, accessed April 5, 2016, http://www.buzzfeed.com/jordanzakarin/brie-larson-the-geekiest-it-girl-ever#.bnoVV63lW6.

213 **Turnbull told me:** Alex Turnbull (founder and CEO of Groove), in an e-mail to the author, October 9, 2015.

214 **when people are grateful:** Barbara L. Fredrickson, "Gratitude, Like Other Positive Emotions, Broadens and Builds," in *The Psychology of Gratitude*, ed. Robert A. Emmons and Michael E. McCullough (Oxford: Oxford University Press, 2004).

214 **Turnbull's blog:** Alex Turnbull, *Groove*, accessed April 6, 2016, https://www.groovehq.com/blog/startup-journey.

216 **Project 333:** Courtney Carver, "Project 333: Simple Is the New Black," *bemorewithless* (blog), accessed April 6, 2016, http://bemorewithless.com.

216 **Lauri Ward:** Lauri Ward, "Design & Decor Tips for Smaller Homes, Chat with Lauri Ward," LogHome.com, accessed April 6, 2016, http://www.loghome.com/chat-with-lauri-ward.

216 **art of decluttering and organizing:** Marie Kondo, *The Life-Changing Magic of Tidying Up: The Japanese Art of Decluttering and Organizing* (Berkeley, CA: Ten Speed Press, 2014).

216 **mouse pad that could be used as a trivet:** "50 All-Time Favorite New Uses for Old Things," RealSimple.com, accessed April 10, 2016, http://www.realsimple.com/home-organizing/home-organizing-new-uses-for-old-things/favorite-new-uses/mousepad-trivet.

216 **bent silverware:** "20 Clever Uses for Everyday Items," RealSimple.com, accessed April 10, 2016, http://www.myhomeideas.com/how-to/household-basics/10-new-uses-old-things/mismatched-silverware.

217 **Play-Doh started as a wallpaper:** "Wonder of the Day #582: Who Invented Play Dough?" Wonderopolis.org, accessed April 10, 2016, http://wonderopolis.org/wonder/who-invented-play-dough.

217  **corkscrew:** Daniel Crow, "The 5 Most Insane Original Uses of Famous Products," Cracked.com, January 12, 2012, accessed April 10, 2016, http://www.cracked.com/article_19644_the-5-most-insane-original-uses-famous-products_p2.html.

217  **Pyrex:** "It Was All Her Idea," ClassicKitchensAndMore.com, accessed April 10, 2016, http://www.classickitchensandmore.com/page_4.html.

217  **baby carrot:** "The Invention of the Baby Carrot," Priceonomics.com, accessed April 10, 2016, http://priceonomics.com/the-invention-of-the-baby-carrot.

218  **Miles Davis:** F. Barratt, "Creativity and Improvisation in Jazz and Organizations: Implications for Organizational Learning," *Organization Science* 9, no. 5 (1998): 605–22.

218  **Weick poses an intriguing question:** Karl E. Weick, *The Social Psychology of Organizing*, 2nd ed. (New York: McGraw-Hill, 1979), p. 133.

219  **Chess960:** Eric van Reem, "The Birth of Fischer Random Chess," ChessVariants.com, accessed April 7, 2016, http://www.chessvariants.com/diffsetup.dir/fischerh.html.

220  **the Babylonians:** Sarah Pruitt, "The History of New Year's Resolutions," History.com, accessed April 5, 2016, http://www.history.com/news/the-history-of-new-years-resolutions.

220  **success rate for making positive changes:** John C. Norcross, Marci S. Mrykalo, and Matthew D. Blagys, "Auld Lang Syne: Success Predictors, Change Processes, and Self-Reported Outcomes of New Year's Resolvers and Nonresolvers," *Journal of Clinical Psychology* 58, no. 4 (April 2002): 397–405.

220  **July Fourth resolutions:** Linda Wasmer Andrews, "Midyear Resolutions You'll Actually Keep," PsychologyToday.com, accessed April 5, 2016, https://www.psychologytoday.com/blog/minding-the-body/201006/midyear-resolutions-youll-actually-keep.

221  **water-filled bottle:** accessed April 12, 2016, http://www.psychologicalscience.org/index.php/news/releases/stumped-by-a-problem-this-technique-unsticks-you.html.

221  **break down a resource:** Tony McCaffrey, "Innovation Relies on the Obscure: A Key to Overcoming the Classic Problem of Functional Fixedness," *Psychological Science* 23, no. 3 (February 2012): 215–18.

221  **effective and practical technique:** Ibid.

222 **worm poop packaged in used Coca-Cola bottles:** Kim Bhasin, "The Incredible Story of How TerraCycle CEO Tom Szaky Became a Garbage Mogul," BusinessInsider.com, August 29, 2011, accessed April 5, 2016, http://www.businessinsider.com/exclusive-tom-szaky-terracycle-interview-2011–8.

223 **General Motors' landfill-free initiative:** "GM's MacGyver Devises Unconventional Uses for Everyday Waste," GeneralMotors.Green.com, accessed April 6, 2016, http://www.generalmotors.green/product/public/us/en/GMGreen/home.detail.html/content/Pages/news/us/en/gm_green/2014/0122-bradburn.html.

223 **hotel was rebuilt at a substantially faster pace:** Mauricio Martinez (general manager of a Luxury Resort in Los Cabos, Mexico), in discussion with the author, December 30, 2014.

## CONCLUSION: YOUR STRETCH

226 **three major financial challenges:** Pew Charitable Trusts, "The Precarious State of Family Balance Sheets," January 2015.

226 **Leisure time:** Mark Aguiar and Erik Hurst, "A Summary of Trends in American Time Allocation: 1965–2005," *Social Indicators Research* 93, no. 1 (August 2009): 57–64.

226 **working parents:** Bureau of Labor Statistics, "Employment Characteristics of Families Summary," April 25, 2014.

226 **had not received any skills training:** Mindflash, accessed April 25, 2016, https://www.mindflash.com/blog/press-release/americans-cite-lack-of-corporate-training-as-1-driver-of-the-skills-gap-today-according-to-national-survey-from-mindflash/.

# INDEX

# INDEX

# INDEX

# INDEX

# INDEX

# INDEX

# INDEX

# ABOUT THE AUTHOR

Scott Sonenshein is the Henry Gardiner Symonds Professor of Management at Rice University. His award-winning research, teaching, and consulting have helped Fortune 500 executives, entrepreneurs, and professionals in industries such as technology, health care, retail, education, banking, manufacturing, and nonprofits. He holds a PhD in management and organizations from the University of Michigan, an MPhil from the University of Cambridge, and a BA from the University of Virginia. He has also worked as a strategy consultant for companies such as AT&T and Microsoft and lived the rise and fall of the dotcom boom while working at a Silicon Valley start-up.